Palgrave Studies in Marketing, Organizations and Society

Series Editor
David W. Stewart
College of Business Administration
Loyola Marymount University
Los Angeles, CA, USA

This book series will focus on the broader contributions of marketing to the firm and to society at large. It takes a focus more consistent with the original reasons the marketing discipline was founded, the creation of efficient systems through with societies provision themselves and match supply with the needs of a diverse market. First, it looks at the contribution of marketing to the firm, or more broadly, to the organization (recognizing that marketing plays a role in not-for-profit organizations, governments, and other organization, in addition to for-profit commercial businesses). Marketing plays a pivotal and unique role in the creation and management of intangible assets such as brands, customer lists and customer loyalty, trademarks, copyrights, patents, and specialized knowledge. Second, the series explores the broader contributions of marketing to the larger society of which it is a part. The societal effect of the modern firm, largely through the development of markets, can be seen in the per capita growth of GDP in Western Europe between 1350 and 1950. During this period, per capita GDP increased by almost 600%, while remaining virtually unchanged in China and India during the same period. Marketing has played an important role in the improvement of the quality of life through increasing the number, nature and variety products and services, the improvement of the quality and convenience of these product and services, and by making these products and services more readily accessible to larger numbers of persons. The series will examine ways in which marketing has been employed in the service of social welfare—to promote healthy behaviors, family planning, environmentally friendly behavior, responsible behavior, and economic development.

More information about this series at
http://www.palgrave.com/gp/series/16292

David W. Stewart

Financial Dimensions of Marketing Decisions

palgrave
macmillan

David W. Stewart
College of Business Administration
Loyola Marymount University
Los Angeles, CA, USA

ISSN 2661-8613   ISSN 2661-8621 (electronic)
Palgrave Studies in Marketing, Organizations and Society
ISBN 978-3-030-15564-3   ISBN 978-3-030-15565-0   (eBook)
https://doi.org/10.1007/978-3-030-15565-0

Library of Congress Control Number: 2019936177

This Palgrave Macmillan imprint is published by the registered company Springer Nature Switzerland AG
The registered company address is: Gewerbestrasse 11, 6330 Cham, Switzerland

Acknowledgments

December 2018

This book, like all books, is the result of an accumulation of experiences. While I take responsibility for the content of the book, I had considerable help in its completion. Of special note is my long association with the Marketing Accountability Standards Board (MASB), which for 15 years has championed the important and necessary links among marketing, analytics, and finance. Much of the content of this book had its genesis in my interactions with MASB project teams and attendees at MASB summits. But for my involvement with MASB, this book would not have been written.

I owe a special debt of gratitude to Margaret (Meg) Henderson Blair, with whom I cofounded MASB. Meg was passionate about the need for managerially relevant, reliable, valid, and precise measurement of marketing outcomes. Meg passed away unexpectedly in early 2018, but her legacy and devotion to marketing accountability live on. I knew Meg for over 40 years during which time she was my friend, coauthor, and mentor. Meg's thinking permeates the content of this book.

Allen Kuse, Frank Findley, and Tony Pace, all members of the MASB staff in addition to being quite accomplished marketers and marketing researchers, also played an important role in influencing the concepts offered in this book. Neal Bendle, at the Ivy School at Western University, and Jim Meier, recently retired from his role as Vice President of Marketing Finance at Miller/Coors, read and provided comments on an early draft of the book. Hugh Taylor read and provided feedback on early drafts of all the chapters and contributed examples, developed spreadsheet illustrations of key concepts, and generally helped me polish the content of the book. Patty Biner at Loyola Marymount University tracked down the copyright permissions required. I thank her for taking on such a thankless task. The publisher of the book, Palgrave, was very helpful in making my words become a book.

I also wish to acknowledge my teachers, students, colleagues, and consulting clients who have presented me with interesting questions and opportunities to interact with and learn about the operations of many diverse businesses in hundreds of market contexts. This book and my life have been enriched by these interactions.

I would be remiss if I did not observe that this book was completed during a sabbatical from Loyola Marymount University and during a visit at the Leeds University Business School. I am indebted to both institutions for their support.

Finally, I thank my wife of more than 40 years, Lenora, who has supported my devotion to the hobby for which I am paid.

Leeds, UK   David W. Stewart

Praise for *Financial Dimensions of Marketing Decisions*

"The next evolution of marketing involves greater linkage of marketing activities to value creation. Dave does a great job of laying that out for marketers who are savvy enough to be early adopters."
—Tony Pace, *President and CEO of the Marketing Accountability Standards Board*

"Dave Stewart's brilliant rendition of this book serves as a marketers' guide for making the case for resources to financial decision makers. The powerful content of measuring brand value and customer value as well as managing risk, real options, and portfolio of products provides the necessary guidance for the financial decision makers. A resourceful book at a compelling time!"
—V Kumar, *Regents Professor, Richard and Susan Lenny Distinguished Chair, and Professor of Marketing, Georgia State University, USA*

"Successful marketers must be prepared to justify their expenditures, activities, and outcomes in terms of their contribution to the financial performance of the firm. Stewart's book is an excellent guide for practicing marketing managers and marketing students who wish to increase their value and credibility by translating marketing actions into financial results."
—Robert W. Palmatier, *John C. Narver Chair in Business Administration and Professor of Marketing, University of Washington, USA*

CONTENTS

About the Author

David W. Stewart, PhD, is President's Professor of Marketing and Business Law at Loyola Marymount University, Los Angeles. He has previously held faculty and administrative appointments at Vanderbilt University, the University of Southern California, and the University of California, Riverside. He is a past editor of the *Journal of Marketing*, the *Journal of the Academy of Marketing Science*, and the *Journal of Public Policy and Marketing*. He is founding chair of the Marketing Accountability Standard Board (MASB). He serves as Vice President, Publications, for the American Marketing Association and has served on the Board of Governors of the Academy of Marketing Science and as Vice President, Finance, and a member of the Board of Directors of the American Marketing Association. He is a past president of the Academic Council of the American Marketing Association, a past chairman of the Section on Statistics in Marketing of the American Statistical Association, a past president of the Society for Consumer Psychology, and a Fellow of both the American Psychological Association and the Association for Psychological Science. He has also previously served as a member and past chairman of the United States Census Bureau's Advisory Committee of Professional Associations.

Dr. Stewart has authored or coauthored more than 250 publications and 12 books. His research has examined a wide range of issues including marketing strategy, the analysis of markets, consumer information search and decision-making, effectiveness of marketing communications, public policy issues related to marketing, and methodological approaches to the analysis of marketing data. His research and commentary are frequently featured in the business and popular press. A native of Baton Rouge,

Louisiana, Professor Stewart received his BA from the Northeast Louisiana University (now the University of Louisiana at Monroe) and his MA and PhD in psychology from Baylor University.

Dr. Stewart has been awarded the American Marketing Association's Award for Lifetime Contributions to Marketing and Public Policy, the Elsevier Distinguished Marketing Scholar Award by the Society for Marketing Advances, and was honored by the Academy of Marketing Science with the Cutco/Vector Distinguished Educator Award for lifetime contributions to marketing. He has also received the American Academy of Advertising Award for Outstanding Contribution to Advertising Research for his long-term contributions to research in advertising.

Professor Stewart's experience includes work as a manager of research for Needham, Harper, and Steers Advertising, Chicago (now DDB), and consulting projects for a wide range of organizations. Among the organizations for which he has consulted are Hewlett Packard, Agilent Technologies, the Coca-Cola Company, Hughes, NCR, Texas Instruments, IBM, Intel, Cadence Design Systems, Century 21 Real Estate, Samsung, American Home Products, Visa Services, Xerox, the US Census Bureau, and the United States Federal Trade Commission, among others. He has served as an expert witness before the Federal Trade Commission, in United States Federal Court, and in State Courts in cases involving deceptive advertising claims and unfair business practices, in matters related to trademarks and intellectual property, and in antitrust actions. Professor Stewart has delivered executive education programs throughout the United States and in more than 20 other nations on five continents. In 1988, he was Marketing Science Institute Visiting Scholar at the General Motors Corporation.

LIST OF FIGURES

LIST OF TABLES

CHAPTER 1

Introduction

It's tempting to consider marketing and finance to be completely separate business disciplines. Marketing is about subjective, edgy, creative things like brands and television commercials. Finance focuses on hard, cold numbers. In reality, as most experienced business leaders know, the two disciplines are deeply entwined in the successful management of a venture. Though it's not the only factor, marketing is one of the most essential drivers of business profitability and high valuations. Marketing is about revenue generation and growth, which is what drives the financial side of the business. For this reason, marketing and finance are two sides of the same issue, both answering the same, fundamental questions that every business must answer: who will buy our product at the best price? How do we get as many profitable customers as possible? How do we keep customers loyal and returning to purchase again and again? This book offers an approach to answering these questions. Blending basic information about both marketing and finance with case examples and thought-provoking exercises, it enables the reader to develop an appreciation for the way marketing drives finance and vice versa.

An Example

Imagine that you work for the Chief Executive Officer (CEO) of Coca-Cola. He asks you for an opinion on a recommendation by the company's Chief Marketing Officer (CMO) to raise their advertising budget from

© The Author(s) 2019
D. W. Stewart, *Financial Dimensions of Marketing Decisions*,
Palgrave Studies in Marketing, Organizations and Society,
https://doi.org/10.1007/978-3-030-15565-0_1

$3.2 billion to $3.5 billion. Should Coke spend an additional $300 million on advertising? The Chief Financial Officer (CFO) is opposed, saying the money would be better spent elsewhere. Alternatively, keeping the ad budget flat will increase earnings and drive the stock price up. The CMO counters that the increase in ad spending is actually an investment in the brand, and one that will result in higher sales and earnings over time as well. This was an actual decision facing Coke's senior leadership in 2013. Already the largest advertiser in the beverage industry, Coke was spending 6.9% of its revenue on advertising at the time (Investopedia 2018).

What should Coke do in such a circumstance? What would you advise the CEO? Is marketing an expense or an investment in an intangible, but extremely valuable, asset known as the brand? Is it both an expense and an investment? How should a company treat marketing from a financial point of view? These are the questions this book seeks to answer. The answers, in turn, are intended to make the reader a better business person and manager with an understanding of how two vital parts of a business, marketing and finance, work together to create value for customers, shareholders, employees, and other stakeholders.

WHY DOES THIS BOOK EXIST?

There is a fallacy that marketing and finance are separate disciplines. In reality, they are closely linked. They often overlap, and they inform one another about the current and future health of the business. This is the case even when the people performing finance and marketing functions either don't know or believe that they're interdependent. This book's goal is to enable you to see marketing from a financial perspective and finance from a marketing perspective. When a business leader can operate with this insight, good things tend to happen in a business and other types of organizations as well.

Looks can be deceiving. Finance appears to be a numbers game, a cold, fact-based area of the business world where money talks and everything else walks. Marketing, in contrast, is often viewed as subjective, an arena for creative, artsy types who love talking about soft-edged concepts like brand aura and emotional engagement with the customer. However, finance is not only about money and marketing is about a lot more than image. In truth, both disciplines are about the same thing: how a business sustainably earns, grows, and increases in value. Marketing is one of the main drivers of earnings, growth, and valuation. Finance is about measuring the effects of marketing—from the decisions to operate in specific markets and serve specific customers to pricing, basic advertising and messaging, product design, and the scope of product lines.

Applying these concepts to the Coca-Cola situation, consider the following conundrum: in the middle of 2018, Coca-Cola's balance sheet showed total assets of $89 billion. Yet, the company's market capitalization, the total value of the company, was $199 billion at that time (Coca-Cola Investors Webpage 2018). Why are the two numbers so different? The $110 billion premium of entity value over the book value of its assets signifies how the market values the Coca-Cola brand. What is it about Coca-Cola that creates such value in the investment community?

Going further, is the Coca-Cola brand worth more than that of its competitors? Perhaps, a look at the ratio between the stock price and the company's earnings (the price-to-earnings ratio or P/E) is instructive. Coke trades at around 33 times its earnings (Google 2018a). In contrast, Pepsi's P/E is just 21 (Google 2018b). Thus, in rough terms, a dollar of earnings generated by Coke's marketing machine is worth $33 to shareholders versus $21 for a dollar of Pepsi's earnings.

But wait. Aren't stock prices based on expectations of cash flow? Yes, they are, give or take various other influences. And there is a connection between brand (powered by marketing) and future cash flows. The value of a brand surfaces in the stock price because of its ability to generate and assure future cash flows. Good products, ubiquitous distribution, television commercials, and a host of other marketing activities transform consumers into cash-generating customers. From this perspective, the intersection between marketing and finance becomes clearer.

Should Coke increase its marketing spending? We still don't know, but this book is intended to frame an informed answer to the question. It delves into the nature of marketing and finance, both as individual disciplines and as synergistic partners. It gives you a way to assess the success of marketing as a generator of cash.

What You Will Get Out of This Book

This book is for you if you want to become a better, more informed business manager. You will only be great at marketing if you understand finance and marketing's effects on financial outcomes. Conversely, you will only be great at finance if you understand marketing and how it affects business financial performance and valuation.

You do not have to be a marketing or finance specialist to benefit from reading this book. General managers need to understand how these two functions affect business operations. Reading this book will equip you to view and perform marketing functions with a financial and strategic mind-set. These skills are essential to steering a business in the direction of strong growth and robust cash flow. Knowing how to work with marketing while applying financial discipline enables the firm to build value for shareholders and will likely make you more valuable as well.

What's Inside

This book begins with an overview of finance and its connections with marketing. Chapter 2 covers the basics of finance, accounting, and financial statements. These are the fundamental tools of the trade, so to speak. Building on these foundations, the book proceeds to business valuation and the relationship between cash flow and stock price. With these concepts in place, the chapter explores the marketing-finance conversation in earnest with a look at marketing budgeting decisions.

Chapter 3 focuses on business models, which define how a firm makes money. The chapter highlights how the value chain works and marketing's role in it. We look at organizational structure, sustainability, and revenue generation and their contributions to the business model. Business models encompass finance and marketing. We continue this investigation in Chap. 4, which offers insights into estimating cash flows. As we saw with the Coke example, this is where marketing connects directly with finance. We will take the discussion much further in this chapter.

Chapters 5 and 6 discuss marketing metrics and the links among business models, marketing metrics, and cash flow. Chapters 7 and 8 address brands and customer equity and develop models for translating these key marketing concepts into financial metrics. Chapter 9 provides a discussion of risk and how it is managed along with a discussion of how marketing creates opportunities for the future. Chapter 10 describes the complexities that arise when a firm offers multiple products. Chapter 11 provides a review of marketing strategy and its relationship with financial results. Finally, Chap. 12 explores the importance of factors beyond immediate marketing and financial results with a discussion of how the firm should consider and report on its efforts to create value over the long term for all of its stakeholders.

There is much to explore. This book is intended as an introduction to the marketing and finance interface. It offers a general discussion of relevant issues, but the amazing diversity of organizations and markets means that the reader will need to go beyond the book to consider many of the details that are unique to specific business situations. Each chapter offers some exercises and points to ponder to help the reader begin the process of application and extrapolation.

Exercise

1. Find a copy of a recent annual report for a publicly traded company. Such reports can generally be found in the investor relations portion of a company's website. Read the CEO's letter to shareholders. How often are terms like cash flow and growth used? How often is marketing mentioned? What might you conclude based on your reading?

Points to Ponder

1. Why do you think marketing and finance seem to be such different disciplines? Can marketing be about numbers? Can finance be creative? What type of person would thrive at the intersection of these two disciplines?

REFERENCES

Coca-Cola Investors Webpage. (2018). https://www.coca-colacompany.com/investors/investors-info-sec-filings

Google. (2018a). https://www.google.com/search?q=market+cap+of+KO+coca+cola&ie=utf-8&oe=utf-8&client=firefox-b-1-ab

Google. (2018b). https://www.google.com/search?q=pepsi+stock+quote&rlz=1C1CHBF_enUS728US728&oq=pepsi+stock+quote&aqs=chrome.0.0l3.5534j0j4&sourceid=chrome&ie=UTF-8

Investopedia. (2018). https://www.investopedia.com/articles/markets/081315/look-cocacolas-advertising-expenses.asp

CHAPTER 2

The Financial Imperative of Marketing

A customer walks into your business. She buys a $20 product and leaves. You put the money in the cash register. The item cost you $10 wholesale. In purely financial terms, you just made $10 in gross profit. Over the course of a month, you'll hopefully make enough gross profit to cover the expenses of running your business so you can take home some net earnings.

What really just happened, though? Where did that customer come from? How did she choose your business and that particular product? Why was she willing to pay $20 for it, rather than $15, $11, or even $9? Is anyone else selling the same product for $9? If so, you might have to drop your price to match that and lose $1.00 in the process.

That hypothetical loss of $1 on gross profit of $10 is entirely a marketing issue, not a financial one. In the case of matching a competitor's low price in the example above, if you don't understand marketing, you will never understand why you just lost $1. This chapter is meant to give you an overall sense of how marketing and finance interact to drive business results—both positive and negative.

Finance and Marketing: A Quick Take

There are important reasons for measuring the performance of a firm in financial terms (Stewart 2009). First, finance is the language of the firm; publicly incorporated firms must report results in financial terms and are

© The Author(s) 2019
D. W. Stewart, *Financial Dimensions of Marketing Decisions*,
Palgrave Studies in Marketing, Organizations and Society,
https://doi.org/10.1007/978-3-030-15565-0_2

evaluated based on financial performance. Second, financial measures are the only way to compare alternative actions across products, markets, and customers.

Often managers must make decisions about investments and activities that are noncomparable. For example, should the firm invest in brand building in Indonesia or in expanding distribution channels in Brazil? Such decisions can only be made if the costs and benefits are translated into comparable terms, and this usually means financial terms. Indeed, the only way to answer questions about the optimal marketing mix is to translate activities and outcomes into financial terms.

Marketing is very much subject to financial measurement. Measuring marketing outcomes in financial terms provides accountability. Financial performance is not a perfect metric, but it is relatively easy to identify success or failure based on it. Finally, measures of financial performance promote *organizational learning* and cross-functional team work by focusing members of the team on a common set of inputs and outcomes. Forcing managers to evaluate past marketing actions in financial terms and future marketing actions in terms of prospective cash flows aligns marketing with the ultimate objectives of the firm, making a profit over time.

The outcomes of marketing expenditures and actions can be quite complex. Some activities may create immediate outcomes, such as immediate sales. Other marketing activities may create both immediate and long-lasting outcomes. For example, an advertising campaign may create awareness and trial of a new product. Combined with a positive product experience, the same advertising campaign may also contribute to product preference and a willingness on the part of customers to pay a price premium and continue to purchase again and again.

If this seems a little confusing, that's because the business world has not entirely reconciled marketing with finance. We're going to address that deficit now. First, though, we need to learn some of the specifics of finance.

THE INCOME STATEMENT

How did Coke "Buy low and sell high" in the second quarter of 2018? Table 2.1, the company's Income Statement, can tell us. Like our hypothetical business that sold a $10 item for $20, Coke sold $8.297 billion worth of beverage products in the quarter and paid $3.252 in "cost of goods sold." Their gross profit for the quarter was $5.675 billion. This is also known as "gross margin."

Table 2.1 Coca-Cola quarterly income statement

Condensed consolidated statements of income	Three months ended		Six months ended	
(In millions except per share data)	6/29/2018	6/30/2017	6/29/2018	6/30/2017
NET OPERATING REVENUES	$8927	$9702	$16,553	$18,820
Cost of goods sold	$3252	$3659	$5990	$7172
GROSS PROFIT	$5675	$6043	$10,563	$11,648
Selling, general and administrative expenses	$2723	$3180	$5264	$6532
Other operating charges	$225	$826	$761	$1116
OPERATING INCOME	$2727	$2037	$4538	$4000
Other income (loss)—net	$156	$587	$178	$131
INCOME FROM CONTINUING OPERATIONS BEFORE INCOME TAXES	$2883	$2624	$4716	$4131
Income taxes from continuing operations	$594	$1252	$1100	$1575
NET INCOME FROM CONTINUING OPERATIONS	$2289	$1372	$3616	$2556

Coca-Cola quarterly income statement for period ending 6/29/2018

What is margin and why is it important? Margin is the direct profit you make on a sale before you have to pay any other expenses. In the case of Coke, they earned a margin of $5.675 billion on sales of $8.927 billion. That's a rate of margin of 63%. Is that high or low? Good or bad? Let's figure out the answer to this most important but subjective question.

Every business has a different margin rate. There are several ways to know if a company's margin is good or bad. For one thing, how does it compare to competitors' margins. If your margin is lower than your competitors' margins, your business may operate at a disadvantage unless there is a deliberate effort to compete on price. If competitors are more profitable, you need to know why. In the case of Coke, their cost of goods consists mostly of sugar and aluminum. If Pepsi can buy either commodity at a lower price, then Coke is at a disadvantage. (This is why companies often merge—so they can have better buying power and increase their margins.)

Then, there is the issue of comparative margins over time. A year earlier, Coke's margin was 62%, so it went up. That's good! Let's explore how this works and why it matters.

MARGINS

Margin is critically important because it demonstrates, quantitatively, the profitability of revenue. A firm can generate large sales revenue but lose money if the sales price does not cover costs. Costs can be classified as *variable* and *fixed*.

Variable costs are costs associated with producing, delivering, and selling an individual unit of a product or service. In Coke's case, the variable costs are from water, sugar, other ingredients, and aluminum for the cans. These costs are variable because they occur as each unit is produced; the total variable costs will be larger when more units are produced and will be smaller when fewer units are produced.

In contrast, total *fixed costs* do not vary with the number of units produced. Sometimes called the "nut" of a business, fixed costs include such things as office space, production plant and equipment, most personnel, and other expenditures that are not a function of the actual number of product units produced.

Note that marketing expenditures can be variable or fixed. For example, a price promotion that provides a discount off the sales price of each unit sold would be a variable cost. On the other hand, a national advertising campaign that involves the purchase of several million dollars of broadcast media would be a fixed cost because the cost of the media does not vary with the number of units sold.

Obviously, a firm must cover both its variable costs and fixed costs and it is important to know both. Assigning variable costs is relatively easy because they are directly linked to sales of individual products or services. Fixed costs, in contrast, cannot be easily assigned to individual products or services. As a result, firms develop rules for allocating fixed costs. For example, a proportion of fixed costs could be assigned to each unit sold. In Coke's case, if the cost of running the canning plant is $100 per year, and the plant produces 10,000 cans a year, Coke will allocate 1 cent of fixed costs to each can it sells. While this rule is simple, it is problematic because the allocation will vary with the number of units sold. Thus, if many units are sold, each unit will be assigned a smaller share of fixed costs than if fewer units are sold.

In a marketing planning context, it is common to compute the *contribution margin* of the product or service, that is, the portion of sales revenue that is not consumed by the variable costs. The contribution margin is often referred to as *gross margin*. Gross margin is computed by subtracting the cost of producing the product (*variable costs*) from the selling price:

$$\text{Gross Margin}(\$) = \left(\text{Selling price}(\$) - \text{Cost of Producing the Product}(\$)\right)$$

However, as has been discussed, there are other fixed costs that need to be accounted for. Accounting for such costs involves computing the *net margin*. Net margin is obtained by subtracting all costs, both variable and fixed, from the selling price. Net margin can vary dramatically depending on how fixed costs are allocated. However, for marketing planning and budgeting purposes, the contribution margin after accounting for marketing expenditures is a particularly useful way to assess the effects of marketing activities and expenditures on financial performance.

$$\text{Total Contribution Margin After Marketing}(\$)$$
$$= \left[\left(\text{Gross Margin}(\$) \times \text{Sales Volume}\right) - \text{Cost of Marketing}(\$)\right]$$

Note that both gross margin and total contribution margin after marketing can also be expressed as percentages:

$$\text{Gross Margin}(\%) = \left[\left(\text{Selling price}(\$) - \text{Cost of Producing the Product}(\$)\right)\right]$$
$$\div \text{Sales Price}(\$)$$

$$\text{Total Contribution Margin After Marketing}(\%) = \left[\left(\text{Gross Margin}(\$) \times \text{Sales Volume}\right)\right.$$
$$- \text{Cost of Marketing}(\$)\left.\right]$$
$$\div \text{Total Sales Revenue}(\$)$$

The unit of analysis for gross margin, whether computed as a dollar amount or a percentage, is the individual product. In contrast, the unit of analysis for total contribution margin after marketing is total sales volume. This is because the cost of marketing cannot be allocated to individual product unit sales but must be spread across all product unit sales.

The contribution margin after marketing can be used to determine how marketing expenditures influence revenue. The focus here is on contribution rather than "profit." The reason for this is that profits or earnings are more of an accounting term that may be influenced by a variety of decisions and factors beyond the control of the marketer: for example, management's decisions to allocate fixed costs to one unit or another. Amazon has rarely reported profits because it has decided to reinvest its very substantial cash flow in growing its business.

What does this have to do with marketing? A lot! For instance, can Coke raise the price of a can of soda if the price of sugar goes up? If it can, it can pass along the sugar price increase and maintain a high margin. This is essentially a marketing question. What price will people pay for soda? Is it "elastic," meaning that people will pay more if the price goes up? If not, then Coke has to eat that sugar price increase and cut its margins. Market research is necessary to predict whether consumers will adapt to higher prices. Conversely, if marketing research reveals that people will buy much more soda at a lower price point, the price increase may not be worth doing, from a margin perspective. This is just one example of the interplay between marketing and finance.

Or, consider the following management issue: if the contribution margin increases after an increase in marketing expenditures, marketing activities are producing positive financial returns to the firm. Of course, analyzing marketing expenditures in the aggregate is not very helpful because there are so many different marketing activities that are available to the firm.

From a planning perspective it would be useful to know what effect a specific marketing activity has on financial performance. For example, does an expenditure on an advertising campaign increase the contribution margin after marketing relative to the contribution margin after marketing without the advertising expenditure? If not, the advertising expenditure is not justified. This is also a way to compare alternative marketing activities to determine which activities contribute more to the contribution margin after marketing. While seemingly simple, the challenge is that it is rarely possible to link a marketing activity directly to margin. Rather, it is usually necessary to establish such a link through measures of marketing outcomes such as brand preference or customer loyalty. Subsequent chapters of this book will examine such linkages.

The Balance Sheet

The income statement measures financial performance, including revenue, expenses, and profits, over a period of time, for example, a month, a quarter, or a year. The balance sheet looks at financial performance from the perspective of assets and liabilities at a specific point in time—essentially how much money is left over at the end of the period. The system actually comes from a very old way of tracking the profits of merchant ships, where an accountant would keep records of sales and then do an accounting of the amounts of products and gold coins in hand. The latter was the balance sheet, literally the "balance" of the gold coins as weighed on a scale.

Table 2.2 shows Coke's balance sheet for the six months ending on June 29, 2018, compared to the year ending on December 31, 2017. We see that Coke had current assets (cash, accounts receivable, and liquid securities) totaling $36 billion. Other assets, including plant and equipment, totaled $43.4 billion. Goodwill and other intangible assets (more on these later) ran around $10 billion for a total of $89.593 billion in total assets.

This represents the pile of gold coins and other property owned by Coke at the end of the six months. It's a snapshot of a financial moment in time. On July 2nd, the snapshot will look different as the company takes in revenue and pays its bills.

What about the other side of the balance sheet? This measures liabilities, including accounts payable (bills to be paid) and other debts. The liabilities count against the assets, resulting in a sort of "Net worth" of the

Table 2.2 Coca-Cola balance sheet

Condensed consolidated balance sheets

(In millions except par value)	Period ending	Period ending
ASSETS	6/29/2018	12/31/2017
TOTAL CURRENT ASSETS	36,024	36,545
Other Assets	43,414	41,582
GOODWILL	9863	9401
OTHER INTANGIBLE ASSETS	292	368
TOTAL ASSETS	$89,593	$87,896
LIABILITIES AND EQUITY		
TOTAL CURRENT LIABILITIES	31,398	27,194
LONG-TERM DEBT	28,063	31,182
OTHER LIABILITIES	7367	8021
DEFERRED INCOME TAX LIABILITIES	2589	2522
Total Liabilities	69,417	68,919
TOTAL EQUITY	20,176	18,977
TOTAL LIABILITIES AND EQUITY	$89,593	$87,896

Coca-Cola balance sheet for period ending 6/29/2018

corporation. Equity, which totals $20 billion, comprises the money the company has earned in previous periods and other shareholder holdings. In a balance sheet, the assets must always equal (or balance) the sum of liabilities plus equity.

We will not get into the accounting behind this, but the main idea is that the balance sheet shows the financial health of the company. If the debt dwarfs the current assets, for example, that spells trouble. That means the company is probably going to struggle to service its debt. Similarly, if the ratio between current assets and current liabilities (the "Current Ratio" which measures how much working capital the company has) deteriorates over time, this can reveal a worsening ability to pay bills that needs attention.

What does the balance sheet have to do with marketing? Marketing strategies determine the look of the balance sheet over time. As we shall see, high margin strategies build cash assets and good branding bolsters intangible assets.

The Statement of Cash Flows

The third major financial statement, the Statement of Cash Flows, is, in some senses, the most important report of all. This is where, as they say, the rubber hits the road. How much cash did the company bring in during the reporting period? Wait, you might be saying. Don't we already know that from the income statement. Oh, grasshopper, let us begin the lesson now.

The income statement is important, but the net earnings it reports are not the same as the actual cash flow (positive or negative) that occurred during that period. This discrepancy is the result of several factors. Depreciation, for instance, one of a company's (fixed) operating expenses, is not a cash expense. It helps reduce earnings for tax purposes, but it doesn't deplete the checking account. Alternatively, a capital investment, such as building a new production facility, may drain a huge amount of cash out of a business, yet appear nowhere on the income statement.

The Statement of Cash Flows pulls all of these transactions together and nets out the actual amount of cash entering or leaving the business during the period. As Table 2.3 shows, the statement starts with net income and then adds back depreciation of $553 million. Then, after subtracting another $1.5 billion in other operating costs, we arrive at a net cash flow from operations of $2.6 billion. The statement then factors in

Table 2.3   Coca-Cola cash flows

Condensed consolidated statements of cash flows	Six months ended	
(In millions)	6/29/2018	6/30/2017
Net income from continuing operations	3616	2556
Depreciation and amortization	553	629
Other	(1561)	157
Net cash provided by operating activities	2608	3342
Net cash provided by (used in) investing activities	2341	(1201)
Net cash provided by (used in) financing activities	(2890)	797
Other net cash provided (used) by business	(63)	199
Net increase (decrease) in cash, cash equivalents, restricted cash equivalents during the period	1996	3137
Cash, cash equivalents, restricted cash and restricted cash equivalents at beginning of period	6373	8850
Cash, cash equivalents, restricted cash and restricted cash equivalents at end of period	8369	11,987
Less: Restricted cash and restricted cash equivalents at end of period	394	269
Cash and cash equivalents at end of period	$7975	$11,718

Coca-Cola statement of cash flows for six months ending 6/29/2018

cash flows from investing and financing, which do not appear on the income statement, to reveal that Coke had a positive cash flow of $1.996 billion in the first six months of 2018.

Why does this cash flow figure matter so much? For investors, cash flow is the most accurate descriptor of a company's performance because it is relatively hard to manipulate. It is the bedrock truth of the company's financial reality. You can have great earnings, but if investment needs or other issues take away cash, that's a real problem for investors.

Cash flow is the basis for entity valuation, in broad terms. A company's valuation (Market Cap) is typically based on the present value of predicted future cash flows. There are many other factors that influence valuation, of course, but the present value of future cash flows is the main driver of valuation and thus stock prices. As a result, when investors predict that cash flows will either go down or stop growing, in the future, the stock price usually falls. So, in our case, if the price of sugar is projected to triple every year for the next decade, you will most likely see Coke's share price drop due to an expected decline in margins.

Here's how it works: cash received today is generally more highly valued than the same amount cash to be received in the future. This is known as the *time value of money*. One reason for this is that money in hand today can be invested at some interest rate, so that the amount grows over time. A dollar in hand today can become $1.10 in a year at an annual interest rate of 10%. This would be the *future value* of a dollar in a year. Alternatively, a dollar to be received a year in the future has a *present value* of 91 cents ($1 ÷ 1.10). Many projects and marketing activities have payoffs at different points in time. Future value and present value provide a means for comparing cash flows that are received on different time schedules. Thus, at a 10% interest rate, a marketing program that generates $100 in a year produces a financial return equivalent to a marketing program that immediately produces $91.

To compute the future value of an investment one needs to multiply the investment by the rate of return in each time period. Thus, if one invests $100 for three years at a 10% annual interest rate, the future value (FV) would be computed as

$$FV = \$100 \times 1.1 \times 1.1 \times 1.1 \text{ or } FV = \$100(1.1)^3 = \$133.1$$

The general form of the equation is $FV = C(r+1)^n$. Where C is the investment, r is the rate of return, and n is the number of periods of the investment.

Present value (PV) is computed by taking a dollar amount at some time in the future and discounting it by a rate of return for each time period between the present period and the future period in which the funds will be received.[1] Thus, when the annual rate of return is 10%, $100 that will be received in three years must be discounted by 10% each year to obtain the PV:

$$PV = 100 \div (1.1 \times 1.1 \times 1.1) \text{ or } 100 \div (1.1)^3 = \$75.13$$

The general form of the equation is $PV = C \div (r+1)^n$. Where C is the amount of money to be received at a future date, r is the rate of return, and n is the number of periods in the future before funds are received.

---

[1] Readers unfamiliar with the notion of discount rate may refer to Appendix at the end of this chapter for further discussion.

BUDGETING FOR MARKETING, WITH AN EYE ON CORPORATE FINANCE

Now that we have a basic understanding of finance and see the connection between cash flow and valuation (stock price), let's move over to the mechanics of how marketing affects these financial activities. Marketing initiatives and budgets arise from a process of planning and approval by senior management. Typically, in a large company, lines of business will submit marketing plans, including a budget and investment proposals for review, discussion, and (hopefully) a green light from senior management. Resources are limited, though, so management cannot approve everything. This section of the book discusses what goes into a successful marketing plan and budget.

The role of senior management is to determine the best set of actions and investments for the firm as a whole. Some of the marketing plans they receive may be for the launch of new products or the expansion of existing products into a new market. Other marketing plans may focus on maintaining current sales levels in the face of a declining market and intense competition.

These many marketing plans include many marketing goals: building product awareness, expanding distribution, product improvement through research and development, and so on. Such goals are necessary and laudable, but they pose a dilemma for decision makers: how to compare many marketing goals and select those that best serve the overall interests of the firm? This dilemma is resolved by creating a common metric, financial results, or, more specifically, the cash flow that each marketing plan is expected to generate.

In well-managed companies, senior management asks for presentations of marketing plans so that they can assess all of the opportunities and threats confronting the firm. Some marketing plans may focus on generating immediate profits from a mature product, while others may focus on the development of a new product in a new market that will not generate profits for several years. In effect, the marketing plans represent a portfolio of potential business investments. The role of senior management is to construct the most profitable portfolio possible from all of the plans presented. Marketing planners can assist senior managers in constructing this portfolio by framing marketing outcomes in financial terms.

The world is not static, so budgets cannot be static. Changes in demand, changes in competitors' behavior, innovations in technology, and costs can all change, sometimes with blinding speed. Well-constructed marketing plans include contingency plans, but potential changes in the environment are not always known or knowable. Even if change can be anticipated, the best response to change is not always apparent in advance. For this reason, well-managed companies, and the marketers who work for them, constantly scan the environment to identify changes that necessitate modification of marketing plans and changes in marketing budgets.

Some changes to which the firm needs to respond are highly localized. They may be specific to a particular market, country, or competitor. Or they may be the result of weather, natural or man-made disaster, or other local conditions. For this reason, in many companies, budgeting is decentralized so that the managers most familiar with the locale can respond quickly to changes in the local environment without going through a long centralized decision-making process. It is also the case that the evaluation of comprehensive marketing plans requires substantial time, effort, and money. It also tends to involve the most senior and most highly compensated managers in the firm. Thus, the amount of review and evaluation of changes in marketing plans and budgets needs to be consistent with what is at stake when making a change.

IT'S ABOUT CUSTOMERS

The process of evaluating marketing plans and budgets is complex, but in one sense, it's quite simple. It all starts with customers. How many can you get? Will they pay top dollar? Will they return and buy more? These are crucial drivers of cash flow that begin and end with marketing.

Successful businesses must have profitable customers. Marketing thus justifies actions that are designed to produce customers in terms of their contributions to the profitability of the firm. Marketing plans and planning are incomplete without specific linkages to financial results in both the short and long term.

Firms make enormous investments in product and market development, in building brands, in creating customer loyalty, in efficient ways to deliver products and services, and in communicating information about products and services to customers. Most of these investments are made with the expectation that these investments will generate cash flows and profits in the long term, as well as in the short term.

Such investments, investments expected to generate cash flows beyond the first year, meet the definition of a capital investment. Capital investment refers to funds **invested** in a business for the purpose of furthering business objectives.

Capital Budgeting

The process of planning and justifying such investments is commonly referred to as *capital budgeting*. Historically, capital budgeting resided in the financial function of the firm and in finance courses in business schools. The process focused on the firm's acquisition of *capital assets* or fixed assets such as manufacturing plants, service delivery systems, machinery, and other tangible assets that were expected to be productive over many years. That is, they were expected to contribute to the profitability of the business over a long time period.

The focus of capital budgeting on tangible assets certainly makes sense for a business. Plants, machinery, warehouses, and other fixed assets are often very expensive, and their utility is premised on their being complete. Unlike an advertising budget, which may be halved in a given quarter without losing the effect of the other half of the budget that is actually expended, there is little value in a half-completed manufacturing plant. In addition, for most of the industrial age, investments in tangible, or physical, assets have been the dominant investments of firms. A firm's value was determined largely by the value of its tangible assets. Thus, it is not surprising that most treatments of capital budgeting have focused on tangible assets.

The Role of Intangible Assets

The world has changed in dramatic fashion over the past several decades. Intangible assets now play a dominant role in the profitability and value of businesses. This change has altered the importance of the marketing, human resources, and sustainability functions of the firm. It has also necessitated the need for a change in marketing planning and budgeting. While many marketing expenditures are certainly intended to have an immediate effect, they also often are designed to produce longer term effects. Brand-building activities and expenditures may have an immediate effect, but the very definition of a brand implies long-term effects. Similarly, investments in customer satisfaction and customer loyalty are, by definition, intended to produce long-term effects.

Marketing, along with research and development and human resource management, is concerned with the creation and management of intangible assets. Intangible assets are assets that are not physical in nature. Physical assets include land, buildings, equipment, vehicles, and inventory. Intangible assets, in contrast, have no physical presence. For example, brand names, such as Coca-Cola, McDonald's, and IBM, are identifiers of companies and products that cannot be touched or held in hand. Nevertheless, these names have value because they influence consumers. Because they have value, they are assets. Firms possess numerous intangible assets.

Table 2.4 lists some examples of intangible assets. Many, but not all, intangible assets are created and managed by marketing. Creation and management of intangible assets require investment. One estimate of 2017 expenditures on just one component of overall marketing expenditures, marketing communications, placed this investment at more than $565 billion (Myers 2017).

Table 2.4   Examples of intangible assets

Brands	Research and development
Trademarks	Patents
Customer loyalty	Copyrights
Reputation	Intellectual property
Contracts	Proprietary processes
Licenses	Franchise rights
Customer lists	Human capital
Organizational models	Software

The size of such investments alone would suggest a need for careful planning by senior management. However, in recent decades the value of the intangible assets of firms has come to dwarf the value of tangible assets. Figure 2.1 illustrates the growth of the value of intangible assets as a percent of the value of the firm over the past 40 years. Under current accounting rules, intangible assets only show up on a firm's balance sheet if they are acquired. Nevertheless, with so much of the value of a firm driven by intangible assets, planning and budgeting should be done with as much care as capital budgeting for physical assets. Well-managed companies require that investment projects, including marketing activities, rest on a viable business model and a strong strategic plan that explicitly considers how marketing expenditures and activities contribute to the financial performance and long-term viability of the firm.

COMPONENTS *of* S&P 500 MARKET VALUE

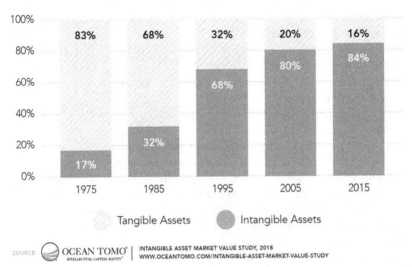

Fig. 2.1   Intangible assets as a percent of the value of firms. (Source: Ocean Tomo 2018)

THE MARKETING BUDGETING DECISION

In recent years, managers have become more sophisticated about the allocation of resources to marketing activities and more concerned about the return on such investments. The growing availability of data on response to marketing programs and the increasing use of analytical tools for the analysis of such data have increased managers' insistence on marketing accountability. As with any budgeting exercise, the ultimate goal of marketing budgeting exercises is maximization of the value of a business. Something is an "asset" only to the extent that it is used to generate cash. An investment in an asset, whether it be a tangible asset like a factory or an intangible asset like a brand, is justified only if it produces a positive return for the owners/shareholders of a business. For this reason, cash flow is the ultimate financial metric. Therefore, investments in marketing need to be justified in terms of cash flow.

Some marketing actions may create future opportunities, sometimes referred to as real options, which the firm may or may not pursue in the future. For example, the creation of a website to provide information to consumers also creates an option to sell directly to consumers through the website. A firm may or may not choose to exercise this new distribution option in the future, but it represents a distribution alternative that the firm would not otherwise have had if the website had not been created. Finally, some marketing expenditures and actions may create immediate results, long-term results, and real options. Figure 2.2 illustrates these three general classes of outcomes and provides examples of specific types of results within each class.

When evaluating the return on any marketing investment, it is important to consider the financial value of all the likely outcomes. Evaluation of only the immediate, or short-term, outcomes may undervalue the return on marketing. For example, empirical research has shown that in many markets, the long-term return on advertising, especially advertising designed to build brand or customer preference, is twice that of the short-term effect (Lodish et al. 1995). Thus, all of the objectives of marketing expenditures and actions should be clearly articulated. Marketing managers must demonstrate how success in achieving these outcomes will be translated into financial terms.

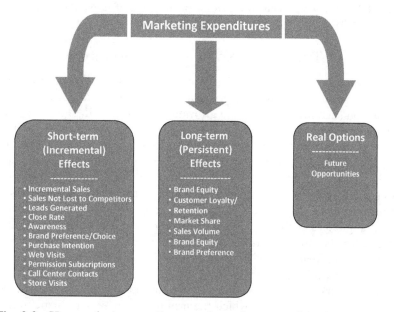

Fig. 2.2 How marketing contributes to the performance of the firm. (Adapted from Stewart 2009)

FACTORING FUTURE CASH FLOWS INTO MARKETING
BUDGETING/INVESTMENT DECISIONS

Marketing activities may have many outcomes. They may create product awareness, build brand loyalty, reinforce existing beliefs about a product, and have a host of other important effects. However, as we noted previously, from the perspective of financial performance, cash is king.

Marketing managers should justify every marketing expenditure and activity in terms of the cash flows they are expected to generate. Such justification requires assumptions, but this is no different than the assumptions required in justifying other types of investments. The decision to build a production facility generally is justified in terms of assumptions about future sales, competitors' actions, and costs and pricing, among other suppositions.

There is always some uncertainty associated with assumptions about the future. Projects and actions where there is greater uncertainty are riskier. The probability of success is lower because there are more unknowns that can affect the outcome. In general, higher risk investments should be expected to produce a greater return than lower risk investments, other things being equal. In other words, a willingness to take greater risk should be compensated for by a higher rate of return. Thus, it is important to evaluate risk and factor risk into marketing planning and budgeting. Chapter 9 of this book will examine approaches for managing risk and incorporating risk into financial performance metrics.

Evaluating the financial return on a marketing investment requires information about the investment required, the cash flow to be generated, the timing of the receipt of the cash, and the amount of risk (probability of success) associated with the marketing activity. Marketing activities differ considerably on these dimensions. This is why it is important to have a method for ensuring the comparability of the outcomes associated with alternative marketing actions. In finance, this method involves discounting uncertain future cash flows to reflect both risk and the time value of money. Subsequent chapters in this book will address approaches for estimating cash flows and for adjusting for the time value of money and the risk of failure.

There are some general principles that arise from these basic elements of financial analysis:

1. Marketing expenditures that have a positive return, that is, a net present value of future cash flows, greater than the investment should be given consideration for action, while marketing expenditures that have a negative return should be rejected.
2. When deciding between two or more alternative actions using the same resources, the actions with the highest risk-adjusted net present value should be given priority. This means:

   (a) Greater weight should be placed on marketing actions that produce cash flows earlier in time;
   (b) All inflows and outflows of cash associated with the marketing action must be a part of the analysis; and
   (c) Other things being equal, riskier marketing actions, for example, those with a lower probability of success, are less desirable.

Some Simple Formulas to Guide Planning

Budgets do not exist in isolation. Marketing expenditures "buy" something that is intended to achieve some objective. For example, the launch of a new product may require expenditures for advertising to build product awareness and trial; without awareness and trial there are no long-term customers. The same new product launch may require incentives to retailers to motivate them to stock the product; consumers do not purchase products they cannot obtain. In such circumstances, marketing budgets should be driven by sales forecasts. These forecasts would consider how product awareness, trial, and distribution influence initial sales, repeat purchases, and cash flow. Indeed, an important equation for predicting marketing success is

$$\text{Market Share} = \left(\% \, \text{aware} \times \% \, \text{available} \times \% \, \text{choosing the product} \right)$$

Stated simply, the expected market share of a product is a function of how many customers in the relevant market are aware of the product (influenced by such marketing communications decisions as advertising and personal selling), how many consumers can obtain the product (influenced by the availability of the product through distribution channels), and choice (influenced by the benefits and quality of the product and its price relative to potential substitutes). Combined with data on the size of the market as a whole, which is often easily obtained from Census data or surveys of consumers, it is not difficult to create a forecast of sales:

$$\text{Sales Volume in Units} = \text{Size of Market in Units} \times \text{Market Share}$$

Knowledge of sales volume can be readily translated to financial performance by multiplying the sales volume in units times the selling price of the product. This computation can become complex when a product sells for different prices in the market because of discounts, add-on features, differential delivery charges, or other product characteristics that may alter the actual selling price. Such complexity, which is often worth exploring in its own right, is often simplified by using the average selling price per unit:

$$\text{Sales Revenue} = \text{Sales Volume in Units} \times \text{Average Selling Price Per Unit}$$

THE MARKETING BUDGETING PROCESS

The marketing budgeting process typically begins with an analysis of forecasts of general market demand based on general demographic, economic, and social trends. Although an individual firm's product or service sales are usually only a fraction of all sales in a product category, it is helpful to know whether overall demand is increasing, declining, or remaining stable. Marketing actions in a growth market are typically quite different from activities in declining or stagnant markets. Growing markets often require expenditures to build product awareness among customers entering the market for the first time and for expanding the availability of the products through new distribution channels. In contrast, a declining market may suggest the need to cut back on marketing expenditures or focus on taking customers away from competitors.

Information about aggregate market demand is then put together with market research and competitive intelligence to assess the opportunities and threats faced by the firm. An assessment of these opportunities and threats then gives rise to the setting of priorities and the identification of potential marketing actions. The effects of these actions on sales and contribution, along with the costs of the marketing activities involving sales forecasts, are then identified and forecasts of sales and contribution margins computed. There may be several alternative marketing actions, and these must be compared and evaluated. This is usually an iterative process and often involves input from key marketing partners such as advertising agencies, distributors, and retailers.

Types of Marketing Plans and Budgets

In a now classic *Harvard Business Review* article, Ansoff (1957) identified four strategies for business growth. These four strategies also identify four basic types of marketing plans and the types of investments and activities associated with each. The strategies are defined by whether the focus is on new or existing products and new or existing markets.

Market Penetration Strategy

When a firm focuses on selling its current products to existing customers, it is pursuing a market penetration strategy. The marketing activities that will dominate in this type of marketing plan are those that emphasize increasing the loyalty of existing customers so that they are not vulnerable to loss to competitors, attracting competitors' customers, increasing the frequency of product use, and converting nonusers into users.

Increasing awareness through marketing communications and increasing availability through expanded distribution are common marketing activities in this type of plan. Identifying new use occasions and new uses for a product may increase usage frequency or convert current nonusers into users. For example, the advertising campaign for orange juice that has the tagline "It's not just for breakfast anymore" was an effort to expand usage. Price promotions might be used to encourage competitors' customers to try the firm's product if there is reason to believe that such a trial will result in repeat purchases. Loyalty programs can be very effective in retaining existing customers. This strategy reduces risk by relying on what the firm already knows well—its existing products and existing customers. It is also a strategy where investments in marketing should pay back more quickly because the firm is building on an existing foundation of customer relationships and product knowledge. Customer acquisition and retention is one of the key elements in revenue generation, a topic that will be explored in greater detail in Chaps. 4 and 8.

Market Development Strategy

The efforts to expand sales by selling current products in new markets are referred to as a market development strategy. Such efforts may involve entering new geographic markets, such as international markets. Creating product awareness and developing distribution channels are key marketing activities. Some product modification may be required to better match the needs of the local market. For example, as fast food restaurants have moved into international markets, they have often changed their menus to better match the food preferences of customers in local markets. Expanding into a new market with an existing product carries some risk because the new market is not well known to the firm and the firm and its products are not well known in the market. The return on marketing investments in such a strategy is likely to be longer than for a market penetration strategy because of the time required to build awareness, distribution, and product trial.

Product Development Strategy

Creating new products to sell to existing customers, a product development strategy, is a common marketing strategy among firms that can leverage their relationships with existing customers. For example, American Express has been able to leverage its relationships with its credit card customers to also sell travel-related services. Similarly, cable television companies have expanded their offerings into Internet and telephone services. Research and development activities play a dominant role in this strategy. The time required to develop and test new products may be long, but once a product is developed, creating awareness, interest, and availability should be relatively rapid because the firm already has a relationship with customers. A product development strategy is also riskier than a market penetration strategy because the necessary product may not be possible to develop, at least at a cost acceptable to customers, or the product developed does not match the needs of customers.

Diversification Strategy

A diversification strategy involves taking new products into new markets. This is really the creation of a completely new business. This is the riskiest of strategies and the strategy likely to require the most patience in waiting for a return on investment. There are circumstances when this strategy makes sense, and subsequent chapters will explore these circumstances.

MARKET AND PRODUCT INTERACTIONS

In many marketing planning and budgeting situations, the marketing activities for one product or service may have implications for other products and services. For example, the ability to obtain shelf space at retail for one product may be dependent on the marketer being able to provide a whole line of products. Similarly, advertising and promotion for an umbrella brand or corporate brand may influence customers' awareness, perceptions, and purchase intentions with respect to multiple products sold under the same brand. Thus, in thinking about marketing planning and budgeting it is important to recognize when such interactions exist and plan accordingly.

There are three general classes of marketing plans. There are independent plans. These are plans where the outcomes of one plan do not influence others and decisions to accept, reject, or modify the plan do not influence the plans for other product and service offerings. For example, a firm may wish to heavily advertise one product while engaging in significant price discounting for another product in a different category. If there is no influence of the advertising on the non-advertised product and no influence of price discounting of the product on the advertised product, the firm could execute both plans, only one plan, or neither of these plans because they have no relation to one another.

In contrast, in the face of limited resources or conflicting objectives, a firm might find that two plans are mutually exclusive. For example, a firm may need to decide between launching a new product and investing in existing products. In offering exclusive distribution for a product to a retailer, the firm's selection of one retailer forecloses the opportunities with other retailers. A firm may need to select from two different advertising campaigns for a product. In the face of such mutually exclusive alternatives it is important for the firm to make a studied comparison using common metrics for evaluation. Such common metrics frequently involve financial metrics such as the net present value of the alternative marketing investments.

Finally, as noted above, there are many circumstances in which the marketing plans, activities, and budgets for one product influence market and financial outcomes of other products. Such interactions are especially common in multiproduct companies where the products share production capacity, distribution, and/or advertising support. A special case of such interactions is the contingency plan. Generally, a contingency plan is one whose acceptance depends on the implementation of another plan. For example, a plan to provide more support for the retail trade may be contingent on the decision to launch a new product. Chapter 10 of this book will focus on the unique issues that arise when managing a portfolio of products and when dealing with contingent plans.

CONCLUSION

This chapter introduced the general topic of marketing planning and budgeting and has suggested that the processes, tools, and metrics commonly employed in traditional capital budgeting exercises be extended to marketing. Such a recommendation is not only logical, it is imperative in light of the contributions of intangible assets to the value of the firm. Because marketing plays a significant, and often determinant, role in the creation and management of intangible assets, it is critical that marketing planning and budgeting be done with the same care and be based on the same standards that have long governed capital budgeting exercises involving tangible assets. The ultimate goal of marketing budgeting is to maximize the market value of the firm. This means that marketing plans, activities, and budgets must be translated into the cash flows they are expected to generate. Because different plans and activities produce cash at different points in time and carry different risks, future cash flows should be discounted. Plans that are riskier and that are expected to produce cash flows that are more distant in the future should be discounted more heavily than less risky plans and those that will produce more immediate cash flows.

Exercises

1. Pick any business. Identify the major tangible and intangible assets of the business. How would you place a value on the tangible assets? How would you place a value on the intangible assets?
2. Compute the future value of a $1,000,000 investment after five years with an annual rate of return of 8%.
3. Compute the net present value of $1,000,000 that will be received in five years with an annual rate of return of 8%.

Points to Ponder

1. Why have intangible assets come to dominate the value of firms in recent years? What does this dominance of intangible assets imply about managing a business? Would management be different for a firm dominated by tangible assets?
2. How does marketing contribute to the creation and maintenance of intangible assets? How would you measure the value of an intangible asset?

APPENDIX: A PRIMER ON DISCOUNT RATES

Throughout this chapter there has been reference to discount rates. For readers who have been exposed to financial management, this discussion is likely to be quite clear. This brief appendix is for readers who have had little exposure to finance.

A simple way to think of the discount rate is as interest the firm incurs to borrow funds. For example, if a small business went to the bank and obtained a loan for the business, the interest rate it pays on the loan would be the discount rate. Obviously, a firm wants a return on the funds it borrows that is larger than the interest rate.

More generally, the discount rate is the firm's "cost of capital" or cost to obtain and use money. The cost to obtain and use someone else's money can be the interest paid for a loan or the return expected by shareholders, or any of numerous other sources of funds. When the cost of the money across all of the sources is weighted to reflect the proportion of total funds from each source and then averaged, the firm obtains its *weighted average cost of capital*.

In reality, the definition of the cost of capital and associated discount rate can be even more complex because another way to think about the cost of capital is in terms of rate of return a firm might expect from other ways of using its own money. For example, Amazon has rarely ever reported a profit because its strategy is to put all earnings back into growing the company. It would be naive and imprudent for Amazon to set its discount rate at zero because it is using its own money. Rather, the discount rate reflects the return Amazon thinks it can generally obtain from its investments in future growth. At minimum, it could just put its money in the bank and draw some interest. In mid-2018, it could buy ten-year U.S. Treasury bonds, guaranteed by the U.S. government and obtain a guaranteed rate of return of about a 2.5% return for ten years. Because this return is guaranteed by the government it is often referred to as the "risk-free rate," that is, the firm has to take virtually no risk and not even undertake much work to obtain this rate.

Well-managed companies expect to be able to earn more than the risk-free rate. Firms generally have some idea of what they currently earn on their investments and what their average return is. Therefore, when they think about the cost of money, they often think in terms of the return the same funds could earn if invested in other ways, or, for convenience, an average return on investment. This is called the opportunity cost of capital because using capital in one way precludes its use to pursue other opportunities. Many firms use the perceived opportunity cost of capital as the discount rate.

Discount rates are often standard across a company and frequently do not change much over time. This makes things simple and computations using it very easy. However, as will be explored in Chap. 9, different activities in a firm—different products, different technologies, different market—often differ in how risky they are. Return and the discount rate should reflect this risk such that the riskier projects should yield more than less risky projects to compensate for the risk. Chapter 9 will explore this risk-return relationship in greater detail.

Because firms differ, their costs of capital, and hence discount rates, should differ. In larger firms, the discount rates among divisions and business units will often differ as well. An unproven start-up firm, which represents a risky venture will have a higher cost of capital and associated discount rate than a very mature company with stable cash flows. Aside from these rather general relationships between risk and return, and the level of interest rates in general, there is no specific formula for determining the "right" discount rate. Establishing the discount rate and adjusting it to reflect relative risk is a subjective exercise. Marketers need to understand that firms recognize the costs of capital and incorporate these costs in their planning. The discount rate is the way this is done in practice.

References

Ansoff, I. (1957). Strategies for Diversification. *Harvard Business Review, 35*, 113–124.

Lodish, L., Abraham, M. M., Livelsberger, J., Lubetkin, B., Richardson, B., & Stevens, M. E. (1995). A Summary of Fifty-Five in-Market Experimental Estimates of the Long-Term Effect of TV Advertising. *Marketing Science, 14*(3) (Part 2 of 2), G133–G140.

Myers, J. (2017). *2017: A Down Year in the Marketing Economy.* Our 25th Annual U.S. Advertising and Marketing Expenditures Report. https://www.mediavillage.com/article/2017-a-down-year-in-the-marketing-economy-our-25th-annual-us-advertising-marketing-expenditures-report/

Ocean Tomo, LLC. (2018, March 15). *Annual Study of Intangible Asset Market Value from Ocean Tomo.* http://www.oceantomo.com//2015/03/04/2015-intangible-asset-market-value-study/

Stewart, D. W. (2009). Marketing Accountability: Linking Marketing Actions to Financial Results. *Journal of Business Research, 62*(June), 636–643.

Business Models: How Firms Make Money

Chapters 1 and 2 introduced the importance of translating marketing outcomes into financial outcomes. More specifically, the chapter argued that the cash flows generated by or expected to be generated by marketing activities should be the measures of marketing performance. Such cash flows need to be appropriately discounted to reflect the time value of money and the relative risk of success or failure. This chapter focuses on how businesses make money. At the most general level of conceptualization, the way a firm makes money is its business model. Marketing plans, activities, and budgets should support the firm's underlying business model.

WHAT IS A BUSINESS MODEL?

A firm's business model describes how it makes money from its operations. A business model is the story about how a business works and how all of its activities come together to produce a profit. In its simplest form a business model could be defined as a producer who makes something that they sell directly to a customer at a profit.

Coke's business model, for example, is that of a manufacturer. It buys low-cost inputs like corn syrup and aluminum and produces and sells a valuable product made from them using proprietary techniques. Netflix has a subscription business model. LinkedIn is a "freemium" business model, and so forth. In many cases, the business model is quite obvious and evident. Other times, it is not so obvious and that can lead to trouble.

© The Author(s) 2019   33
D. W. Stewart, *Financial Dimensions of Marketing Decisions*,
Palgrave Studies in Marketing, Organizations and Society,
https://doi.org/10.1007/978-3-030-15565-0_3

If a firm does not possess a viable business model, it cannot be a successful business in the long run. Many firms are able to raise start-up capital and investment, sometimes on repeated occasions, but over time the operations of the business must generate a profit and provide a return on investment. What the firm produces and sells and how production and selling are done must eventually produce a profit.

Ventures flounder when managers have not identified or don't understand the underlying business model (or when there is no business model at all). This may sound silly, but it happens all the time. For instance, if you are operating a retail business using the "low-touch" model, as is the case with Ikea or Walmart, then you make money by selling many products at low prices, accompanied by minimal customer service and retail support. If you hired people to be "high-touch" sales people in a low-touch model, you would quickly go broke.

Unpacking a "Simple" Business Model

Let's examine the seemingly simple business model of a farmer who grows vegetables and sells them directly to consumers from a roadside stand. This stands in contrast to the traditional farm business model of selling crops in bulk to commodity buyers. Closer examination reveals that even this simple model is quite complex.

To be successful, the farmer must have customers who value and will pay for what he produces. This raises the question of what the farmer should produce. What's the most profitable: tomatoes, beans, milk, beef, or something else? What are customers willing to pay for different items? What the farmer decides to grow has implications for resources and activities that are required for production and sales, as well as questions about how to obtain these resources and carry out these activities. Growing tomatoes is very different from raising dairy cows.

Whatever the farmer decides to produce, he must decide how to organize the production process. The farmer could attempt to do everything himself or hire others to carry out some of the necessary activities. The farmer could buy land or lease it from someone else. Of course, resources and activities have costs, so the farmer must consider both what costs to incur and how these costs compare to what customers value and are willing to pay. To be financially successful the price customers are willing to pay the farmer must exceed the farmer's costs. Finally, the farmer must consider how he will keep customers coming back over time and why customers will purchase his products rather than those of other farmers.

The story of the farmer can be applied to any business, and that story is the business model. Many businesses are far more complex than that of the farmer, which makes analysis of the business model more difficult. Firms often serve different types of customers with different products or services. Different types of customers may differ in what they value and how much they are willing to pay. Different products and services may have different cost structures.

Firms may, in fact, be composed of many different businesses with different business models. For example, Disney makes movies, operates theme parks, manages broadcast and cable television networks, runs a cruise line, and licenses and sells various consumer products, among other businesses. These businesses have different business models; they make money in different ways.

Managers often lose sight of a firm's business model as they attend to day-to-day activities. Operations worries about production quotas and/or service delivery; sales focuses on making sales; marketing works on branding; human resources hires and trains personnel; and so forth. Nevertheless, the success of a business, or any organization, and effective long-term planning for the business require an understanding of how the various activities and resources of the firm and its partners are organized and managed.

THE VALUE CHAIN

The collection of activities and resources required for a business to deliver something of value to a customer is commonly referred to as the **value chain** (Porter 1985). Some of these resources and activities may exist within a single firm. Often, though, some also exist outside of any one firm. For example, a manufacturer may produce a product but partner with a retailer to distribute the product to consumers. The manufacturer and retailer are different companies, different businesses with different business models. But, they are part of the same value chain if they serve the same end-user customer. Frequently, the value chain is illustrated as a linear chain of organizations that perform specific types of activities, as shown in Fig. 3.1.

A more useful way to think about the value chain is as sets of activities that add value for the end customer, that is, increases what a customer will

Fig. 3.1   The value chain

pay for a product or service and carry some cost. Thus, the value chain can be conceptualized as two equations, a revenue equation and a cost equation, as illustrated in Fig. 3.2. Each activity can be conceptualized in terms of its added value, the incremental revenue it will generate, and the costs associated with the activity. When illustrated in this form the elements and story of the business model emerges.

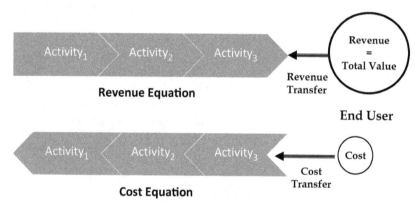

Fig. 3.2   The revenue and cost chains

ELEMENTS OF A BUSINESS MODEL

Every business model has four elements: (1) the served market, (2) a structure for organizing all of the activities and resources necessary for addressing the served market, (3) a method for generating revenue from the served market, and (4) a means for sustaining the revenue stream over time. This last one refers to a way to keep members of the served market coming back to make more purchases. Every element revolves around the customers in the served market. This is the reason a deep understanding of customers is necessary for identifying and implementing a successful business model.

The Served Market

At the heart of any successful business model is a set of customers who value and will pay for something the firm has to offer. This is the served market. The business model, and the business itself, should be defined by a statement of the value provided by the product or service offering of the firm. This statement is the *value proposition*. A value proposition describes how a product or service solves problems or provides benefits for a specific group of customers. When described in this way, the value proposition identifies the served market in terms that customers can understand, evaluate, and place a value on. In other words, the value proposition states who will buy the firm's offering and how much these customers should be willing to pay. It also defines the size of the market—how many customers need to buy the firm's offering and are willing to pay a given price.

A value proposition is not an advertising slogan or a technical description of the product or service. It is a statement of who is it that values the firm's offering and what they value about it. Few businesses, if any, can serve everyone profitably because customers differ. Some customers have a specific need while others do not have this need. Parents with infants need diapers; most other consumers do not. People who own pets buy pet food; people who do not own pets are unlikely to do so. Some customers value customization, and they will pay for it. Other customers desire a simple product that works and want to pay the least amount possible to obtain a basic benefit. The value proposition defines the business in terms of an explicit set of customers who are purchasing for a specific reason and at a specific price. Thus, the value proposition answers an important strategic question: which customers will the firm serve? Table 3.1 provides some examples of value propositions.

Table 3.1 Examples of value propositions

Company	Value proposition
BMW	"The Ultimate Driving Machine"
Dollar Shave Club	"A Great Shave for a Few Bucks a Month"
Intuit	"Simplify the Business of Life"
Lyft	"A Ride in Minutes"
Netflix	"Watch Anywhere, Cancel Anytime"
Ritz	"Ladies and Gentlemen Serving Ladies and Gentlemen"
Target	"Expect More, Pay Less"
Zillow	"Find Your Way Home"

An Organizing Structure

Once the served market and value proposition have been defined, it is possible to identify all of the activities and resources required to serve the market and deliver the promised value. These activities and resources also define the cost of serving customers. Most organizations do not try to provide all of these activities and resources themselves. One reason is that specialization is frequently more efficient than doing all things. Thus, a firm that is very good at manufacturing may focus on this function while partnering with retailers to distribute products to consumers.

A firm that seeks to do everything required to deliver value would be completely *vertically integrated*. For example, a firm selling shoes to consumers would be vertically integrated if it owned and managed the farm on which cows were raised for leather, the tannery, the fashion design house, the shoe manufacturer, and the retailer who sells the shoes to the end user. These various organizations engage in very different activities and the skills required to efficiently complete each activity are quite different. A firm might choose to focus its own talent and resources on design and manufacturing, while partnering with other firms that supply leather on the one hand and distribute and sell shoes to the consumer on the other. For example, the fashion company Benetton has historically focused on design and branding while partnering with other firms who do manufacturing and distribution (Camuffo et al. 2001).

If an activity or resource is necessary for providing value to a customer, it must occur or be obtained. The question is how to do so: what activities will the firm do itself and which activities will it outsource to other firms? If some activities are to be outsourced, which alternatives are the best partners, and how will the relationship(s) with these partners to be managed? Embedded within these questions are issues related to how revenue and costs will be divided among all of the partners in the value chain. Also included within the scope of these questions are issues related to assuring the reliability and quality of whatever activities are carried out by partners.

The organization and management of the value chain is associated with a second strategic question for the firm: on which activities will the firm focus and which activities will be delegated to partners in the value chain? In other words, where in the value chain will the firm focus? The answer to this question has implications for both revenue generation and costs.

Revenue Generation

The third element of a business model is the means by which the firm will generate revenue. This is not just about the price to be charged; it is also about how the price will be charged. For example, Apple sells music by the song or album that customers pay for and download to their computers or phones. Apple also sells a music subscription service that provides unlimited access to streaming music for a monthly fee. The benefit to the consumer, the ability to listen to music, is virtually identical, but the way the benefit is delivered to the consumer and the way the consumer is charged differ.

Consumers often differ in their preferences for payment or even in their ability to pay in a particular manner. For example, the cost of purchasing early Xerox machines was prohibitive for many organizations. To make acquisition more affordable, Xerox offered an option for a monthly lease and per copy charges (Brooks 2014). Similarly, Honeywell made it possible for school districts to complete energy retrofitting of buildings by creating a pricing structure that allowed schools to fund facility improvements through the energy and operating savings the upgrades produced. Honeywell even guaranteed the savings so the work did not impact school budgets.

Pricing and pricing strategy are also strategic decisions. They influence how and when the firm realizes revenue and can even change the economics of key elements of a business. In the Xerox example, ink is a cost, because the charge is per page. In contrast, for Hewlett Packard, ink is a major source of revenue, because users must pay for the ink they use. The benefit to the end user is the same, printed ink on a page, but the revenue generation strategy changes the cost in one context, Xerox, to a source of revenue in another context, Hewlett Packard.

Sustainability

Most businesses are not content to make one sale, even at a profit. Rather, firms look for ways to sustain their revenue stream over time by attracting new customers and by repeating sales to existing customers. This means delivering the promised value, or benefit, to the customer and doing so in a way that avoids loss of customers to competitors. In the face of competition firms must find ways to differentiate themselves in meaningful ways that are not easily duplicated. Such differentiation might take the form of superior quality or service, lower price, or greater convenience, but service, price, and convenience are relatively easy for competitors to copy unless there is some other advantage. For example, the firm with the lowest cost structure has an advantage when competing on price because it can make a profit at a lower selling price than any of its competitors.

Sources of differentiation that contribute to the sustainability of a firm's revenue stream often take the form of intellectual property such as patents, copyrights, and brands or relationships with customers that create loyalty. Indeed, part of the power and value of a brand is that it is both protected by law and defines a relationship with a customer. Ideally, the source of differentiation is in itself valued by the customer, so that the customer will not only purchase but also pay a premium over an undifferentiated competitor. (Remember "no frills" cola? Yeah, me neither.)

It is important to appreciate the fact that business models are successful and sustainable in a context. A business model that is or was successful at one point in time or in one market may not be successful at a different point in time or in a different market. Kodak was a very successful company for more than 100 years before filing for bankruptcy in 2012. Its success was based on a business model that involved selling inexpensive cameras that used consumables, like film, paper, and chemicals, which were sold at high margins. In the mid-1970s, Kodak sold 90% of the film and 85% of the cameras in the United States (Lucas 2012).

Unfortunately, Kodak was unable to successfully change its business model in the face of digital technologies that reduced the demand for film. Similarly, Disney's business model for its highly successful amusement park operations in the United States did not translate well into the European market because European consumers are different from American consumers (Spencer 1995). These two high-profile examples, and countless others, serve as a reminder of the importance of regularly revisiting the underlying assumptions of a business and of the need to be vigilant in identifying threats to the sustainability of the model.

There is also a broader dimension to sustainability that focuses on the broader role of resource availability. The very successful whaling industry in the first half of the nineteenth century ultimately proved unsustainable as a result of overfishing and the resulting decline of the whale population. Henry Ford's decision to pay his workers higher wages helped expand the market for automobiles, thereby contributing to the success of his business. Chapter 12 of this book will examine some of the issues related to the larger issues of the planet and people in the sustainability of business models.

FINANCIAL DIMENSIONS OF BUSINESS MODELS

Business models can take many forms and can range from simple to complex, but they must ultimately define a sustainable way to make a profit. This definition requires a compelling and cohesive story about how the business works and a quantitative financial analysis that demonstrates the economic viability of the business over the long term. A useful conceptual tool for describing how business models are linked to financial performance is the DuPont model (van den Berg and Pietersma 2015). Developed by F. Donaldson Brown for the DuPont Corporation in 1919, the model helps analyze the relationships among key activities of the firm and financial metrics, at least at a very high level of conceptualization. The Dupont model is built on three factors that contribute to revenue: *profit margins*, *velocity* (or asset turnover), and asset *leverage*.

Margin

As discussed in Chap. 2, *margin* is simply the ratio of the profit on sales and total sales revenue. It is computed as

$$\text{Profit Per Unit }(\$) = \text{Sales Price }(\$) - \text{Cost of Production }(\$)$$

$$\text{Total Profits }(\$) = \text{Profit Per Unit }(\$) \times \text{Number of Units Sold}$$

$$\text{Total Sales Revenue }(\$) = \text{Sales Price }(\$) \times \text{Number of Units Sold}$$

$$\text{Profit Margin }(\%) = \text{Total Profits }(\$) \div \text{Total Sales Revenue }(\$)$$

The size of profit margins reflects the value customers place on the product of service. Such value judgments may rest on product quality or convenience or on such intangible assets as patented innovations or brand reputation.

Velocity

Velocity (or asset turnover) is associated with how many sales occur in a specified time period, usually how many times a company turns over the value of its inventory in a year. It is computed as the ratio of sales revenue and the value of assets devoted to the business. Assets include cash, accounts receivable, property and equipment, inventory, and other things the firm owns or controls. It is computed as

$$\text{Velocity} = \text{Total Sales Revenue} \div \text{Assets}$$

Intangible assets may also contribute to velocity. For example, business processes, which may or may not be patented, may enable a firm to be more efficient in producing, delivering, and selling its products or services. This is important to remember in businesses with numerous intangible assets, because intangible assets are rarely accounted for in the analysis of velocity.

While both margins and velocity influence the profitability of a business, some business models are more heavily influenced by margins, while others are more heavily influenced by velocity. For example, Apple's margin is about 21% (Wieczner 2017). In contrast, Walmart's margin is less than 2% (Gurufocus 2018). However, Walmart is able to turn over its inventory, a substantial portion of its tangible assets, more than eight times per year. Thus, it is effectively obtaining its 2% margin eight times each year. Companies with large margins, like Apple, operate business models that emphasize innovation, customization, fashion, and other activities for which customers will pay a premium price. In contrast, companies like Walmart focus on making many sales quickly through such activities as distribution, inventory assortment and control, transportation and logistics, and other activities that efficiently move large numbers of product from producers to buyers.

Return on Assets (ROA)

Margin and velocity can be used to compute a common accounting metric, return on assets (ROA):

$$\text{ROA} = \left(\text{Total Profits} \div \text{Total Sales Revenue}\right) \times \left(\text{Total Sales Revenue} \div \text{Assets}\right)$$
$$= \text{Total Profits} \div \text{Assets}$$

ROA is often used as an indicator of how efficient a company is at using assets to generate earnings. ROA is a measure of how well a business can generate earnings from invested capital (assets). ROA can vary substantially from company to company and is highly dependent on the industry.

Leverage

Some business models enable a business to multiply earnings on assets by using someone else's assets to generate earnings. This is leverage. While leverage is most often thought of in terms of financial assets, that is, borrowing money, it may also apply to the assets of the firm. For example, when Disney introduces a new character in a movie, it often licenses the rights to make toys featuring the character to other companies. These other companies use their own assets, production facilities, distribution networks, and so on to produce and sell the toys while paying Disney a licensing fee. In effect, Disney uses someone else's assets to make money. Note that the source of this leverage, a copyrighted character, is an intangible asset. This is the third factor in the Dupont model, a measure of leverage or an equity multiplier:

$$\text{Leverage} = \text{Total Assets} \div \text{Equity}$$

Where total assets are all of the assets involved in the business and equity represents the assets actually owned by or invested in by the firm.

Another way to obtain leverage is to borrow money to invest in additional assets. Financial leverage obtained through borrowing can also increase return on investment and may have some tax advantages, but it also creates a liability and risk, because lenders expect to be repaid. In contrast, leveraging an asset such as a movie character, a piece of music, a brand, or other property through licensing arrangements can create leverage without the financial risk associated with a loan. Similarly, most franchising models involve an effort to create leverage by using the assets of the franchisee.

Thus, the Dupont model consists of three terms: margin, velocity, and leverage:

$$\text{Profit margin} \times \text{Velocity} \times \text{Leverage} = (\text{Profit} / \text{Sales Revenue})$$
$$\times (\text{Sales Revenue} / \text{Total assets})$$
$$\times (\text{Total assets} / \text{Equity})$$

Canceling terms in the equation produces another useful indicator of the health of a business, return on equity (ROE):

$$\text{ROE} = \text{Profits} \div \text{Equity}$$

Return on Equity (ROE)

ROE expresses the income earned by a business as a percentage of owners'/ shareholders' equity. ROE measures how efficient a business is by revealing how much profit the company generates with the equity invested in it.

In addition to providing useful measures of the effectiveness and efficiency of a business, the Dupont model also identifies three generic business models: (1) one dominated by margins, (2) one dominated by velocity and (3) one dominated by leverage. While most businesses include all three components of the model, it is usually the case that one element is the most critical factor in generating profits for a business. There are, of course, many business models but at the heart of all are the three components of the DuPont model. In planning marketing actions, it is important to link these actions, and investments in them, to the ability to generate margin, increase velocity, or improve leverage and thereby improve return on investment. Chapters 4 and 6 will explore the linkages of marketing actions to financial results in detail.

Types of Business Models

There are many forms of business and many types of business models. Two firms in the same business can be based on quite different business models, as the comparison of Xerox to Hewlett Packard makes clear. Firms may be successful in competing against firms by using a superior business model or by executing the same business model in a superior manner. Competitive strategy should always be informed by knowledge of competitors' business models and the economic implications of these models. Success in serving a market is not just about being better in executing the same model. Success can also grow from being different—employing a different business model from the ones used by competitors.

It is also important to recognize that the business model is part of the offering to customers. Customers not only have preferences for products and services; they also have preferences for the way(s) in which they wish to shop and do business. Some customers prefer to purchase products online, while others prefer shopping in a bricks and mortar store. Some customers prefer to buy online and pick up the product at a retailer, while others prefer to shop at retail stores and buy online for home delivery. Indeed, the same customer may prefer to purchase some products online while preferring to purchase other products in a retail store. Thus, a business model defines not only how a firm makes money but also the business itself.

There are numerous lists and descriptions of business models. Table 3.2 provides one such list. The examples identified in the table are largely successful businesses. There are, of course, many other models, and there are

Table 3.2 Examples of business models

Business model	How it operates	An example
Brokerage	Match buyers and sellers and charge a fee to one or both parties	Real estate broker
Direct sales	Selling a product directly to a customer for a fee or commission	Tupperware
Razor/ blades	Provide a high-margin product at a low cost in order to obtain recurring future sales of necessary supplies	Printer and ink cartridges
Freemium	Give away a basic service; charge for premium services	LinkedIn
Subscription	Charges a fixed fee for access to a product or service	Magazines
Leasing	Rent rather than sell access to a product or service	Automobile leasing
Project work	Sell a completed project as a unit at a fixed price	Home remodeling

also many examples of firms using one of the business models identified in the table that have not been successful. Execution matters. Nevertheless, every successful business must be based on a viable business model and every marketing action should be justified in terms of how it supports the business model.

CONCLUSION

This chapter has introduced the concept of a business model, that is, the means by which a firm makes money from its operations. A business model is characterized by four elements: (1) the served market, (2) the means for revenue generation, (3) the way the value chain is organized, and (4) the means by which the business model will be sustained over time. Different business models have different implications for marketing activities and budgets and it is critical to the success of a business that marketing activities are consistent with and supportive of the underlying business model.

Exercises

1. Assume that you were given a cow. List all of the ways one could make money from owning this asset. Pick one of these ways to make money. State the value proposition and identify the business model: (1) what market would you serve?, (2) how would you generate

revenue?, (3) what activities, resources, and partners would be required to generate revenue?, and (4) how would you sustain the business over time? What are the costs of owning a cow? Is it an asset or a liability if you cannot make money using it?

2. Select one of the business models in Table 3.2. Analyze the business model: (1) what market is served?, (2) how is revenue generated?, (3) what activities, resources, and partners are required to generate revenue?, and (4) how has the business sustained itself over time?

Points to Ponder

1. Why is it important that the served market be clearly identified by a business? What are the consequences of not identifying the served market or of defining it very broadly?

2. Why is it important for a firm to think about the value chain in which it participates rather than focus only on its own business activities? Can different businesses in the same value chain have different business models?

3. Consider the proposition that the revenues and costs generated by a value chain do not need to be divided up equally among all participants in the value chain. In fact, revenues and costs do not need to be divided in the same way. What are the implications of this observation for the organization and sustainability of a value chain?

References

Brooks, J. (2014). Xerox, Xerox, Xerox, Xerox. In *Business Adventures* (pp. 166–200). New York: Open Road Media.

Camuffo, A., Romano, P., & Vinelli, A. (2001). Back to the Future: Benetton Transforms Its Global Network. *Sloan Management Review, 43*(1), 46–52.

Gurufocus. (2018). https://www.gurufocus.com/term/netmargin/WMT/Net-Margin-Percentage/Walmart%20Inc

Lucas, H. C. (2012). *The Search for Survival: Lessons from Disruptive Technologies.* Santa Barbara: ABC-CLIO.

Porter, M. E. (1985). *Competitive Advantage: Creating and Sustaining Superior Performance.* New York: Simon and Schuster.

Spencer, E. P. (1995). Educator Insights: Euro Disney—What Happened? What Next? *Journal of International Marketing, 3*(3), 103–114.

van den Berg, G., & Pietersma, P. (2015). *Key Management Models: The 75+ Models Every Manager Needs to Know* (3rd ed.). London: FT Publishing.

Wieczner, J. (2017, June 7). The Fortune 500's 10 Most Profitable Companies. *Fortune.* http://fortune.com/2017/06/07/fortune-500-companies-profit-apple-berkshire-hathaway/

Estimating Cash Flows

The previous chapter introduced the concept of a business model, which defines how a firm makes money or, more specifically, the way cash flows are generated through operations. Chapter 2 suggested that the success of marketing activities should be measured in terms of their contribution to the generation of cash flows. This chapter focuses on how to estimate cash flows.

Cash flow estimates are a necessary input for the evaluation of marketing plans, activities, and budgets. Estimating cash flows that are attributable to marketing activities is the most important input into the evaluation of marketing activities. Yet, it is also the most difficult part of the task of evaluation. The reason is this: for purposes of investment decisions, such as expenditures on specific marketing activities, total cash flow is not the focus of interest. Rather, the relevant question is how much *change* in cash flow can be attributed to expenditures in specific marketing activities. Adding to the complexity is the fact that some marketing activities can increase cash flow, while other marketing activities are more defensive and help prevent reductions in cash flow that might otherwise have occurred as a result of changes in the market or competitors' actions. In the latter case the question becomes how much cash flow would decline if the marketing action(s) did not occur.

© The Author(s) 2019
D. W. Stewart, *Financial Dimensions of Marketing Decisions*,
Palgrave Studies in Marketing, Organizations and Society,
https://doi.org/10.1007/978-3-030-15565-0_4

How Marketing Generates Cash Flow

Firms generate cash in numerous ways. They may obtain funds from investors who take a share of the company, borrow from lenders who expect to be repaid at some interest rate, or sell assets, such as a piece of equipment when that equipment is no longer needed. However, there are only three ways that a firm can generate revenue through its operations and all involve marketing activities. Table 4.1 lists these sources of revenue and, ultimately, cash flow.

Customer Acquisition and Retention

Among the most common means for generating revenue are the acquisition and retention of customers. While this may seem obvious, this process is more complex than you might imagine. Revenue translates into cash flow, or profits, only when customers are willing to pay more for a product or service than the cost to produce, deliver, and sell it.

Again, duh, right! Not so fast. When you sign up for a credit card, for example, the bank has likely spent a lot of money trying to reach you. Think of the endless commercials you see for credit cards and the dozens of mailers you get telling you the time to get a new credit card is now! A marketer somewhere is spending a fortune on these. By the time you take the bait, the bank's "cost of customer acquisition" could be in the hundreds of dollars per card holder. If the bank doesn't earn more from you than that amount in interest over the lifetime of the card, they've lost money on you.

Marketers have historically focused on revenue, largely because they had greater control over revenue than costs and because most often they were evaluated and compensated based on revenue generation. However,

Table 4.1   How marketing generates cash flow

Source of revenue

Customer Acquisition and Retention: obtaining new customers and holding current customers (increasing and managing the customer base)
Share of Wallet within Category: increasing the frequency of purchasing relative to competition and or increasing category consumption (e.g., increasing market share or size of category)
Share of Wallet across Categories: selling additional products/offerings to existing customers (new offerings for existing customers; cross selling)

Adapted from (Young et al. 2006, p. 101)

not all customers are profitable. Thus, the key to financial success is acquiring and retaining profitable customers. There are also significant costs associated with acquiring new customers, so retaining customers is as important, if not more important, than acquiring new customers, at least for established businesses. Chapter 8 will examine the role of customer selection, acquisition, and retention in greater detail.

More Sales from Existing Customers

Another way for a firm to generate revenue is to obtain more sales from existing customers within the product or service category. There are two ways to do this. One approach is to take sales from competitors, that is, to increase market share within the relevant category. This can be an expensive proposition because competitors are unlikely to remain idle in the face of falling sales. A firm needs to think carefully about whether it can profitably take customers, and market share, from its competitors. Only when there is some point of superiority that is valued by customers will customers who switch from a competitor remain loyal customers. Otherwise, efforts to take share from competitors can degenerate into a price war that may reduce revenues for all competitors in the category.

Alternatively, a firm may be able to increase the frequency with which customers buy a product. Reminding customers about the product, such as was done in the "Got Milk" advertising campaign, or suggesting new uses or use occasions can be effective in increasing consumption. In another example, Arm & Hammer was able to increase consumption of what was once just a baking product, baking soda, by suggesting such new uses as carpet cleaning, deodorization of refrigerators, and polishing silverware, among others. Such a strategy may be especially effective for products that already have a very high market share in the product category. Clorox, which has a market share of almost 60% in the bleach category, would likely benefit more from increases in the use of bleach than from taking share from smaller competitors.

Share of Wallet

The third way in which a firm may generate revenue is to obtain a greater share of customers' overall spending, often called "share of wallet." This approach to revenue generation involves the identification of additional products and services that can be sold to existing customers. Thus, Allstate sells homeowners insurance, automobile insurance, motorcycle insurance, marine insurance, life insurance, and business insurance, as well as estate planning and wealth management services. An advantage of this approach is that many potential customers for these product and service offerings are already doing business with the firm. Thus, the firm does not need to incur the costs of building awareness and customers who are satisfied with one of the firm's offerings are likely to be more receptive to additional offerings from the same company.

There are limits to "share of wallet" strategies. It is important to avoid polluting a brand by extending it into areas where there is a lack of core organizational competencies. A great insurance company might harm its reputation if it offered substandard estate planning.

These three approaches to revenue generation are not mutually exclusive and many firms employ all three. Because these three approaches are the only ways in which a firm can generate revenue from its operations, every marketing activity needs to be justified in terms of its cash contribution to one of these approaches.

Revenues, Contribution, Cash Flow, and Profits

Marketers often focus on revenue because marketing activities are designed to increase the cash coming into the firm. They usually have less influence over the cash going out of the firm (e.g., expenses). Thus, it is not surprising the marketers would care more about what they can influence. However, firms are generally more interested in profits, and profits and revenue are not the same thing (Bendle and Bagga 2016). Sometimes, increases in revenue lead to increases in profits, but this is not always the case.

Even the term "profit" is problematic. Profit can mean many different things and can be influenced by many factors. It is certainly the case that the accounting profits reported by firms are not very useful for planning purposes because there are many accounting reporting decisions that can influence the amount of profits reported (Sherman and Young 2016). This is the reason this book introduced the concepts of contribution and cash flow. The reported profits of a firm are generally not helpful in making decisions about specific marketing activities and budgets, but cash flow is.

Total Versus Incremental Cash Flows
and Cannibalization

It is also important to distinguish between total and incremental cash flows. Total cash flows represent the aggregate effects of all of the firm's efforts including all marketing outcomes. In marketing planning, the relevant question is how much more cash will be generated by a particular marketing activity relative to not implementing the marketing activity or implementing a different marketing activity. In addition, there are other reasons why total cash flow may differ from incremental cash flow.

Some marketing actions can simultaneously increase revenue from one source while diminishing revenue from another source. Such an effect is known as cannibalization. For example, by one standard Coca-Cola's introduction of Diet Coke was an enormous success because it soon became the best-selling diet soft drink in the United States. However, the success of Diet Coke resulted in a loss of sales of Tab, another Coca-Cola diet drink. It is frequently the case that a firm's new product introduction in the same product category will reduce sales of the firm's other similar products. Thus, the effects of such product introductions, which may make good business sense, need to account for such cannibalization effects; the incremental revenue produced by the new product needs to be reduced by the loss of revenue from other products.

Another common context in which cannibalization occurs is price promotion. In many product categories, a temporary price reduction has the effect of changing the timing of consumers' purchases, but not the amount of product purchased (Mela et al. 1998). For example, a consumer may have planned to purchase laundry detergent next week, when he or she needs to replenish the household's supply. However, while shopping in a store for other products, the customer may see a price promotion for her favorite brand and decide to buy it then rather than wait a week.

In such a circumstance, the purchase would have occurred anyway. The price promotion did not increase sales volume, but it did change the timing of the purchase. Thus, the sales due to the price promotion cannibalize future sales, and in this example, actually reduced revenue. This does not mean that all price promotions are poor investments. Some promotions may increase total consumption. While this is not likely for laundry detergent, it may be the case for products like snack foods and soft drinks, when having the products on hand encourages consumption. Nevertheless, it is important to determine whether a short-term increase in revenue is really incremental or merely a change in timing of receipt of revenues.

Cannibalization effects are sometimes very obvious, but not always. For example, in the promotion example above, the marketer may not know what would have happened had a competitor offered a price promotion the following week. If a competitor's price promotion would have resulted in the loss of sales the firm would otherwise have obtained, then the price promotion did create incremental sales. Similarly, placing a new product in the market may offset sales that would have been lost to competitors.

Estimating Revenues and Cash Flow

At a conceptual level, the estimation of revenues generated by marketing programs is relatively straightforward. Unfortunately, as will be developed in subsequent chapters, it is not so simple in execution. Nevertheless, it is possible with some effort, and the effort is usually worthwhile in the context of managing a business and marketing programs.

Figure 4.1 provides a conceptual description of a process for revenue estimation. As has been observed earlier, marketing activities may have numerous effects that can be directly linked to revenues and cash flow.

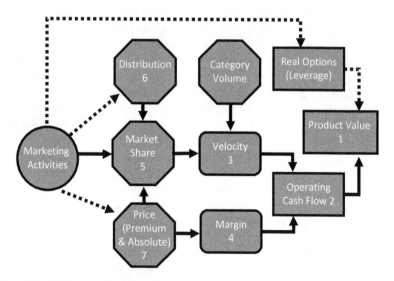

Fig. 4.1   Linking marketing actions to cash flow. (Adapted from: Meier et al. 2018)

Marketing activities may influence sales and *market share* (5 in Fig. 4.1). Such activities also influence *distribution* (6 in Fig. 4.1) in numerous ways. They may increase or decrease the number of points of distribution, the amount of coverage and shelf space within individual points of distributions, and the behavior of distributors related to such things as displays, features, sales training, advertising, and other behavior. Distribution, in turn, may have an effect on sales volume and market share. Finally, various marketing activities may influence both the *absolute price* and any *price premium* a firm may be able to command relative to competitive products (7 in Fig. 4.1). Thus, in planning and budgeting marketing activities it is important to justify marketing expenditures in terms of their effects on one or more of these outcomes.

Market demand for the product, *category volume*, along with market share influences *sales velocity* (3 in Fig. 4.1), that is, sales volume in a given period. The price of the product, in turn, influences *margin* (4 in Fig. 4.1). Velocity and margin determine *operating cash flow* (2 in Fig. 4.1). Finally, the *value of the product or service* to the firm can be determined by the operating cash flow that will be generated over some defined period of time plus the value of any real options (potential opportunities) that are associated with the product or service.

Each of the various elements in Fig. 4.1 can be readily estimated. Each of the numbered elements can be computed by a simple equation. Table 4.2 provides these equations. In most markets, category volume can be obtained from various syndicated information services, such as Nielsen and IRI, or through primary marketing research.

PRODUCT VALUE AND NET PRESENT VALUE

The value of a product to a company is determined by the net present value of the cash flows it produces over some period of time (Eq. 1 in Table 4.2). This is a common way in which companies are valued with some added value related to the value of any real options plus a terminal or residual value for the firm at the end of the relevant time period over which the net present value is computed.

Net period cash flows (Eq. 2) are simply product revenues minus product costs. The former, product sales, is a function of category volume, market share, and average unit costs (Eq. 3). Product costs are the variable costs of producing and selling the product, plus any allocated fixed costs (Eq. 4). Unit share can be estimated using some measure of consumers'

Table 4.2   Predictive equations & terminology

NPV calculations and financial ratios for Fig. 4.1

(1) Net present value = $\sum$ {net period cash flows/$(1 + r)^t$} + terminal value
(2) Net period cash flows = Product sales – product costs (margin: profit/sales)
(3) Product sales = Category size × average unit price × unit share (velocity: sales/assets)
(4) Product costs = Costs associated with producing sales and selling for the product
(5) Unit share ~ Purchase intention × distribution factor/relative price factor
(6) Distribution factor = f (B0 + B1 × ln (distribution))
(7) Price ratio = f (B2 × average product unit price/average category unit price)

Adapted from: Meier et al. (2018)

purchase intention, which can be tracked with survey research, plus estimates of distribution coverage, for example, how many consumers can readily obtain the product, and price relative to competition (Eq. 5).

Obtaining unit share requires some statistical estimation, but the input for this estimation exercise is relatively easy to obtain. Similarly, the influence of distribution requires statistical estimation, but in most product categories, distribution coverage is available from syndicated information providers. Finally, the influence of relative price must be estimated statistically but the information about prices in the category is readily available.

The aggregate value of all marketing activities can be determined by estimating sales and cash flow if no expenditures were made on marketing. This is unrealistic because no firm would want to cut all marketing expenditures to see what happens. Such an analysis would not be very helpful for planning and budgeting in any case. A more useful analysis would focus on the incremental value (incremental cash flow) associated with specific marketing activities and expenditures. Such an incremental analysis is illustrated conceptually in Fig. 4.2. The equations would change only to reflect the incremental effects rather than aggregate outcomes.

CASH FLOW AND PRODUCT VALUE ESTIMATION EXAMPLE

Let's look at an example to see how this works in actual dollars. Imagine you're coming out with a new cosmetic product. Table 4.3 provides the basic assumptions for estimating cash flow for the product and the overall value of the product.

So, breaking this down, you're selling a product for $10 and earning $5 gross margin. Your cost of production is $2 per unit, so the gross margin

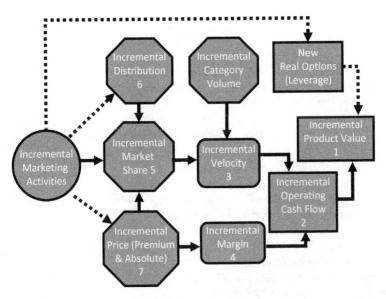

Fig. 4.2 Linking marketing actions to incremental cash flow. (Adapted from: Meier et al. 2018)

Table 4.3 Assumptions for cash flow and product valuation example

Example: New cosmetic product		
Retail price		$10.00
Gross margin	50%	$5.00
Cost to produce product		$2.00
Net margin (AKA "Gross Contribution": gross margin − cost to produce)		$3.00
Net margin (as percent of retail price)		30%
Category size (all products of this type sold in market per year)		50,000,000
Distribution coverage (baseline = 50%)		50%
Market share		10%
Total products sold by company per year		5,000,000
Total annual gross contribution (units sold × gross contribution3/ unit)		$15,000,000
Marketing launch and support		$5,000,000
Net contribution before overhead—year 1 (gross contribution— marketing launch and support)		$10,000,000

(also referred to as gross contribution) is $3 per unit. If you sold 100 units, your gross contribution would be $30. However, the total market for this product category is 50,000,000 units! Your market share is 10%, so you're selling 5,000,000 units per year. Distribution coverage is 50%, meaning you're reaching half the possible distribution potential of the product in the entire market.

Table 4.4 provides a summary of the calculations of cash flow. In terms of financial performance, the gross annual contribution is $15,000,000 (5 million units × $3/unit = $15 million). But, you're spending $5,000,000 per year on marketing and support. Your cash flow from this product is $10,000,000 per year. Over the projected ten-year life of the product, you will bring in $100,000,000 in cash. But, remember, we use a discounted cash flow method to estimate actual value.

Using a discount rate (sometimes called the "cost of capital"), we can show the present value of cash flows in later years. With this modeling technique, the present value of the $10,000,000 you receive in year 5, for example, is just $7.47 million. The net present value of the ten-year life of the product is around $78,000,000. That's what the product is worth.

Why does this matter? Well, for one thing, the value of the product contributes to the value of the business. If you had, say, three products of this type, your business would be worth around $210,000,000. The value of the product is also important for determining whether it's a project worth pursuing. For instance, what if the product had a patent that you had to buy for $78,000,000 up front. Is that worth it? Probably not since the rights to the patent alone equal the total expected revenue over ten years, and there would still be production and marketing costs to cover. This modeling process is also extremely revealing of the ways in which seemingly small changes in assumptions can affect value.

Discount Rate Change

The discount rate determines the present value of future cash flows. These values are inversely related to the discount rate. If the discount rate goes from 6% to 7%, for example, the net present value of the product drops from $78,000,000 to $75,000,000. Why? The reason is because $10,000,000 in the future is worth less if it could be earning more (a higher discount rate) in a different investment. This is why stock prices tend to drop when interest rates go up. Interest rates are one of the key factors in determining discount rates for net present value models.

Table 4.4 Computation example for cash flow and product valuation

Year		0	1	2	3	4	5	6	7	8	9
	Cash flows and NPV				*6%*	*Discount rate*					
Cash flow		$10,000,000	$10,000,000	$10,000,000	$10,000,000	$10,000,000	$10,000,000	$10,000,000	$10,000,000	$10,000,000	$10,000,000
Discount factor		1.00	0.94	0.89	0.84	0.79	0.75	0.70	0.67	0.63	0.59
Discounted cash flow		$10,000,000	$9,433,962	$8,899,964	$8,396,193	$7,920,937	$7,472,582	$7,049,605	$6,650,571	$6,274,124	$5,918,985
Net present value of product	$78,016,923										

Changes in Price and Margin

If you change the retail price from $10 to $11, the value of the product over ten years jumps from $78,000,000 to over $97,000,000. The retail price increase makes the gross margin and gross contributions go up. In turn, future cash flows go up. Even a one cent price increase makes a difference, adding over $200,000 to the lifetime value of the product. Changing the cost of the product from $2.00 to $1.95 pushes the net present value of the product up by $1,000,000. Based on this illustration, you can start to understand why companies are so eager for even small, incremental changes in price and cost.

Changes in Market Share and Distribution

Selling more product is good for the product's value to the firm. How much? The model shows that increasing market share from 10% to 11% results in a product value of $89.7 million. Similarly, changing distribution coverage from 50% to 51% adds $2 million to the product value.

The model here is relevant because it gives you a tool to evaluate marketing decisions. Imagine that an advertising agency comes to you and says they can increase your market share by 5% for $25,000,000. Is that worth doing? The model says that if you can grow to a 15% market share, your product value will be a whopping $140 million. Your gain in product value will be $62 million ($140 million–$78 million). Factoring in the $25 million cost of the ad campaign, you will be ahead of the game by $37 million in net present value.

INCREMENTAL EFFECTS

The incremental effects of specific marketing activities and expenditures can be examined in several ways. It is possible to use historical data and compare sales and cash flow in periods when the focal marketing activities occurred with periods when the focal activities either did not occur or occurred at different levels. Alternatively, the firm might engage in experimentation by selectively implementing or selectively eliminating specific marketing activities in a few markets and determining the effect of such changes relative to markets where there is no change.

ESTIMATING COSTS[1]

In some ways, marketing budgeting is easier than traditional capital budgeting involving tangible assets. Under current accounting rules, most marketing expenditures are expensed in the year they occur. You can usually ignore issues related to depreciation and other accounting consequences, such as tax incentives or disincentives associated with specific types of expenditures in marketing planning and budgeting. Even so, determination of costs, especially fixed costs, can be daunting. Even the cost of producing, delivering, and selling a product may change based on factors like transportation costs related to distance to the market from the point of production, tariffs, and so forth. Nevertheless, it is important to assign all of the costs actually associated with the production, delivery, and selling of the product to the product.

As noted earlier, it is also common to attribute various types of fixed costs, or overhead, to products. While this is often defended as convenient, and rationalized by the need to cover fixed costs, such allocation rules can seriously distort the costs and, hence, the cash flow attributable to a particular product or service. Many of these overhead items are far removed from an individual product: utilities, rent, legal services, staff, and so on. Good decisions about marketing activities and about the business more generally should allocate only the expenses associated with producing, delivering, and selling a product when estimating product contribution and cash flows. This does not mean that fixed costs should be entirely ignored, but for purposes of marketing planning it is important that they do not distort the financial picture related to the outcomes of marketing expenditures and activities.

BREAK-EVEN VOLUME AND REVENUE

One of the more informative uses of contribution is in helping marketers understand whether their investments will make money, that is, whether contribution will be positive or negative. A key concept relevant to this understanding is *breakeven*, that is, the level of activity needed to pay for the costs of the activity (but not make any profit). Breakeven can be expressed in terms of volume or revenue:

---

[1] Readers who have not had an exposure to cost accounting may refer to Appendix of this chapter for a brief introduction.

> Break-even Volume = The number of units that must be sold to cover marketing expenditures and other fixed costs.

It is calculated like this:

$$\text{Break-even volume} \left(\# \text{ of units}\right) = \text{Fixed Costs} \left(\$\right)$$
$$\div \text{Contribution per unit} \left(\$\right)$$

For example, if a can of coke generates 10 cents of gross profit contribution, the break-even volume for fixed costs of $1 will be 10 cans of coke.

$$10 \text{ cans} = \$1 \left(\text{fixed costs}\right) \div 10 \text{ cents} \left(\text{contribution per unit}\right)$$

> Break-even Revenue = The level of dollar sales required to break even.

Break-even revenue is computed as

$$\text{Break-even Revenue} \left(\$\right) = \text{Break-even Volume} \left(\# \text{ of units}\right)$$
$$\times \text{Contribution per unit} \left(\$\right)$$

In our example, if each can of Coke sells for 50 cents, then the break-even revenue for $1 in fixed costs will be $5 ($10 \times 50$ cents).

$$\$5 \text{ break-even revenue} = 10 \text{ cans Break-even Volume} \left(\# \text{ of units}\right)$$
$$\times 50 \text{ cents revenue Contribution per unit} \left(\$\right)$$

Calculation of breakeven requires computing the contribution per unit, that is, the amount each sale generates after covering variable costs and the level of fixed costs including marketing expenditures. Clearly as fixed costs increase, more units must be sold to reach break-even volume and with greater contribution per unit fewer units need to sell to break even.

Of course, companies rarely wish to merely break even, but failure to break even is a clear indication that decisions need to be reconsidered. Break-even volume and revenue also provide a reality check for marketing decisions that is easy to compute. If break-even volume or revenue seems unrealistic and daunting, it may be necessary to reconsider plans. In the extreme case, break-even volume might be found to exceed the total demand in the market. Such a finding would clearly suggest that moving forward with the product makes no business sense.

Break-even analysis can also be used to evaluate individual marketing actions. In such circumstances the question is whether the incremental sales, in units or revenue, generated by the marketing action covers the cost of the proposed marketing action. Thus:

$$\text{Break-even Incremental Volume for Proposed Marketing Program}$$
$$= \text{Cost of Marketing Program} \div \text{Contribution per unit} (\$)$$

And

$$\text{Break-even Incremental Revenue}$$
$$= \text{Break-even Incremental Volume} (\# \text{ of units}) \times \text{Contribution per unit} (\$)$$

Break-even volume and break-even revenue are often used as starting points for marketing planning and are frequently used to set sales volume, revenue, and profit targets. Such targets can be very helpful for marketing planning and operations planning and establish goals for marketing managers, sales personnel, and others in the organization. They function as vital reality checks on marketing ideas. For instance, it may sound like an amazing idea to book today's biggest music superstar to advertise your product for $1 million. But you better be able to explain how you will break even from that million-dollar marketing expense. It's an easier trap to fall into than you might imagine. Break-even analysis is a great cure for wishful thinking.

One way this is done is to set a target profit level and use this to calculate the volume necessary to achieve the desired profit. To achieve the target profit, the company will need to achieve a total contribution equal to fixed costs plus the target profit. Given the target profit and the contribution per unit, the volume needed to achieve this target is

$$\text{Target Volume} (\#) = \left(\text{Fixed Costs} (\$) + \text{Target Profits} (\$) \right)$$
$$\div \text{Contribution per Unit} (\$)$$

And

$$\text{Target Revenue} (\$) = \text{Target Volume} \times \text{Price per Unit}$$

Subsequent chapters will describe specific examples of the estimation of cash flows and break-even volumes and revenues in the context of brand building, creating and maintaining customers, and advertising and promotion campaigns.

Pitfalls in Estimating Cash Flow

All efforts to forecast the future, including the estimation of cash flows, are based on assumptions. Some of these assumptions are specific to the marketing activities being contemplated such as the characteristics of the product or service, the price that will be charged, the type and amount of advertising and promotion, and the level of distribution that may be obtained. However, there are also general environmental assumptions that should be made explicit. These environmental assumptions include expectations about the state of the general economy, actions by competitors, and, in some cases, even the weather forecast. All assumptions about factors that may influence the success and outcomes of marketing actions should be identified and documented. It is tempting to assume that the world of tomorrow will be the same as the world of today. While such an assumption simplifies the forecasting and estimation challenges, it is almost never correct. Markets change, sometimes quickly. Competitors respond. Indeed, if a firm is successful in the market with a new product, it is likely to attract competition, which may improve on the offering and/or place downward pressure on prices. Similarly, in the face of a successful advertising campaign, competitors may step up their own advertising expenditures or engage in price promotion.

Identification and documentation of assumptions enables sensitivity analysis. Forecasts and estimates can be tested against changes in assumptions. Such testing can help identify factors to which forecasts and estimates are especially sensitive. These factors would be closely monitored for changes and contingency plans developed in advance, thereby reducing the likelihood of surprise and the need to decide on and make changes in a hurried fashion.

Sunk Costs

Future investments are sometimes justified by pointing to investments already made. For example, further investment in development of a specific product may be rationalized by the prior expenditures on the development of this product. In reality, once an investment is made it is a sunk cost which should have no influence on future decisions. If information suggests that future investment will not pay out, it makes no sense to make that investment, no matter how much has already been expended. There is a human tendency to become emotionally attached to projects in which time and money have been invested. As a result, the greater the investment in something, the harder it becomes to abandon it. This tendency needs to be resisted even when there is a feeling of loss associated with walking away from sunk costs.

Optimism Bias

Another bias in decision-making that is rooted in emotion is the tendency to be optimistic about the outcomes of decisions. A marketer who develops a creative idea or a manager who has put a great deal of time and effort into planning a marketing campaign often develops an emotional attachment to the idea that leads to overly optimistic assumptions and a tendency to ignore nonconfirmatory information. This bias tends to become an organizational bias because optimistic forecasts and estimates are likely to be more highly valued than more realistic forecasts and estimates. Of course, it is only possible to differentiate optimistic forecasts from realistic forecasts after the fact.

Many organizations are also overly optimistic about what they can achieve with existing resources, personnel, and competencies as well as how they compare to competitors. This bias is especially problematic when the firm is undertaking something that is relatively novel and where it has little or no prior experience.

While it is inevitable that such optimism biases will exist, it is helpful for managers to be aware of them. In addition, there are things an organization can do to reduce the effects of such biases. Documentation and examinations of assumptions and sensitivity analysis can often reveal optimism. The creation of an organizational review process that includes decision-makers without emotional vesting in proposed plans and investments can also reduce bias. A competitive review process that pits competing investments against one another to obtain resources can also create a system of checks and balances within the organization.

Selection Bias

There is almost always some error in forecasting sales and estimating cash flow. Even if the model for forecasting and estimation is perfect, the future cannot be perfectly known. Even reasonable and defensible assumptions may not hold. Thus, some estimates of cash flow will be too high and some will be too low. However, investments with higher returns, higher net present value, are more likely to be selected. This creates a selection bias because investment opportunities that overestimate net present value are more likely to be selected than investment opportunities with a lower projected net present value. This is another reason to conduct post investment reviews that may help identify reasons for and the size of such over-estimates and discover potential corrective measures.

The Need to Review Previous Efforts

Finally, management should routinely review the results of investments and compare forecasts and estimates with what actually occurred after implementation. Such reviews are a potential source of learning for the organization: what worked?, what did not work?, was success for the reasons anticipated?, why were we not successful?, what do the results suggest about better ways to plan and budget in the future? Over time, they may also help identify systematic biases, such as a manager or business unit that is consistently overly optimistic or pessimistic.

CONCLUSION

This chapter described three approaches for the generation of revenue and suggested that marketing expenditures should be justified based on their contribution to cash flow, that is, the revenue generated minus costs of production, delivery, and marketing. It is important to understand the profitability of actions controlled by marketers. A key way of doing this is to look at the contribution generated by marketing activities. The chapter also presented a conceptual framework for estimating the cash flows generated by marketing activities and examined some of the rules and techniques for estimating the cash flows associated with specific marketing activities. A fundamental principle for the analysis of cash flows generated by marketing activities is that only incremental cash flows should be used to justify marketing expenditures. Incremental cash flows are the difference between cash flows with the marketing expenditures and cash flows without the marketing expenditures. The chapter also introduced the concepts of break-even volume and revenue and discussed their use in decision-making. Finally, the chapter explored several biases associated with forecasting sales and estimation of cash flows and suggested some approaches for minimizing these biases.

Exercises

1. A retail store sells 10,000 products at $9.99 per unit. Each unit costs the retailer $8.00 to sell. The retailer's merchandising manager is compensated for meeting a revenue target and receives a 5% bonus if revenues exceed $100,000. The merchandising manager proposes a price cut to $8.99 on grounds that the price cut will boost sales to 12,000 units while leaving costs the same. Assuming that the numbers are correct should management approve the price cut? Does this price cut make sense for a retailer seeking to increase its profits? What do you think of the compensation plan for the merchandising manager? Is the merchandising manager's recommended price cut rational?

2. A small business owner sells bicycles for $600 each. The owner's variable costs are $300 per bicycle. The owner pays $15,000 per month to rent store space and pay utilities. What is the contribution of each sale? What is the monthly break-even volume? What is the monthly break-even revenue? If the owner had a target of $5000 for profits each month, how many bicycles would the owner have to sell.?

3. The same small business owner is considering advertising in a local community newspaper. The total cost of placing a daily ad for a month will cost $2500. What is the break-even volume required to justify this expenditure on advertisings? What is the break-even revenue?

Points to Ponder

1. Look at the conceptual framework in Fig. 4.2. What obstacles can you identify in applying this framework? Are there other factors that you think should be considered that are not captured by the framework?

2. If you were asked to use the conceptual framework in Fig. 4.2 to evaluate an advertising campaign costing $5 million dollars over the next quarter, what information would you need to determine whether this investment is justifiable?

APPENDIX: A PRIMER ON COST ACCOUNTING

Readers who have had some exposure to accounting, either in practice or through formal course work will appreciate the role of accountants. Firms are required to report to external constituencies, such as investors and government regulators, and must do so using very specific, if not always logical or internally consistent, rules. Financial accountants play an important role in getting these external reports right (and by doing so, inform current and potential investors and help firms avoid large fines and even jail time for managers if the reports are not right). Marketers should appreciate the high stakes associated with generating these external reports, which are largely about financial performance. There are very good reasons to focus on financial performance.

Other accountants manage internal reporting within the firm, that is, the reports that go to operating managers who must allocate resources and who are responsible for resource allocation. To most people, a cost is an easy and very tangible thing to understand. People go to the store and pay for a product. There is a simple link between the cost (what is paid) and what is received. Even in households, where multiple people live, there is rarely an effort to allocate the cost of a meal to each individual at the dinner table or the cost of a cable television subscription based on how many hours each member of the household watches television. The reasons for this are simple. There is nothing much to be gained, and potentially a lot to lose, in such efforts at allocation.

The world of business is different. There are often large and very real costs that are difficult to allocate. The costs of producing a specific product may be easy to determine, but how are the costs of utilities to be allocated in a building shared by people who manage, produce, and market many different products. In fact, even allocation of the costs of production of a product can differ depending on whether the specific product was the first one produced or the 50 millionth product produced. Nevertheless, there are very real costs associated with buildings, people not directly involved in the production or sale of identifiable products (like the cleaning crew, accountants, and human resources professionals) whose costs must be covered. There must be rules for the allocation of such costs. The contribution of any individual product or service can be made large, small, or even negative based on how such costs are allocated. The role of managerial accountants or cost accountants is to try to come up with fair rules for the allocation of such costs and for applying these rules for the analysis of expenditures within the firm. There is no allocation of "unallocated" costs that is "correct." Various rules are applied in an effort to be fair. So, the more employees who work on a particular product and are located in a specific building, the more the costs of that building may be assigned to that product based on square footage occupied by the staff dedicated to the product who have offices in the building.

Most allocation rules employed by accountants are an attempt to be "fair," that is, to avoid advantaging or disadvantaging any particular business activity in the firm. The "rules" they establish rarely capture the value of a resource and there are few "rules" for capturing value. Thus, the office occupied by the chief loyalty officer, who spends all day assuring that otherwise long-term, loyal customers who have had a poor experience are not lost, is allocated the same cost as the person hired to deal with parking. The cost allocation rule may be fine, but there must be an off-setting value for the contribution to the business and its business model. It is important that marketers make clear the value being created by their activities, even as they accept cost allocation rules.

Many internal reports fail to include the value of such assets as brand, customer relationships, and loyalty. Marketers would do well to remind others in the organization of the value being created by the costs for which they are responsible. In addition, marketers need to be aware of how costs are being allocated. Good management accounting systems allow users to examine in depth the drivers of specific costs. Reports can be wrong and, even if nominally correct, allocation rules may create a misleading picture. Many costs are not readily obvious and how they are allocated is often subjective. Frequently, costs are reported without a link to revenue. An increase in costs that is accompanied by an even larger increase in revenue is usually a good thing.

It is also important to recognize that different firms allocate costs in different ways. This is further evidence that there is no right answer when it comes to the allocation of costs. In fact, what is considered marketing, and therefore a marketing cost, can vary widely across firms. However, there should be consistency within a firm. For example, the cost of a promotion involving a price reduction could be viewed as a marketing cost. On the other hand, the price reduction could be viewed as a lowering of price with a consequent reduction in revenue. Either approach is justifiable, but a firm should not treat some promotions as a marketing cost and other promotions as a price reduction.

Marketers need to understand costs because the costs they are assigned or allocated can make a big difference in how the outcome(s) of marketing actions and expenditures appear. In addition, costs can behave in unusual ways that really do change the economics of market offerings. The cost of increasing production is often not identical to the cost savings associated with decreasing production by the same amount. A production line or service operation that is already at full capacity may require additional machinery and/or additional personnel just to meet the demand of one additional sale. Such circumstances can create steep malfunctions in costs. Insofar as the role of marketing profitably matches supply and demand, an understanding of such cost structures is critical for the success of marketing.

A common approach to managing costs is *Activity-Based Costing* (*ABC*). ABC seeks to explicitly link costs to the activities that produce them. For some costs, this is easy. It is clear that the costs of purchasing media for advertising is a marketing cost that should be assigned to whatever product(s) are being advertised. But what is to be done with the CEO's salary and bonus?

ABC classifies costs into different buckets: direct costs, indirect costs, and allocated fixed costs. Direct costs are generally easy to assign because there is a clear link to an activity. For example, if a bakery puts two eggs into every cake it makes, the cost of the two eggs is a direct cost associated with producing the cake. However, even direct costs can be complex because there are often multiple ways to define an activity. For example, should costs be assigned based on each sale or based on managing the overall relationship with a customer who buys many different products? While either approach can make sense, one or the other must be adopted. Generally, the choice would, or should, be driven by the definition of the activity most relevant to the creation of value for the customer and the firm. For example, if there is little interaction with customers beyond the individual sales transaction, the better definition of the relevant activity is likely to be the individual sale. On the other hand, if there is a great deal of interaction associated with account management and some or much of this activity is not tied to a specific sale, it is likely more appropriate to define the activity as account management.

In contrast, there are indirect costs, that is, costs that are not easily assigned to any particular activity, product, or service encounter. These costs are often called overhead and dismissed. But, like direct costs, there are identifiable drivers of these costs. The problem is that it is not so easy to link these costs to specific revenue-generating activities. It is not difficult to count the number of people in a customer service center and determine their salaries. However, it is often difficult, if not impossible, to assign the time spent on an individual call to a specific product or service. As discussed above, accountants try to create fair and meaningful rules for the allocation of such costs.

A special case of indirect costs revolves around the allocation of fixed costs, that is, costs that will be incurred regardless of sales. Most firms must have office space, furniture for employees, utilities, and a host of other things regardless of how many sales are made. Again, accountants generally try to come up with fair and meaningful rules for allocating these costs, but such allocation always includes political dimensions.

The lessons for marketers are (1) don't ignore costs, (2) understand how costs are allocated, (3) include an understanding of cost drivers in planning marketing actions, (4) push back on allocation rules that seem unfair, and (5) whenever possible in internal reports, link revenue generation and profitability to the costs that generated them.

REFERENCES

Bendle, N. T., & Bagga, C. K. (2016). The Metrics That Marketers Muddle. *Sloan Management Review, 57*(Spring), 73–82.

Meier, J., Findley, F., & Stewart, D. W. (2018, May). *Applying the MASB Brand Investment & Valuation Model*, Marketing Accountability Standards Board White Paper. https://themasb.org/wp-content/uploads/2018/05/MWP_ApplyingBIVModel_MeierFindleyStewart2018.pdf

Mela, C. F., Kamel, J., & Bowman, D. (1998). The Long-Term Impact of Promotions on Consumer Stockpiling Behavior. *Journal of Marketing Research, 35*(2), 250–262.

Sherman, H. D., & Young, S. D. (2016). Where Financial Reporting Still Falls Short. *Harvard Business Review*, (July–August), 3–9.

Young, R., Weiss, A., & Stewart, D. W. (2006). *Marketing Champions: Practical Strategies for Improving Marketing's Power, Influence and Business Impact.* New York: Wiley Interscience.

CHAPTER 5

Intermediate Marketing Outcome Measures and Metrics

Nextdoor.com, a social network for neighborhoods, raised $110 million in venture capital in 2015, a move that valued the company at $1.1 billion. At that time, Nextdoor had no revenue. Indeed, the company had been operating for a decade without revenue or profit, relying on over $200 million in investor money to survive. How was this possible?

Either the investors were incredibly stupid and naive (always a possibility) or they understood that pure financial metrics alone do not always reveal the value of a business. In the case of Nextdoor, the company had succeeded in connecting people in 160,000 communities around the world. With that one-of-a-kind user base, a collection of communities with a high degree of user-to-user trust, Nextdoor was positioned to offer advertisers unique placement opportunities.

They forecast[1] that they could achieve advertising click-through rates of 5–7%. The industry average is 2%. This potential led investors to believe the company was worth over a billion dollars despite having none of the traditional financial characteristics of a regular business in the same valuation league. What's going on?

Previous chapters have made the case that marketing outcomes should be linked to financial performance. However, financial metrics are not the

---

[1] https://www.sramanamitra.com/2017/08/25/billion-dollar-unicorns-valuation-without-revenue-nextdoor-trying-to-monetize/

© The Author(s) 2019
D. W. Stewart, *Financial Dimensions of Marketing Decisions*,
Palgrave Studies in Marketing, Organizations and Society,
https://doi.org/10.1007/978-3-030-15565-0_5

only measures of marketing outcomes. There are many measures of marketing outcomes in use today. Online advertising click-through is just one example. This chapter explores some common measures used to assess the performance of marketing and the effects of marketing actions. It also places these measures within a conceptual framework that identifies how various measures may, or may not, be useful and when they may be helpful. Chapter 6 will link these marketing performance measures to financial performance.

OVERVIEW OF INTERMEDIATE MARKETING OUTCOME MEASURES AND METRICS

Marketing activities may not produce an immediate effect on sales, revenue, or cash flow. However, this does not mean there are no effects or that the effects of a marketing activity cannot be measured. An advertisement may persuade a consumer that a particular brand is superior to its competitors, but the consumer may not purchase that brand until they have a need for it. A sales call may create interest in the services of a company, but that interest may not translate into a sale until it is time for contract renewal.

It is for this reason that there are many measures of marketing outcomes that can provide insights into the success of marketing activities. These measures are often referred to as *intermediate measures* because they represent more immediate outcomes that are potentially related to future financial outcomes. Intermediate measures are important because they can provide feedback about the success of marketing activities in advance of actual sales and revenue generation. Such feedback is helpful, of course, only if there is a link between the intermediate outcome and financial results. Chapter 6 will address the identification of such links. This chapter will focus on intermediate marketing outcomes.

The marketing discipline has developed a rich array of measures and metrics. Whole books have been devoted to cataloging and defining marketing measures (see, e.g., Davis 2018; Kozielski 2018; Bendle et al. 2016). Indeed, one book identifies almost 200 metrics in the context of digital media alone (Rappaport 2015). The Marketing Accountability Standards Board (MASB 2018) maintains a *Common Language Marketing Dictionary* that provides standard definitions for many measures of marketing outcomes (http://www.marketing-dictionary.org).

Measures and metrics related to the outcomes of marketing activities take numerous forms depending on both what is measured and how the measure is used. The same "number" may be used differently in distinct contexts, so it is important to know not only how a measure is defined but also how it is being used. For example, product awareness, as measured by a survey of consumers, may be descriptive if it refers to the number or percent of consumers who are currently aware of the product or it may be predictive if it refers to an expected future outcome of an advertising campaign.

It is useful to consider the various ways in which measures and metrics can be conceptualized beginning with the difference between measures and metrics. Table 5.1 lists some common types of intermediate marketing measures. The table is by no means exhaustive but does serve to illustrate some of the specific measures and metrics used by marketers. Note that these measures and metrics can often be operationalized in multiple ways.

You can go through Table 5.1 and connect the effects of these intermediate measures and metrics with eventual financial outcomes. Ad recall, for example, usually predicts a higher likelihood of product selection at the point of sale. Thus, increases in ad recall suggest that revenue will increase. It's not an exact science. However, knowing nonfinancial measures and metrics and comparing them to earlier periods and to those of competitors can tell you a lot about how your business is doing—or is going to do—in dollars.

Measures Versus Metrics

The terms "measure" and "metric" are often used interchangeably, but they actually represent distinct concepts. A measure is a single point of data obtained at a specific point in time. A measure is rarely useful when taken alone. Unit sales in the past week is a measure. Such a measure indicates little about how well the business is doing, however. This measure does not indicate where sales are good or poor.

To be useful for assessing how well a business is performing it is necessary to put the measure in context. A measure in context is a metric. For example, sales this week versus sales last week can indicated whether sales are increasing or declining, and by how much in unit, dollar, and percentage terms. Similarly, the number of visits to a website in the current quarter is a measure, while the number of visits in the last quarter compared to the number of visits in the current quarter is a metric. In other words, a measure is just a number; a metric transforms a measure into an indicator of performance.

Table 5.1 Common intermediate marketing measures and metrics

Advertising wearout	The rate of decline in the effectiveness or selling power of an advertisement after exposure to the target audience
All commodity volume	The total annual sales volume of retailers that can be aggregated from individual store-level up to larger geographical sets. This measure is a ratio, and so is typically measured as a percentage (or on a scale from 0 to 100). The total dollar sales that go into ACV include the entire store inventory sales, rather than sales for a specific category of products—hence the term "all commodity volume"
Brand equity	A measure of the value of a brand often operationalized as the incremental revenue that the brand earns over the revenue it would earn if it were sold without the brand name
Brand awareness	A measure of familiarity frequently obtained by asking questions such as "have you heard of brand X or "what brands come to mind when you think of 'luxury cars'? The former question is a recognition measure; the latter question is a recall measure
Brand preference	The percent of those who are aware of a brand and prefer it over your competitors under the assumption of equality in price and availability
Brand image	A measure of the perception of a brand in the minds of persons. The brand image is a mirror reflection (though perhaps inaccurate) of the brand personality or product being. It is what people believe about a brand—their thoughts, feelings, expectations
Brand loyalty	A measure of the degree to which a consumer generally buys the same manufacturer-originated product or service repeatedly over time rather than buying from multiple suppliers within the category. The degree to which a consumer consistently purchases the same brand within a product class
Carryover effect	A measure of the effect of a marketing action beyond a single time period (i.e., a lagged effect). The rate at which the effects of a marketing action diminishes with the passage of time
Clickthrough	A measure of the number of users who clicked on a specific internet advertisement or link
Customer lifetime value	The monetary value of a customer relationship, based on the present value of the projected future cash flows from the customer relationship
Customer equity	Customer equity is the total combined customer lifetime value (CLV) for all of a company's customers
Customer satisfaction	A measure of customers' perceived satisfaction with their experience of a firm's offerings. It is generally based on survey data and expressed as a rating. It is measured at an individual level, but it is almost always reported at an aggregate level. Customer satisfaction is generally measured on a five-point scale, ranging from "very dissatisfied" to "very satisfied"

(*continued*)

Table 5.1 (continued)

Day-after-recall	A method of testing the performance of an ad or a commercial whereby members of the audience are surveyed one day after their exposure to the ad or commercial in a media vehicle to discover how many of the audience members remember (unaided and aided) encountering that specific ad or commercial
Distribution coverage	A measure of the availability of products sold through retailers—usually as a percentage of all potential outlets—and reveal a brand's percentage of market access
Frequency	The average number of exposures received by the portion of the defined population that was "reached" (i.e., received at least one exposure to the advertising or campaign) being assessed during a given time period
Gross rating points (GRP)	Measures the size of an audience (or total amount of exposures) reached by a specific media vehicle or schedule during a specific period of time. It is expressed in terms of the rating of a specific media vehicle (if only one is being used) or the sum of all the ratings of the vehicles included in a media schedule. It includes any audience duplication and is equal to the reach of a media schedule multiplied by the average frequency of the schedule. Target rating points express the same concept, but with regard to a more narrowly defined target audience
Impression	A measure of how many times an advertisement is viewed. Also called exposures and opportunities-to-see (OTS), all refer to the same metric: an estimate of the audience for a media "insertion" (one ad) or campaign. In an Internet context an impression is a single display of online content to a user's web-enabled device. Thus, it is the number of times the ad is displayed, whether it is clicked on or not. Theoretically, an impression is generated each time an advertisement is viewed and the number of impressions achieved is a function of an ad's reach (the number of people seeing it) multiplied by its frequency (number of times they see it). Note that impressions do not account for the quality of the viewings, or even whether the consumer actually "sees" the ad: an opportunity to view the ad, a glimpse or a detailed viewing all count as one impression
Intention	An attitudinal measure of customers' stated willingness or plan to behave in a certain way. A common operationalization is purchase intention, the stated plan to purchase a specific product or service at some point in the future

(*continued*)

Table 5.1   (continued)

Inventory velocity or inventory turnover	A measure of the time period starting with receipt of raw materials or purchased inventory and ending with the sale of the finished goods to the customer (the period over which a business has ownership of inventory). It is measured by dividing the cost of goods sold by the average inventory on hand
Leads to closing ratio	A measure of the number of sales made divided by responses to a given marketing activity
Market share	The percentage of a market (defined in terms of either units or revenue) accounted for by a specific entity
Media mentions	Number of product or service mentions or appearances per medium per month and whether those mentions were positive or negative
Price sensitivity	A measure of the degree to which demand for a given product is affected by a change in its price
Rating point	A rating point is defined as the reach of a media vehicle as a percentage of a defined population (for example, a television show with a rating of 2 reaches 2% of the population)
Reach	Also called net reach, this measure is the number or percentage of individuals in a defined population who receive at least one exposure to an advertisement. The number of different persons or households exposed to a particular advertising media vehicle or a media schedule during a specified period of time. It is also called cumulative audience, cumulative reach, net audience, net reach, net unduplicated audience, or unduplicated audience. Reach is often presented as a percentage of the total number of persons in a specified audience or target market
Recall (aided and unaided)	The percentage of people who remember a given ad or commercial in a survey situation when asked generically and specifically about what they recall
Referrals by customer/per customer	Number of customers willing to refer new customers and number of referrals by each customer
Sales per customer	Number of sales made by a given customer in a given time frame
Sales by channel	Number of sales made through a specific distribution channel in a given time frame
Willingness to recommend	The percentage of customers who indicate that they would recommend a brand to friends

Definitions are adapted from the Common Language Marketing Dictionary, Marketing Accountability Standards Board (2018)

There are many potential metrics related to the performance of a business. Some are more important than others in terms of the information they provide about performance. Some metrics mean more in a given business category. For example, changes in the number of visits to an e-commerce site might be a much more significant metric than visits to an informational site.

Companies tend to identify a small number of critical metrics that they monitor closely. Such metrics are often referred to as *Key Performance Indicators* (KPIs). KPIs indicate how effectively a company is meeting its business objectives. They may exist at multiple levels within an organization. For example, changes in cash flow over time may be an important, high-level KPI for the firm as a whole, while lower level KPIs may exist for specific functions or departments within the firm, such as advertising and sales.

Identification of an appropriate set of KPIs for a business requires a clear understanding of the firm's business model and the processes by which revenue, and ultimately cash flow, is generated. The selection of KPIs requires being able to tell the story of how the business works at the level of the customer.

Descriptive Versus Predictive Measures

As noted above, some measures and metrics may describe the current state of the market. Product awareness, purchase intention, customer satisfaction, and market share, among many others, may be obtained for a specific point in time and a specific group of customers to provide a snapshot of how the firm is performing on these measures. Many firms engage in *tracking studies*, which involve the continuous collection of measures over time so that they can identify changes that occur over time. Such changes may be in response to the firm's own actions, the actions of competitors, or general shifts in the environment, such as a major change in the overall economy.

The same measures, which are retrospective when used descriptively, can also be used for predictive purposes. For example, consumer purchase intentions are known to be related to future purchases (Douglas and Wind 1971; Morwitz et al. 2007). Therefore, many firms monitor purchase intentions as a way to forecast future sales. Thus, purchase intention can be descriptive if used to describe the current moment or predictive if used to forecast the future.

Diagnostic Versus Evaluative Measures

Measures and metrics are often used to determine the extent to which a course of action was successful. Such measures are evaluative. They provide information about whether or not the objectives of a marketing activity or program have been attained. Thus, if the goal of an advertising campaign is to increase unit sales over some time period, the metric of change in sales would be appropriate.

Such *evaluative measures* are clearly important for assessing whether marketing goals are attained. However, such metrics usually do not provide much information about why a goal was or was not attained. Diagnosing the reason(s) some activity did or did not work, or why it worked as it did, requires different types of measures—*diagnostic measures*. The purposes of diagnostic measures are to answer the question "why?" and to suggest potential actions for improving an evaluative metric.

In the advertising example, it may be useful to measure such things as the reach of the advertising, that is, the number of people who saw the advertising, recall, the number of people who remember seeing the advertising, and the persuasiveness of the advertising. A study of these diagnostic measures might show the campaign reached few people, in which case a different advertising schedule and greater expenditures on media may improve performance. On the other hand, a measure such as recall might suggest that the advertising is gaining the attention of consumers or a measure of persuasiveness might reveal that the advertising message is not compelling.

Rarely is it sufficient to simply conclude that a marketing activity or program failed to work or did not achieve the intended results. Usually, when this happens there is a need to diagnose the reasons for a lack of success and the types of changes that can change the outcome. This is the role of diagnostic measures and metrics.

Process Performance Versus Outcome Metrics

Financial outcomes associated with product and service sales are typically the culmination of many steps in a process. The customer moves from recognition of a need to awareness of products that might meet the need, to evaluation of alternatives, and, finally, to purchase. The process through which consumers move through these stages is referred to as the *customer journey*. From the marketers' perspective, these stages are often

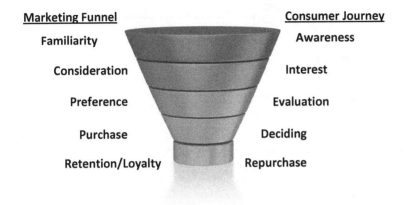

Marketing Funnel

Familiarity

Consideration

Preference

Purchase

Retention/Loyalty

Consumer Journey

Awareness

Interest

Evaluation

Deciding

Repurchase

Fig. 5.1 Two sides of the same process: the customer journey and sales funnel

referred to as the *marketing or sales funnel*. Figure 5.1 provides an illustration of the two perspectives. Obviously, there are many potential variations in such processes that vary in the number and types of steps. For example, for a product purchased in a bricks and mortar retail store, one step would involve the consumer visiting the store, while for a product purchased online, one step would be visiting a website.

There are intermediate marketing measures that can track consumers' progress in their journey and the success of marketing activities in moving consumers through the various stages in this process. Indeed, it is possible to profile a market in terms of the number and percentage of consumers at each stage. The measures that track consumers' progress through their journey are referred to as process performance metrics.

Performance metrics are ongoing measures that indicate whether a process is or is not working to achieve specific goals related to moving consumers from one stage to the next. Examples include the percent of consumers who are aware of the product, numbers of inquiries, leads generated, store or website visits, and daily sales among many others. Figure 5.2 provides an illustration of how a market might be profiled in terms of where customers and potential customers fall in their customer journey, or in the marketing funnel, at one instant in time.

A customer journey like the one depicted in Fig. 5.2 is useful for planning marketing activities and expenditures. It shows where there is the

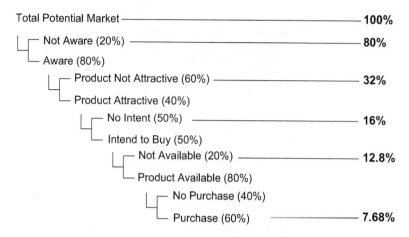

Fig. 5.2 A snapshot of a market based on stage in the customer journey

greatest opportunity to influence consumers in their journey toward purchase. In this example, consider the impact of product awareness. If we hypothesize that the market is worth $10 million, then the 80% measure of awareness translates into an effective market size of $8 million. The other metrics then show how that $8 million shrinks as product attractiveness, buying intention, availability, and so forth affect the final purchasing volume. Table 5.2 provides the computations for this example.

Investing in one stage of the customer journey could have an impact on purchasing volumes. The question, of course, is where should you invest? Not all stages of the journey are the same in terms of financial impact. Continuing with our example, if we were able to raise product awareness from 80% to 85%, purchases would increase from $768,000 to $816,000, a delta of $48,000. Alternatively, if we could increase availability from 80% to 90%, sales jumps to $864,000, a delta of $96,000.

Which one is better to try? That depends on the level of the investment. If it will cost a million dollars to increase your product availability from 80% to 90%, it's not a good move. If you can increase awareness for nothing, which might be possible with a co-op advertising program, for instance, that would make a lot of sense.

Process performance metrics may be contrasted with outcome metrics that are obtained at the end of some process defined by a specific time interval, such as sales revenue or market share in the last quarter. The

Table 5.2   Computational illustration of customer journey

	Measure	Effect on customer journey	Market in dollars
Total potential market	100%	100%	$10,000,000
Awareness	80%	80%	$8,000,000
Product attractiveness	40%	32%	$3,200,000
Intent to buy	50%	16%	$1,600,000
Product availability	80%	13%	$1,280,000
Purchase	60%	7.68%	$768,000

diversity of consumers, products, and markets means that there may be many different consumer journeys, and in turn, a seemingly overwhelming number of performance-related intermediate marketing outcomes.

Fortunately, for any particular product or service there tend to be only a few variations in the purchase process, and therefore, a relatively small number of performance metrics that are likely to be important. A key to identifying and understanding these metrics is to map the customer journey. Such mapping is relatively easy to do by talking with customers. Formal treatments of how to study the purchase process abound and range from qualitative research to survey research.[2] Marketing process management software tools, sometimes called customer relationship management software programs, are also available for tracking markets based on the percent of customers in any given stage at a particular point in time.[3]

Linking marketing activities and expenditures to financial outcomes is nearly impossible without an understanding of the customers' journey, the metrics that illuminate where customers are in their journey, and the influence of marketing activities on these metrics. Chapter 6 will discuss making such linkages.

DIRECT VERSUS DERIVED MEASURES

A direct measure or metric is one you can obtain directly from objective, available information. You can count social media likes or the dollar amount of sales. You can ask consumers directly about the importance of particular

---

[2] Textbooks of marketing research and the customer journey are numerous and widely available.

[3] Such firms as Salesforce.com, Surado CRM, Oracle, and many others offer suites of software programs for such purposes.

product attributes. Other times, you need to take an indirect approach and derive a measure from other sources of data. The results of these calculations are known as derived measures. For example, *Market Share* is derived by dividing the sales of a given firm by total sales in the category. This computation can be done for unit sales, sales revenue, or both.

Research designed to determine the relative importance of individual product attributes offers another example of derived measures in marketing. While it is possible to ask consumers about the relative importance of attributes, consumers are sometimes not very accurate in offering such information (Green et al. 1981). Thus, it works better to derive the importance of product and service attributes through statistical estimation based on consumers' choices among alternatives with various configurations of attributes.

An important limitation of derived measures resides in the fact that these are constructed or computed measures based on multiple other measures. This means that any error in the component measures magnifies the error in the ultimate derived measure. Chapter 6 will consider the implications of this limitation for business and marketing planning.

ABSOLUTE VERSUS RELATIVE MEASURES

Marketing activities do not occur in isolation. Rather, the behavior of consumers occurs in a context. For instance, what may seem like a large marketing budget in an absolute sense can actually be quite small compared to what competitors are spending. It is often useful, therefore, to examine marketing actions and outcomes relative to the market as a whole or relative to competitors.

Consider market share, which represents a firm's sales relative to the sales in the entire category:

$$\text{Market Share} = \text{Sales of Firm} \div \text{Sales in the Category}$$

$$\text{For example, } 50\% \text{ Market share} = \$5000 \text{ Sales of Firm} \div \$10,000 \text{ Sales in the Category}$$

Market share can be computed based on unit sales or based on sales revenue. It can be computed for an individual product or brand or for all products the firm offers in a given category. Similarly, market share can be computed by individual market or geographic region. Market share is widely used as a measure of a brand's competitiveness, that is, how well the brand is doing relative to its competitors. It has the advantage of separating brand effects from category effects, so it is a measure of customers' choices among alternatives rather than whether the category as a whole is growing or declining.

Increases in market share have been shown to be linked to cash flow (Buzzell and Gale 1987), but there are marketing decisions that can increase market share while decreasing cash flow. For example, as shown in Table 5.3, lowering price may grow market share, but reduce cash flow. This is one reason why it is important to explicitly link intermediate marketing outcomes to cash flow rather than judge success only in terms of marketing outcomes.

Table 5.3 illustrates the tension between price, market share, and cash flow. In order to see the effect, it's necessary to understand a few assumptions about this kind of financial/economic modeling. We will assume that the total market size in units is fixed, for example, there are only so many units of this product that will ever be sold. There is also a correlation between price and unit sales, meaning that a reduction in price will translate into higher unit sales for a firm.

Thus, if the firm lowers its unit price from $10 to $9, its unit sales will increase from 2500 to 2625. (To get this figure, we've made a further assumption that the unit sales increase will be one half of the percentage of the price reduction. A 10% price drop results in a 5% sales increase.) This price drop makes the firm's market share go up, from 25% to 26%. However, sales revenue drops accordingly, from $25,000 to $23,625.

When examining relative measures, such as market share, it is important to be clear about how the market is defined. Coca-Cola's share of the soft drink market is very different from its share of the beverage market.

Table 5.3 Increasing market share does not always increase revenue

	Before price change	*After price change*	
Total market size in units	10,000	10,000	
Unit price charged by firm	$10.00	$9.00	
Price increase/decrease			10%
Impact of price change on unit sales			5%
Units sold by firm	2500	2625	
Total revenue for firm	$25,000	$23,625	
Market share for firm (units)	25%	26%	

Similarly, a dry-cleaning business may have a large market share in the small town in which it is located but have an extremely small share in the national dry-cleaning market. Thus, it is important to determine the most relevant point(s) of comparison.

MEASURES OF EFFICIENCY VERSUS MEASURES OF EFFECTIVENESS

Finally, it is important to distinguish between measures of efficiency and measures of effectiveness. Measures of efficiency focus on the resources required to obtain a particular result. Cost per thousand (CPM) is a measure of how many thousands of impressions or viewers can be obtained for a given cost. Thus, if a particular magazine delivers an advertisement to 2 million subscribers and charges $50,000 for the advertising placement, the cost per thousand would be

$$CPM = \$50,000\,(2,000,000 \div 1000) = \$50,000 \div 2000 = \$25.00$$

Measures of efficiency are useful for planning and budgeting because they provide a means for comparing the relative cost, or efficiency, of obtaining some result, such as delivering a specific advertisement to 2 million subscribers to a magazine. However, it is important to recognize that efficiency is not the same as effectiveness. If the 2 million subscribers to the magazine in the example are not in the market for the product being advertised, the advertisement will not be effective in communicating a message to potential buyers. Similarly, it may be less costly to produce one television commercial as compared to another, but if the less costly commercial fails to persuade consumers it is ineffective. The lesson is that measures of efficiency are useless in the absence of evidence of effectiveness. An ineffective action is never efficient.

BEWARE OF MEASURES BEARING THE SAME NAME

When using a measure of intermediate marketing outcomes, it is important to know how the measure was constructed and obtained. There are many measures that differ in their construction that are called by the same name. This is true for even seemingly simple measures. Consider brand awareness, a measure of whether consumers are familiar with the brand.

Awareness can be measured in many different ways. It can be measured by showing the brand to the consumer and asking if he or she recognizes it. Alternatively, the consumer might be asked what brands come to mind when they think of the product category, for example, what brands come to mind when you think of toothpaste? It is no surprise that these measures of "awareness" produce different results. It is not that either approach is right or wrong, but it is important for planning purposes and for evaluation of outcomes that there be an understanding of what is measured and how what was specifically measured is related to other measures and outcomes.

The marketing discipline is replete with names of measures and outcomes that have the same name, but are really operationally different measures: brand loyalty, persuasion, and customer satisfaction, among many others. The decisions about which intermediate marketing measures to use and the operational form of those measures should not be left to marketing researchers and analysts, though such professionals can clearly be helpful. Rather, the marketing strategist needs a deep understanding of measures: what is measured, how the measurement is done, and how particular measures are related to one another and ultimately financial performance.

Selecting the Right Measures and Metrics

Measurement is critical, but the process requires time, resources, and discipline. It is neither possible nor economical to try to measure everything. It is important to select a few key measures that can guide planning and provide feedback on the outcome of marketing activities. Different activities often require different metrics. Planning for advertising involves different measures compared to planning distribution. Planning for a price promotion requires different information from that required for executing a sports sponsorship program. However, all of these activities must ultimately roll up to the firm's business model and the financial performance of the firm. Intermediate outcome measures associated with individual marketing activities need to be justified in terms of their contribution to financial performance.

No measure is perfect. Even seemingly "hard" numbers, like inventory counts, are often estimates. It is a fact that there is some error in most measures. But some measures are better than others. Particularly when dealing with intermediate marketing measures that involve collection of data from consumers through observation of behavior, surveys, and other marketing research methods, the amount of error can be large. Thus, in selecting particular measures it is important to select those that minimize error. There are three key characteristics that should be considered when selecting measures to minimize error: reliability, validity, and precision.

Reliability Reliability refers to the overall consistency of a measure. A measure is reliable to the extent that it produces the same result under consistent conditions, that is, if the measure is taken a second time and nothing has changed, the measure should produce the same value. Reliability is generally measured by the correlation of a measure with itself, when the measure is taken two or more times in the same situation. Thus, reliability ranges from zero, no reliability at all, to 1.0, which is perfect reliability.

There are numerous forms of reliability, but in marketing, the two forms that are most common and useful are *test-retest reliability* and *inter-rater reliability*. Test-retest reliability simply means that the measure is taken at least twice in the same or very similar circumstances and the two results compared. Inter-rater reliability is a measure of the agreement between two or more observers of the same phenomenon.

As an example, consider a measure of customer satisfaction obtained from a survey of consumers. Reliability could be determined by randomly splitting the survey sample in half and comparing the results obtained for the two samples. A reliable measure would produce very similar results for each sample. It is easy to see why reliability would be important for a measure of customer satisfaction. If a firm is interested in tracking real changes in customer satisfaction over time, or wishes to compare satisfaction with service received at different locations, it is important that the measure of satisfaction be reliable. This is because any changes or differences in the measure should reflect actual differences in customer satisfaction rather than random error.

Validity Validity refers to the extent to which a measure actually reflects what it is supposed to reflect. For example, a measure of purchase intention should, in fact, be related to real purchases that will occur in the future. While there are numerous forms of validity, in marketing practice, the most common and useful form of validity is *predictive validity*. Predictive validity is established by showing the degree to which a measure predicts something else of interest. In the case of purchase intention, a valid measure would have a strong and known relationship with future purchases.

It is important to note that the validity of a measure revolves around the purpose or use of the measure. Measures are valid for a particular purpose and they may not be valid for other purposes. A bathroom scale may be a valid measure of weight, but is unlikely to be valid as a measure of intelligence. The validity of a measure for a specific purpose is an empirical question.

Like reliability, validity is measured on a scale that ranges from zero, no validity, to one, perfect validity. Rather than a correlation coefficient, which defines the degree of reliability, a regression equation is usually used to establish validity, that is, the measure of interest is empirically demonstrated to be predictive of some criterion:

$$\text{Criterion} = \alpha + \beta \left(\text{Measure} \right)$$

Or, in the case of the purchase intention measure:

$$\text{Actual Purchase} = \alpha + \beta \left(\text{Purchase Intentions} \right)$$

It is useful to note that a measure can be no more valid than it is reliable, that is, a measure cannot predict something else better than it can predict itself.

Many intermediate marketing measures are used to predict future outcomes. In the context of forecasting the influence of marketing actions and expenditures on future cash flows, it is critical to use valid intermediate measures. The more valid the intermediate measure, other things being equal, the more accurate the forecast will be. Chapter 6 will provide an example of how the validity of a specific measure is determined.

Precision Precision refers to how accurate or exact a measure is. Stated in other words, precision refers to the confidence that can be placed in the specific value, or number, obtained using a particular measure. In a statistical sense, precision refers to the size of the confidence interval around a given value. A large confidence interval means a measure is less precise, while a small confidence interval means a measure is more precise. Other things being equal, it is preferable to use more precise measures because greater precision reduces error both in describing a current circumstance and in predicting future outcomes.

In marketing, a common contributor to precision when collecting data from consumers is the size of the sample used. Larger samples usually result in greater precision, though at a higher cost. In general, more reliable, more valid, and more precise intermediate marketing metrics are desirable because these characteristics of measures can dramatically influence the accuracy of predictions of future marketing outcomes and cash flow.

A SIMPLE ILLUSTRATION

To see the power of intermediate marketing measures, consider a very simple forecasting model that is informed by three measures: consumer awareness, product availability (distribution coverage), and consumers' purchase intentions. Consumer awareness is defined as the percentage of consumers in the market for the product category who name a particular brand in response to a question about what brands in the category come to mind. Distribution is defined as the percentage of consumers who can easily obtain the product, that is, the brand is readily available to them. Finally, purchase intention is defined as the percentage of consumers who state that they plan to purchase a particular brand in the category on the next purchase occasion. All three of these measures can be obtained from a relatively simple survey of consumers.

These measures reflect a model of aggregate consumer behavior that posits that sales are the result of consumers being aware of a brand, are able to easily obtain the brand, and purchase the product that best meets their needs. Using this model, market share can be estimated by the following equation:

$$\text{Market Share} = \text{Percent Aware} \times \text{Percent Available} \times \text{Purchase Intention}$$

Thus, for a brand with 80% awareness, 80% distribution coverage, and 50% purchase intention:

$$\text{Market Share} = 80\% \times 80\% \times 50\% = 32\%$$

Such a simple model can provide powerful insights. For example, if the size of the category is known, the revenue of the firm can be obtained by multiplying market share by the total size of the market in terms of revenue. If margins are known, the contribution before marketing expenditures and overheads can be obtained by multiplying total units sold in the category times market share times margin on each unit:

$$\text{Gross Contribution} = \text{Size of Market} \left(\text{in units}\right) \times \text{Market Share} \times \text{Unit Margin}$$

The model can also be a powerful diagnostic tool that can suggest potential marketing actions for improving sales. Table 5.4 illustrates three different scenarios in which the factors that influence market share are broken out. Looking at the model in each situation reveals an opportunity to expand market share by advertising to raise awareness in scenario (1), by expanding distribution in scenario (2), and by improving the product in scenario (3).

Table 5.4 Using measures to diagnose a marketing opportunities and problems

Percent aware of product	Percent for which product is available	Percent intending to purchase	Market share	Potential action
(1) 10%	80%	50%	4%	Advertise to raise awareness
(2) 80%	10%	50%	4%	Expand distribution
(3) 80%	80%	1%	>1%	Improve product

Obviously, to be useful such a model cannot be static. The values of awareness, availability, and purchase intention parameters need to be continuously updated and there is a need to identify how quickly changes in these parameters are reflected in sales and changes in market share. Nevertheless, the model is a simple but powerful tool for marketing planning and for linking marketing actions and expenditures to cash flows.

CONCLUSION

This chapter has provided an introduction to the many intermediate marketing measures and metrics used in marketing planning and performance evaluation. It is important that measures and metrics be linked to the business model of the firm and that a small number of critical measures, KPIs, be identified for close monitoring because they reflect the health of the business. Measures may serve many purposes and it is important to select the measure(s) that best serve these purposes. It is also important to select intermediate measures that possess adequate reliability, validity, and precision. Finally, the chapter provides an illustration of the power of intermediate marketing measures in a simple model of market share forecasting.

Exercises

1. Do an Internet search on each of the following three intermediate marketing measures: brand loyalty, customer satisfaction, and engagement. How many different definitions of these measures did you find? Compare and contrast any two measures in each category. Do they really measure the same thing? Could you find information on reliability, validity, and precision for the measures you found in your search?
2. Identify any three measures in Table 5.1 that you think would be good KPIs. Why did you select them? Under what circumstances and in which businesses would these measures be useful KPIs?
3. Consider the simple model illustrated in Table 5.3. How might you use the model in scenario (1) to determine whether a firm could justify a $5 million advertising campaign?

Points to Ponder

1. Why are intermediate marketing measures and metrics necessary? Why isn't it possible to go directly from marketing actions and expenditures to financial results? If you could go directly from marketing actions and expenditures to financial results, would there still be a need for intermediate measures? Why or why not?
2. Obtaining measures and metrics requires time, effort, and resources that could be devoted to other activities, such as research and development, advertising, social media, personal selling, and support for distribution. How would you justify time, effort, and resources for measurement? How might you determine how much should be invested in measurement?

REFERENCES

Bendle, N. T., Farris, P. W., Pfeifer, P. E., & Reibstein, D. J. (2016). *Marketing Metrics: The Managers Guide to Measuring Marketing Performance* (3rd ed.). Upper Saddle River: N. J. Pearson.

Buzzell, R. D., & Gale, B. T. (1987). *The PIMS Principles: Linking Strategy to Performance*. New York: Free Press.

Davis, J. A. (2018). *Measuring Marketing: The 100+ Essential Metrics Every Marketer Needs* (3rd ed.). Boston: Walter de Gruyter.

Douglas, S. P., & Wind, Y. (1971). Intentions to Buy as Predictors of Buying Behavior. In D. M. Gardner (Ed.), *Proceedings of the Second Annual Conference of the Association for Consumer Research* (pp. 331–343). College Park: Association for Consumer Research.

Green, P. E., Goldberg, S. M., & Montemayor, M. (1981). A Hybrid Utility Estimation Model for Conjoint Analysis. *Journal of Marketing, 45*(1), 33–41.

Kozielski, R. (2018). *Mastering Market Analytics, Business Metrics – Practice and Application*. Bingley: Emerald Publishing.

Marketing Accountability Standards Board. (2018). *Common Language Marketing Dictionary*. http://www.marketing-dictionary.org

Morwitz, V., Steckel, J. H., & Gupta, A. (2007). When Do Purchase Intentions Predict Sales? *International Journal of Forecasting, 23*(3), 347–364.

Rappaport, S. D. (2015). *The Digital Metrics Field Guide: The Definitive Reference for Brands Using the Web, Social media, Mobil Media, or Email*. Amsterdam: BIS Publishers.

CHAPTER 6

Linking Marketing Outcomes to Financial Performance

Next time you go to the drugstore, stand in the dental care aisle for a few minutes and watch people select a brand of toothpaste. Some shoppers will likely grab the brand they've always bought. If you ask them why, they might not even know why they prefer it over a competitor. (Hint: it probably has to do with thousands of brand exposures over many years.) Other shoppers genuinely don't know. They have no preference other than perhaps the one that's on sale.

One group, however, will have a specific, marketing-driven reason for their selection. They will deliberately choose Colgate over Crest. Within these groups, some may even prefer anticavity protection over whitening. Why? What is driving these choices? The short answer is marketing. It might be a commercial on television. It could be a coupon they received in the mail. Or it might be an in-store display.

Each of these campaigns will likely affect an intermediate marketing measure. The commercial, for example, might increase brand awareness. The in-store display might increase brand preference. The coupon might influence purchase intent. Following up on the previous chapter, which described the important role of intermediate marketing outcome measures and identified a number of specific examples, the focus of this chapter is the identification of the links between these intermediate measures and measures of financial performance.

© The Author(s) 2019
D. W. Stewart, *Financial Dimensions of Marketing Decisions*,
Palgrave Studies in Marketing, Organizations and Society,
https://doi.org/10.1007/978-3-030-15565-0_6

How does a specific marketing action (and the money it costs) affect sales? Linking marketing activities and expenditures to cash flow requires three things: (1) the story of how marketing activities and expenditures influence sales or margins; (2) a baseline that indicates what sales would be without marketing activity and expenditures; and (3) a set of intermediate outcome measures that are reliable predictors or antecedents of financial results.

How Marketing Influences Sales and Margins

As noted in Chap. 4, there are only three sources of operational cash flow: (1) acquisition and retention of customers; (2) growth of product or service use within the category through increasing market share or frequency of use (share of category); and (3) expansion of the number of the firm's products and services that are purchased by customers (share of wallet). The firm's business model is the conceptual framework that explains how the firm manages these three sources of cash flow. Thus, any effort to link marketing outcomes to financial performance requires a detailed and comprehensive understanding of the firm's business model and how the various sources of cash are activated within this model.

It is not possible to put numbers to a business model until the business model itself has been identified and described in detail. This is about telling the story of how the business is supposed to work. It is surprising how often marketing managers have difficulty telling the story. Often, the story includes implicit or implied assumptions that are not articulated or that leave the story incomplete because the story stops with the intermediate marketing outcomes. Such incomplete stories of the business are reminiscent of the cartoon in which the explanation includes the phrase "and then a miracle occurs." Whether miracles occur or not, such explanations lack credibility and make linkages between marketing actions and expenditures and financial performance impossible to identify and test.

Finding the Baseline Sales Level

Estimating the impact of a marketing activity requires knowing the baseline level of sales. *Baseline* sales are those that would occur in the absence of marketing activities or in the absence of a change in marketing activities.

Except for truly new products, some sales are likely to occur without any marketing activity, at least in the short term. The influence of a change in marketing activities must be evaluated against what would have happened without the change.

The value of marketing resides in the degree to which it can change the baseline. In the extreme case, the baseline might be sales that would occur in the absence of any marketing activity. More often, baseline represents sales that would occur in the context of an ongoing set of marketing activities. In the latter case, the question for analysis is the incremental contribution to sales, relative to the baseline, of additional marketing activities and expenditures.

A simple way to think of baseline is that it represents what would have happened anyway had there been no marketing activity or no incremental marketing activity. Baseline can be expressed as a formula:

$$\text{Baseline} = \text{Total sales} - \text{sales attributed to marketing}$$

While the formula suggests that a baseline is easy to measure, it is often difficult to determine in practice. Few firms are willing to stop all marketing activities to see what happens. Firms do often change, reduce, or stop specific marketing activities altogether or in specific markets in order to gauge the effects of such changes. Such experimentation provides a sense of the baseline.

Further complicating determination of baseline is the fact that changes in sales occur for reasons other than those associated with a firm's marketing activities. Competitors' actions may influence the responses of customers, retailers, and others in the marketplace. The strong marketing campaign of a competitor may reduce a firm's sales, just as a competitor's product quality problem may increase a firm's sales. Customers may continue to praise a product or service even in the absence of formal marketing efforts. In some product categories, sales may increase or decline regularly based on factors such as the time of year (often referred to as seasonality), weather, and the general economic climate. All of these types of factors need to be accounted for when determining baseline.

Establishing a baseline provides the means to do two important things. First, it allows the determination of the incremental impact of marketing activities and expenditures. The goal of such a determination is to identify how much of any change in sales is attributable to marketing. Second, it provides a means for explaining variations in sales over time when there have been no changes in marketing activities. Thus, if sales increased by 20% over the last quarter it is useful to know that half of this increase was attributable to specific marketing actions and the other half was due to general growth in the size of the market. Such analyses provide powerful support for marketing actions and expenditures and also reduce the likelihood that marketing will be blamed for changes that result from external factors that are not within the control of the marketing function.

It is important to recognize that a baseline is not static; rather, it will vary over time depending on external conditions, competitors' actions, and the firm's own marketing efforts. This means that determination of baseline must be a continuous process. Making such estimation continuous is important for two reasons. First, it permits the identification of the immediate effects of marketing actions. Second, it provides a means for discovering the longer term effects of marketing actions described in Chap. 2. Thus, an increase in market share that persists over time may be an indicator of a successful marketing campaign. Similarly, a branding campaign built around an improvement in the quality of service may enable the firm to charge a higher price without loss of sales, which would change the baseline for revenue.

It is tempting to attribute any change in baseline, up or down, to marketing actions. This is both wrong and unfair. Changes in baseline attributable to external factors and to changes in customer behavior among those not exposed to the firm's marketing efforts do not provide insight into the effects of marketing activities and expenditures. It is important to account for non-marketing factors that influence baseline.

Finally, analysis of the baseline should reflect all of the identifiable factors that contribute to changes in sales, revenue, market share, or other outcomes of interest. This means that there is a need for a deep understanding of the factors that drive demand for a product or service in the marketplace. Just as knowledge of the firm's business model is critical to linking marketing to financial performance, so too is a deep knowledge of customer behavior.

Marketing Outcomes Versus Baseline Case Example: Toothpaste at Retail

To get a handle on how marketing outcomes connect to financial results, we will quickly run through a case example featuring the business model at work in the toothpaste aisle. The rest of the chapter will then flesh out the concepts explored in this initial case. We will look at the business model from the toothpaste manufacturer's perspective. The retailer also has a separate business model, and while it's interesting to see how they intersect, we will keep it nice and simple for now.

First, let's focus on the basic relationship between a marketing outcome and a financial result. In Table 6.1, we're positing that a 1% increase in brand awareness, an intermediate measure, will translate into a 5% increase in unit sales volume. How do you increase brand awareness? There are many ways, including advertising, direct mail coupons, and so forth.

Working with this simple model, which is shown in the spreadsheet in Table 6.1, we see that a $40 marketing expenditure will get the desired 1% increase in brand awareness. (This is not realistic, but it's useful for illustrative purposes here.) An outlay of $1500 will result in a 38% jump in brand awareness. At 5% of unit sales growth per 1% of increase in brand awareness, the marketing activity generates a 190% growth in unit sales (38% × 5%).

The "baseline" unit sales—the level of sales that occurs without any marketing influence—is 1000 units per month. After the marketing spend, unit sales go up to 2875 units based on the effects of increased brand awareness. Gross profit contribution grows from $1000 to $2875, and the net contribution after marketing is $355. The $1875

Table 6.1 Outcomes versus baseline example

Intermediate measure to unit sales calculation	
If you increase brand awareness by	1.00%
Unit sales volume will increase by	5.00%
Financial model of increase in intermediate measure	
Cost to increase brand awareness by 1% (through marketing)	$40
Expenditure on increasing brand awareness	$1520
Increase in brand awareness	38%
Baseline unit sales	1000
Unit sales after increase in brand awareness	2875
Gross profit contribution per unit sold	$1.00
Baseline gross profit contribution	$1000
Gross profit contribution after increase in brand awareness	$2875
Increase in gross profit contribution	$1875
Increase in contribution after accounting for marketing	$355
Return on investment in increasing brand awareness	23%

gain in gross profit translates into a return on investment (ROI) of 25% for the $1500 marketing spend.

Now, let's apply this approach to the toothpaste example. The manufacturer buys the ingredients, things like calcium carbonate and dicalcium phosphates, and processes them into toothpaste. In a large plant, the manufacturer places the toothpaste in tubes, boxes the tubes, and ships them to retailers. Imagine that each tube of toothpaste costs the manufacturer ten cents to produce. The wholesale price paid by the retailer is $1.10 per tube. The manufacturer makes $1 per tube in gross profit.

So far, so good. But do we think the retailer puts the manufacturer's toothpaste on the shelf out of kindness? Certainly not. The manufacturer pays for the shelf space in the store. The retailer charges the manufacturer a "rent" for a space on the shelf for the manufacturer's product, a fee sometimes called a "slotting fee" or "listing fee." Many retailers make their money by renting out their shelves. Their actual margins on retail sales are often quite slim.

The retailer charges the manufacturer $100 per month per shelf to "slot" the toothpaste. The position on the shelf is also not an accident. The retailer sells premium space, that is, at eye level, for more than he charges for floor level. The slotting fee and product position are indicated on a chart called a "planogram."

A practical question for planning: How many tubes of toothpaste does the manufacturer need to sell per month to break even on the slotting fee? We can calculate that by dividing the slotting fee by the gross margin (contribution) for each tube sold. That looks like: $100 slotting fee ÷ $1 per tube gross margin contribution = 100 tubes per month break-even volume.

The modeling example illustrated in Table 6.2 shows the effects of marketing activities on toothpaste sales. The model assumes a gross margin contribution of $1 per tube sold; the baseline sales volume (before marketing) is 250 units per store per month. With the wholesale price of a tube of toothpaste at $1.10, the baseline monthly revenue—for the toothpaste manufacturer—is $275 per store. Monthly gross profit is $250. Net of the $100 slotting fee, each store is contributing $150 per month to the company. Selling in 1000 stores, the toothpaste generates $275,000 in revenue, $250,000 in gross margin contribution, and $150,000 per month in gross margin net of slotting fees.

Table 6.2 Modeling ROI

Manufacturer business model	As is	After marketing activity
Manufacturing cost per tube of toothpaste	$0.10	$0.10
Wholesale price (to retailer) of tube	$1.10	$1.10
Gross margin (contribution) per tube	$1.00	$1.00
Slotting fee (per month/per store)	$100	$108
Baseline sales per month (tubes sold per store)	250	280
Baseline wholesale revenue—per store	$275	$308
Baseline gross profit—per store	$250	$280
Gross profit per store net of slotting fee	$150	$172
Number of stores where toothpaste is sold	1000	1000
Slotting fees for all stores	$100,000	$108,000
Sales per month (tubes sold in all stores)	250,000	280,000
Wholesale revenue—for all stores	$275,000	$308,000
Gross profit—for all stores	$250,000	$280,000
Gross profit store net of slotting fees	$150,000	$172,000
Predictors	Impact of activity on unit sales	Cost of activity
Effect of marketing activity on unit sales	5.00%	$10,000
Effect of slotting position change on unit sales	7.00%	$8000
Total costs of marketing activities		$18,000
Delta in gross profit from promotion	$22,000	
Cost of promotion	$18,000	
ROI of promotion	22%	

Now, let's model the impact of two marketing activities. One is a promotion of some sort, like a TV commercial, that drives customers to the stores. The other is a change in slotting, a shift in positioning so the toothpaste is more visible to the buyer at the point of sale. They cost $10,000 and $8000, respectively. The promotion pushes unit sales up by 5%, while the slotting change pushes sales up by 7%.

The combined effect of the $18,000 spent on promotion and the slotting change causes unit sales to go from 250 tubes per month to 280. Revenue and gross profit go up as well. Net of the $18,000 spent on the promotion and slotting change, the activities have resulted in an increase of gross profit of $22,000. The ROI of these activities is 22%.

RELIABLE AND VALID MEASURES OF INTERMEDIATE MARKETING OUTCOMES

Chapter 5 explored the role of measures of intermediate marketing outcomes and identified a number of examples of such measures. These measures take many forms, have many different uses, and vary considerably in their reliability, validity, and precision. It is often tempting to select the most convenient and least costly measures of marketing outcomes. Doing so reduces the value of such measures and makes linking to financial performance difficult if not impossible. Given what is at stake in most marketing decisions, an extra resource to assure that measures are reliable and valid is a wise investment. No amount of statistical analysis, no matter how sophisticated, can compensate for error-filled measures.

When selecting intermediate outcome measures it is important to use measures that map into the story of the firm's business model. Some marketing outcomes are necessary but not sufficient for producing financial results. For example, it is usually necessary that consumers are aware of a product or service, but awareness alone does not produce a sale. Indeed, awareness can be high for the wrong reasons. Thus, it is critical to not only identify the right measures but also develop an understanding of how measures are related to one another and ultimately to financial performance. Outcomes often have a cascading effect with lower level outcomes feeding higher level outcomes.

Figure 6.1 provides a conceptual illustration of such cascading outcomes. Lower level outcomes, like awareness, product knowledge, and preference, feed higher order outcomes like brand loyalty and purchase intention, which, in turn, drive sales and margins. There may be a relationship between measures like awareness and financial performance but it is likely to be small because there are so many intervening factors. However, it would be expected that changes in lower level outcomes should influence higher order outcomes. Thus, higher order outcomes are contingent on lower order outcomes, but achieving the lower order objectives does not assure achieving the higher order objectives.

Figure 6.2 provides a real-world example of such contingent outcomes. The figure shows the relationships among the following:

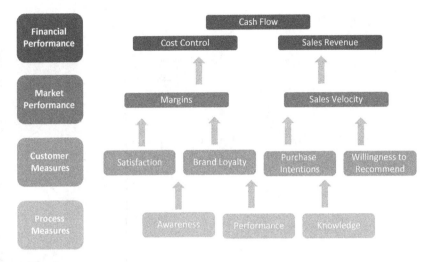

Fig. 6.1   Cascading outcomes

- Advertising recall
- Comprehension of the main message of the advertising
- Characteristics of the advertised product
- Whether new or mature
- A characteristic of the advertising message
- Whether there is a brand-differentiating message
- How the interaction of these effects influences the likelihood of switching to the advertised product

Figure 6.2 summarizes an analysis of 1059 television commercials. Note that the greatest likelihood of switching occurs when recall of the commercial is above average, comprehension of the commercial's message is above average, the message differentiates the advertised product, and the product is new. More than three-quarters of consumers switched from another brand to the advertised brand in this condition. In contrast, at the other end of the spectrum, commercials with below average recall, below average message comprehension, and no brand-differentiating message for a mature product induced switching in only 20% of the cases. If one were to look at the direct relationship of recall to brand switching, the relationship would be small, but when placed in the context of other metrics and

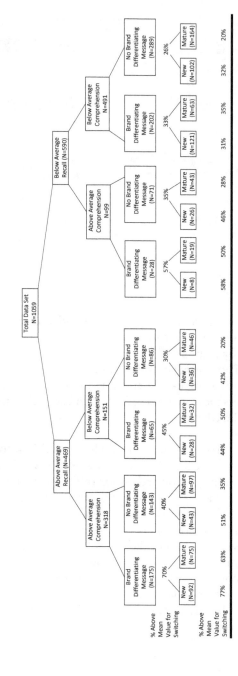

Fig. 6.2 Contingent relationships among marketing outcomes. (Source: Stewart and Furse 1986)

characteristics of products and advertising messages, it is clear that recall matters. However, it is clear that the intermediate outcome measure, recall, is not especially helpful outside of the context of other factors.

Marketing Mix Modeling

A quantitative approach to identifying relationships among marketing activities and intermediate marketing outcomes and between such outcomes and financial performance is known as *marketing mix modeling (MMM)*. In the context of digital marketing, MMM is often called attribution modeling. This term arises because the analysis seeks to "attribute" effects, like sales, to specific marketing activities. MMM involves the use of statistical analyses to explore the effects of specific marketing activities on intermediate marketing outcomes and ultimately on financial performance.

Multivariate regression, time series analysis, and structural equation modeling are common statistical tools used in MMM. These tools are applied to historical data and/or the results of marketing experiments to quantify the impact of marketing activities and expenditures on sales or other measures of interest. Once a relationship between a marketing activity and outcome is identified, the relationship, expressed as a mathematical equation, can be used to simulate the effects of various alternative marketing actions through "What-if" analysis. MMM is often used to examine product and service design alternatives, media and advertising decisions, trade promotions, distribution, and competitors' potential actions.

The outcome measure of interest is referred to as the dependent variable and the marketing activity of interest is the independent variable. A typical MMM equation might take the following form:

$$\textbf{Sales} = \alpha + \beta\left(\textbf{Purchase Intention}\right) + \varepsilon$$

where Sales is the dependent variable
Purchase Intention is the independent variable
α is the intercept
β is a weight applied to the independent variable
And ε is an "error" term that represents unexplained variability

MMM can be used to establish the validity of an intermediate marketing outcome variable as a predictor of another marketing outcome variable or a measure of financial performance. For example, in the equation above, purchase intention is used to predict actual sales. If the relationship is strong, purchase intention can be used for forecasting the outcome of a marketing action. For example, the effect of an advertisement could be examined to determine whether and how it changes purchase intention among those exposed to the advertisement. This change could then be extrapolated to the larger market as the advertisement was rolled out into the larger market.

MARKETING RETURN ON INVESTMENT

A common use of MMM is to analyze the *marketing return on investment (MROI)* or *return on marketing investment (ROMI)*. MROI or ROMI is the contribution to profit attributable to marketing (net of marketing spending), divided by the marketing invested. It is not like other "return on investment" metrics because marketing is not the same kind of investment. Chapters 10 and 11 will explore these differences in detail. Instead of moneys that are "tied" up in plants and inventories, marketing funds are typically "risked." Usually marketing spending will be deemed as justified if the return is positive (MASB Common Language Marketing Dictionary 2018).

Conceptually, MROI is simple. It is computed as follows:

$$\text{MROI} = \left[\begin{array}{l} \text{Incremental Financial Value} \\ \text{Gained as a Result of the} \\ \text{Marketing Expenditure} \end{array} - \begin{array}{l} \text{Cost of the} \\ \text{Marketing} \\ \text{Activity} \end{array} \right] \div \begin{array}{l} \text{Cost of the} \\ \text{Marketing} \\ \text{Activity} \end{array}$$

In reality, computing return on marketing investments is difficult. It requires separating the specific effects of marketing from all other factors that influence sales, including the general economic climate and competitors' actions. When determining the return of marketing investment for a specific marketing activity, it is also necessary to separate the effect of the individual activity of interest from the effects of all other marketing actions.

The utility of MMM is limited by the availability and quality of the data used in the analysis. Better data always results in greater insight than the most sophisticated statistical analysis of weak, error-filled data. MMM has also been most useful in examining the short-term effects of marketing activities and can under-represent longer term effects. This is because many models fail to include such effects as brand equity and customer loyalty. Chapters 7 and 8 address the role of these two marketing outcomes in detail.

Another limitation is that MMM is not very useful when expenditures are used as the independent variable. Simply spending more or less money provides little insight into how marketing activities influence sales. What the expenditure buys is important. The same amount of money can buy greater or lesser change in awareness and purchase intention depending on the effectiveness of the message and the media employed for transmitting the message to consumers.

Finally, at some point, there will be decreasing returns to additional investment. This tends to be true for spending on individual marketing activities as well as for the total marketing budget. Consider an example related to advertising. Figure 6.3 shows two typical response functions for advertising expenditures. One, the concave function, is typical of markets in which there is relatively little competitive advertising. In such markets advertising expenditures have an immediate effect starting with the first expenditure. The other response function, the S-shaped function, is more typical of markets characterized by substantial competitive advertising where there is a need for a minimum amount of spending to break through competitors' advertising and information clutter (McDonald 1995; Berger and Weinberg 2014). Note that the two response functions are identical except for the threshold at the bottom of the "S."

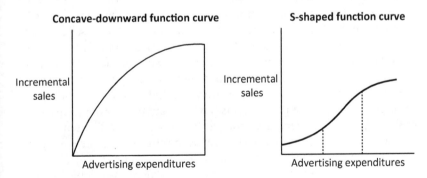

Fig. 6.3 Typical advertising response functions

Careful examination of these two curves makes clear that the return on additional spending on advertising (the ROI) is very much dependent on where a firm is on the curve. There is a very large impact of advertising on sales, and therefore a larger ROI, at the bottom of the curves (or at the end of the threshold for the S-shaped function). However, the impact of incremental additional advertising expenditures on sales becomes less and less as one moves up the curve, until at the top the curves flatten out where there is no incremental effect on sales of additional spending on advertising. Thus, determining ROI in advertising requires knowing where the firm is on the curve. This is another reason why it is important to know the baseline from which the firm is working. Similar response curves and the same issues related to where the firm is on the curve exist for a variety of other marketing activities.

Accounting for the Timing of Sales

Another issue that may arise when determining return on marketing expenditures, or the impact of marketing on sales more generally, is that sales in one time period are often not independent of sales in the preceding and/or subsequent periods. This issue is particularly problematic in the context of price promotions where a price discount may encourage a consumer to purchase earlier than they had planned. For example, a consumer planning to purchase laundry detergent next week, when they know their current supply will be depleted, sees their favorite brand on sale while in a store shopping for other items. Being a conscientious and frugal consumer, the shopper decides to buy their favorite brand while it is on sale rather than wait a week. On the surface, this would appear to be a successful outcome for the price promotion because it creates an immediate sale. However, note that this sale came at the expense of a future sale, the one that would have occurred a week later in any case, and at a lower price than the consumer would have paid otherwise without the price discount. It is just for this reason that marketing analyses have repeatedly shown that most price discounts do not pay out (Abraham and Lodish 1990; Srinivasan et al. 2002). The same problem arises with many trade promotions, price deals offered to retailers and other distributors, who will often use the occasion of a price promotion to do forward purchasing of inventory at a discounted price rather than order later at a regular price.

This does not mean that promotions have no merit. As will be discussed in Chaps. 7 and 8, some types of promotions can build loyalty and create a willingness on the part of consumers to pay a price premium. Airline frequent flyer programs are a good example of such promotions. There are also tactical reasons for using price promotions such as responding to a competitor's price discount to avoid losing sales. It is usually better to make a sale at a modest discount rather than lose it altogether to a competitor. Other justifiable purposes for price promotions are related to the need to clear obsolete inventory and end-of-season items that will be replaced with newer products.

The price promotion problem illustrates the problem with a short-term (one period) revenue-driven plan. The rise in sales associated with a price promotion may increase revenue in a given period. Indeed, such spikes in sales in response to a price discount are easy to measure. The longer term effects require a more complete picture of how customers shop and how retailers buy over time. Price discounts, especially those that occur with regularity, divert customers' attention from other product and service attributes, like quality and brand, and encourage customers to make purchase decisions based on price. Over the long run, this diminishes the ability of the marketer to charge a price premium that might otherwise be justified by the product offering.

Putting the Pieces Together

The preceding discussion makes it clear that it's difficult to link marketing activities and expenditures, intermediate marketing outcomes, and financial performance. Difficult is not the same as impossible, however. In addition, the effort required to develop such linkages can pay off handsomely through more effective and efficient marketing programs and greater revenue associated with higher unit sales and larger unit margins. The ability to tell the story of marketing's contributions and tie these contributions to financial performance also creates credibility for marketing and a stronger justification for marketing resources.

Putting the pieces together is not the responsibility of marketing research or marketing analysts, though these functions have an important role to play. Rather, the ultimate responsibility rests with the marketing manager. For this reason, even if the manager is not a specialist in statistics or MMM, the marketing manager must understand and be able to ask questions about such factors as baseline, marketing response curves, and customer purchase cycles.

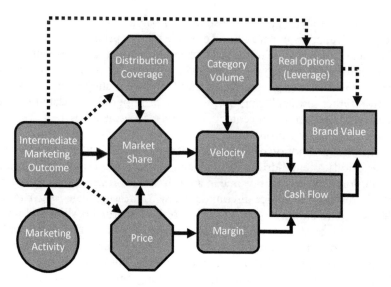

Fig. 6.4 Linking marketing outcomes to financial performance. (Adapted from: Meier et al. 2018)

Figure 6.4, which was first introduced in Chap. 4, provides a structure for linking marketing and financial performance. It assumes that there is an identified marketing activity and expenditure that is intended to influence a well-defined outcome that can be evaluated using a measure that is known to be a reliable predictor of a market outcome that influences cash flow. Thus, the framework shown in Fig. 6.4 could be used to evaluate the financial outcome associated with an advertising campaign designed to increase customers' purchase intentions. The advertising campaign is the focal marketing activity, and the intermediate marketing outcome measure is the customer's purchase intention, which is measured through a survey of customers.

To make the example concrete, the information in Table 6.3 can be used to fill in real numbers. Such information is readily available in most organizations or through third-party market information providers. Assume that purchase intention has been shown to be a strong predictor of market share through a series of validation studies. The firm conducts a marketing experiment in which it shows advertising from the campaign to a sample of representative consumers in the relevant target market. Purchase intention is measured before exposure to

Table 6.3 Assumptions about an advertising campaign to increase customer purchase intentions

Cost of the advertising campaign = $2 million
Price of product per unit = $99
Gross margin per unit = $50
Market size (category volume) = 5 million units
Distribution coverage = 80%
Baseline purchase intention = 40%
Increase in purchase intention created by advertising

the advertising and after exposure to the advertising, and after exposure, purchase intention increases from 40%, the baseline, to 50%, a 10% increase. Note that this information can be obtained in a relatively inexpensive marketing research project before spending large sums on media placement for the advertising. In fact, even the advertising itself could be tested in rough form without the expense of polished, finished production.

Assuming nothing else changes, such as distribution coverage, price, and gross margins, it is a simple matter to extrapolate the results of the experiment to the larger market and derive a measure of the financial return of the advertising campaign. Figure 6.5 replaces the conceptual framework with numbers. The advertising campaign costs $2 million and, to capture all costs, assumes the marketing experiment costs $40,000. The experiment revealed that the advertising increases purchase intention from 40% to 50% for a net increase of 10%. Since purchase intention is a valid predictor of market share it might be assumed that market share would increase by 10%. However, the firm only has distribution that covers 80% of the relevant market. Thus, the increase in market share needs to be reduced to 8%.

Now the math gets easy. Eight percent of a market of 5 million units is 400,000 units. This is the incremental unit sales attributable to the new advertising campaign. The gross margin on each unit is $50. Thus, 400,000 units × $50 per unit is $20,000,000 in incremental cash flow before accounting for the cost of the advertising campaign. This is a pretty good ROI on advertising and testing. The marketing ROI would be computed as

$$MROI = [\$20\,million - \$2.04\,million] \div 2.04\,million = 8.8$$

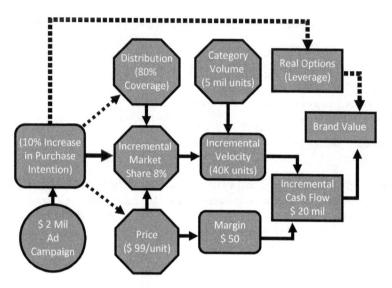

Fig. 6.5 An illustration of linking marketing outcomes to financial performance. (Adapted from: Meier et al. 2018)

The incremental cash flow resulting from the campaign is for the next purchase of the product by consumers. Suppose it is assumed that the increase in purchase intention is permanent, or at least as permanent as such changes are in competitive markets. Assuming the product is purchased once a year and the increase in purchase intention lasts five years, it is not unreasonable to use the net present value of this incremental cash flow as a measure of the increase in brand value attributable to the advertising campaign.

The power of the conceptual model shown in Figs. 6.4 and 6.5 extends to the opportunity to engage in various types of "what-if" analyses. Suppose in response to the advertising campaign, new distribution became available and distribution coverage increased to 90%. Now the campaign would generate 22.5 million in incremental cash flow before accounting for the cost of the advertising campaign. Or, suppose the campaign allowed the firm to sell the product at a higher price and obtain a larger margin without diminishing purchase intention or market share.

While such "what-if" exercises can be a useful guide to planning, even when they are based only on assumptions, in many cases the assumptions can be tested against actual data. However, even in the absence of hard data there is no reason to apologize for making assumptions during planning exercises, as long as the assumptions are clearly identified as such. Assumptions are a part of almost all capital budgeting exercises, for example, the new plant will have a usable life of ten years and it will be able to produce 40,000 units a month. While there is often data to support such assumptions, the future is never certain. Marketing budgeting and planning are no different in this respect.

From Marketing Activity to Marketing Plan

In developing an annual marketing plan or a launch plan for a new product or service, the exercise illustrated above would need to be repeated many times. Each marketing activity would need to be identified, the costs determined, and the likely financial return computed. In some cases, data that already exists or that is collected specifically for the purpose of planning would inform the analysis. In other cases, simply making some assumptions and running the numbers may be sufficient to determine whether a marketing action makes sense. Some assumptions may be based on information obtained from other units in the organization. For example, the sales department might report how many trade shows they plan to attend over the course of a year and how many leads they forecast will be generated by this activity. This information might be transmitted to sales management who apply information about sales conversion rates to obtain financial projections.

The ultimate objective of these exercises is to identify resource needs, that is, the marketing investments required to produce a given set of marketing and financial outcomes, and the bottom line financial outcome of cash flow. Everything in between is important and necessary, but insufficient for the purpose of managing an enterprise that is expected to produce financial results.

It is important to keep in mind, however, that short-term returns can often reduce or handicap long-term returns. A critical function of marketing is that of a shepherd of intangible assets which have long-term value but are easily damaged by actions designed to produce short-term gains. Chapters 7 and 8 will examine two specific intangible assets, brands and customer equity, respectively, that have long-term value for the firm.

Finally, it is worth noting that not all marketing actions produce incremental gains. A market leader in a category is almost always the subject of attack by competitors. Sometimes the best result for such firms is to hold their position against competitors' attacks. A market leader with a 70% market share in its category has twice as many customers who can switch to a competitor compared to the customers of all other competitors who might switch to the market leader. Such market leaders might best expend marketing resources on expanding the frequency of use of products and services within the category or in expansion to new categories. Indeed, firms with large market shares and significant margins are often blind-sided by new technologies and business models. As recently as the late 1990s, Kodak was a dominant and very profitable firm with numerous high market share products commanding substantial margins. Five years later it was decimated by the rise of digital photography. A lesson to be learned!

CONCLUSION

It is imperative that we understand the profitability of actions controlled by marketers. Key ways of doing this are to look at the contribution generated by marketing activities and predict the level of marketing activity necessary to achieve profit targets. This is only possible by creating a causal nexus that links marketing actions and expenditures to intermediate marketing outcomes and through these outcomes to measures of financial performance. While this is simple in concept, it is difficult to implement without an understanding of baseline, that is, what would happen without marketing activity, the temporal dimensions of customer purchase behavior, and where the firm is with respect to customer response to its past and current marketing activities.

Exercises

1. Using the framework presented in Fig. 6.4, determine the incremental return to the firm if the advertising campaign expanded the category by 20%.
2. Using the framework in Fig. 6.4, determine the incremental cash flow minus the cost of the advertising campaign, if distribution coverage was 100% but gross margin before marketing was 10%.
3. Using the framework in Fig. 6.4, what would happen if a competitor reduces the price by 10%? How might you determine this?

Points to Ponder

1. "Baseline" is a vexing concept. Why is it so hard to define? Given the difficulty in defining baseline, what does this suggest about communicating with financial managers?

2. Marketing planning can be a complex exercise, even in relatively small organizations and can be overwhelming in large organizations, where there are many products and services competing for resources. How might the framework in Fig. 6.4 facilitate this process, or do you think it is not helpful? What process (meetings, presentations, analyses) would help a senior manager who must decide among competing investments in different products and markets?

REFERENCES

Abraham, M., & Lodish, L. M. (1990). Getting the Most Out of Advertising and Promotion. *Harvard Business Review, 68*(May–June), 50–60.

Berger, P. D., & Weinberg, B. D. (2014). Concave or S-Shaped Sales Response to Advertising: Does It Really Matter? A Mathematical Model Modifies Conventional Wisdom About Ad Budgeting. *Journal of Advertising Research, 54*(December), 388–392.

Marketing Accountability Standards Board (MASB). (2018). Marketing Return on Investment. *Common Language Marketing Dictionary*. http://www.marketing-dictionary.org/Return+on+Marketing+Investment#cite_note-1

McDonald, C. (1995, April). What Do We Know About Advertising Response Functions? *Admap Magazine, 31*. https://www.warc.com/content/paywall/article/admap/what_do_we_know_about_advertising_response_functions/3724

Meier, J., Findley, F., & Stewart, D. W. (2018, May). *Applying the MASB Brand Investment & Valuation Model*, Marketing Accountability Standards Board White Paper. https://themasb.org/wp-content/uploads/2018/05/MWP_ApplyingBIVModel_MeierFindleyStewart2018.pdf

Srinivasan, S., Pauwels, K., Hanssens, D., & DeKimpe, M. (2002). Who Benefits from Price Promotions. *Harvard Business Review, 80*(September), 22–23.

Stewart, D. W., & Furse, D. H. (1986). The Moderating Role of Recall, Comprehension, and Brand Differentiation on the Persuasiveness of Television Advertising. *Journal of Advertising Research, 26*(April/May), 43–47.

CHAPTER 7

Creating and Measuring Brand Value

Complete the following sentence: "I don't always drink beer, but when I do ..." Did you say, "I drink Dos Equis"? If you hear the word "Coors," do you imagine the Rocky Mountains or perhaps Burt Reynolds? How about "Heinz"? What is the meaning of Heinz to you? If it's not ketchup, you're in a very small minority.

Why do we know these names so well? Because ... they're brands, among the most important assets of a firm. Brands rarely appear on the balance sheet of businesses, but they represent the face of the firm in the market. They differentiate products, serve as the basis for customers' choices, and often enable the firm to charge a premium price for its products.

For instance, think fast: Coke or Pepsi? Budweiser or Miller? Crest or Colgate? Which ones do you prefer? Do you feel a sort of instinctive preference for one cola, beer, or toothpaste? It's a common sensation, the visceral reflex to choose one product over another. That's no accident. It's the power of branding and the result of enormous marketing expenditures over decades. The spending and brand impact are so profound that they tend to operate below our conscious minds—exactly where brand marketers want them to.

This chapter introduces the concept of a brand, describes how the value of this intangible asset can be measured, and illustrates how the financial value of a brand may be determined. A brand can be one of the largest assets that a company owns. Brands are indeed big money. In 2015, Heinz

© The Author(s) 2019   117
D. W. Stewart, *Financial Dimensions of Marketing Decisions*,
Palgrave Studies in Marketing, Organizations and Society,
https://doi.org/10.1007/978-3-030-15565-0_7

merged with Kraft Foods to create a company valued at more than $80 billion (Gelles 2015). In the context of that merger, the Kraft brand was valued at just over $41 billion (Crowe 2016).[1]

Similarly, when Molson Coors completed the acquisition of MillerCoors in late 2016, MillerCoors was valued at approximately $21 billion. Of this $21 billion, almost $13 billion was attributed to the value of the MillerCoors brands (MolsonCoors 2016). Clearly, brand plays a major role in the success of these businesses. Understanding the role of brands and assuring that brands are well-managed and appropriately valued is a necessity for a healthy business.

What Is a Brand?

There are many publications that treat the subjects of brand and branding (see, e.g., Johnson 2016; Keller 2013; Aaker 1991, 1996a, b; Aaker and Jochimsthhaler 2009). The Common Language Marketing Dictionary defines a brand as a "name, term, design, symbol, or any other feature that identifies one seller's good or service as distinct from those of other sellers" (http://www.marketing-dictionary.org/Brand). In fact, a successful brand is much more than an identifier. Another definition of brand is "the internalized sum of all impressions received by customers and consumers resulting in a valuable, distinctive position in their mind's eye based on perceived emotional and functional benefits" (Knapp 2000, p. 7).

A strong brand is characterized by a rich set of associations: perceptions, beliefs, attitudes, feelings, intentions, and behaviors that differentiate and add value to a product or service in the marketplace. Brands tell stories and have personalities, for example, the "Marlborough Man." They have memorable mascots like the Pillsbury Doughboy, the Michelin Man, and the Geico Lizard.

These devices build connections in the mind. The brand becomes a friend, a familiar tale you carry with you into the store. From a business perspective, it is the differentiation and value added that make a brand so important. These characteristics mean that customers will pay more for the product or service with the brand than without.

---

[1] In the United States, the economic value of a brand is systematically evaluated only when a merger or acquisition necessitates placing a value on such assets as part of the justification for the sales price or in the context of an "impairment," in which a firm writes down the value of a brand and takes a loss because of some event that is thought to have damaged the brand.

Advertising Is Not Branding

There is little debate that brands are assets that, when managed well, can have very long lives. However, branding is not the same as advertising. Advertising involves a set of expenditures and actions, much like operations, production, R&D, and other business activities. The outcomes to which advertising contributes are not the same as the activity, just as the outcome(s) to which other business activities contribute are not the same as these activities. A critical and necessary element of successful brand building is positive consumer experience. No matter how effective the advertising, a poor product or service, that is, one that fails to deliver a satisfactory experience to the consumer, will not result in a successful brand.

Advertising and other marketing activities that serve to initiate a series of repeat purchases will appear to have a long-term effect, even if the repeat purchases are driven by positive product experience. A study of four food products, dishwashing detergents, chocolate biscuits, and toothpaste carried out by Givon and Horsky (1990) found that changes in market share over time were accounted for by consumers' product experience; there was no evidence of a long-term carryover effect of advertising. Similar results have been obtained for durable goods by Horsky and Simon (1983) who report that advertising has an immediate effect on innovators, but thereafter, the transmittal of experience from adopters to potential adopters (imitators) is the driver of sales. The lesson to be learned is that a positive consumer experience builds brands; advertising and other marketing activities just create awareness and reinforce this experience.

Brands are inarguably among the largest assets a company owns, but they are difficult to value accurately. Unlike tangible assets like factories, equipment, and inventory (which are often quantified in the form of line items on a balance sheet), a brand's financial value often goes unrecognized and unreported. It's there, but it's not there. MillerCoors is worth a lot more than the sum of its factories and other assets. The brand is what makes those physical assets worth so much. This has become a significant issue as the contribution of intangibles, such as brands, to the value of firms has increased from less than 20% in the 1970s to more than 80% today (Sinclair 2016).

A number of commercial firms provide information about the value of brands: *BrandZ, Brand Finance, Tenet/Core Brand, Eurobrand, Forbes, Prophet*, and *Interbrand* among others. Unfortunately, these various firms differ in what they measure and how they measure, with the result being that the value they assign the same brand is often different. Indeed, they often differ even with respect to the direction of change in brand value over time (Cayanyab 2012). In addition, many of these brand valuations are backward looking. They summarize what has been achieved by past marketing efforts but have less to contribute to management in the future.

Such valuations are still useful. They provide directional guidance and provide a general understanding of a firm's successes and failures in managing brands. However, it is not easy to determine what should actually be done in the future or what actions (or inactions) may have contributed to a particular outcome. It is for this reason that intermediate measures of marketing outcomes that influence brand are important. Such measures can be classified into one of two categories: measures of brand health (brand evaluation) and measures of the economic value of a brand (brand value).

Measures of Brand Health

Given that brands involve associations, it is not surprising that many of the most common measures of brand health are related to such associations. These include measures of awareness and perception, that is, what the consumer believes about the product or service. They also include more global attitude measures and judgments. Some products and services also evoke strong emotions and feelings. Finally, there are measures of preference. Table 7.1 lists some of the more common measures of brand health.

Most measures of brand health do not have a strong, direct relationship to what the customer ultimately purchases. Nevertheless, these measures are very important for diagnostic purposes. Sales may be low because a product

Table 7.1 Common brand health (evaluation) measures

Awareness measures	**Judgements**
Brand recognition	Quality
Unaided recall	Superiority
Aided recall	Value
Knowledge and perception measures	Uniqueness
(image measures)	Satisfaction
Characteristics and features	**Emotions and feelings measures**
Benefits	Liking
User profile	Attachment
Purchase/use occasions	Warmth
Attitude measures	**Preference measures**
Evaluation	Consideration
Trust	Purchase intention
	Preference

lacks sufficient awareness among consumers even though awareness alone may not have much direct impact on purchase decisions. Similarly, consumers' beliefs about the features of a product or service may not predict purchase, but understanding that consumers believe a market offering is inferior to competitors on key features is a helpful piece of information. The consumer perceptions and beliefs that these measures represent are frequently necessary, but not sufficient to drive consumers' purchases. Thus, these measures are examples of the contingent, cascading measures discussed in Chap. 6.

These measures often serve as a leading indicator of problems or opportunities in the future, even if they do not have strong, immediate predictive power. For this reason, it is important to monitor them on an ongoing basis in the context of a systematic brand management process. Indeed, the International Organization for Standardization (ISO) adopted standards for brand evaluation in 2018 (ISO 2018). This standard emphasizes brand management as a continuous process of improvement. Note that customer-centric and market measures are not the only factors that influence the health of a brand. Changes in the legal, economic, political, and financial environment, among others, can also influence the health of a brand.

Figure 7.1 indicates that the brand evaluation process should feed brand valuation. Continuous measurement of brand health is not a substitute for rigorous evaluation of the monetary value of a brand. Indeed, the ISO has adopted and published a specific standard for brand valuation (ISO 2010). This standard identifies three broad approaches for determining the value of a brand: (1) the cost approach, (2) the market approach, and (3) the income approach. The *cost approach* values a brand based on what it would cost to replicate the brand at the time of the valuation. Past expenditures on brand development can inform the cost of reproducing the brand, but the current value of a brand may be more or less than past expenditures.

The market approach bases the value of a brand on what a purchaser of the brand might reasonably be expected to pay to acquire the brand. The market approach is based on information about the sales of similar brands. Finally, there is the *income approach*, which values a brand based on the income it is expected to generate over the life of the brand. In other words, this approach seeks to estimate the net present value (NPV) of the cash flows generated by the brand. There are a number of variations for this approach and one of these will be illustrated in the remainder of this chapter.

Regardless of the approach used to value a brand, the valuation process should be clear and well-documented. Assumptions need to be identified and carefully articulated. In addition, measures of brand

BRAND EVALUATION   BRAND VALUATION

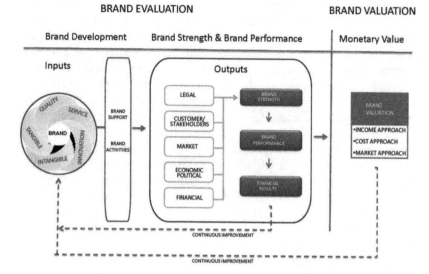

Fig. 7.1   ISO standard for brand evaluation (ISO/TC 289). (Source: ISO 2018)

health or brand evaluation should support the valuation. Table 7.2 provides a listing of the characteristics required for a defensible brand valuation exercise as defined by the ISO standard.

Table 7.2   ISO requirements for brand valuation (ISO 10668; p. 2)

3.1 Transparency: monetary brand valuation processes shall be transparent. This requirement includes disclosure and quantification of valuation inputs, assumptions and risks as well as, when appropriate, sensitivity analyses of the brand value to the main parameters used in the valuation models

3.2 Validity: a valuation shall be based on valid and relevant inputs and assumptions as of the value date

3.3 Reliability: if a valuation is repeated, it shall reliably give a comparable and reconcilable result

3.4 Sufficiency: brand valuations shall be based on sufficient data and analysis to form a reliable conclusion

3.5 Objectivity: the appraiser shall conduct the valuation free from any form of biased judgement

3.6 Financial, behavioural and legal parameters: when performing a monetary brand valuation, financial, behavioural and legal parameters shall be taken into account, the aforementioned parameters forming part of the overall assessment. The monetary brand valuation shall be conducted on the basis of the findings from the financial, behavioural and legal modules

Adapted from ISO (2010)

MEASURING BRAND VALUE

In theory, measuring the value of a brand should not be difficult. You can readily project information about current unit sales and margins per unit into the future. Computing the net present value of this cash flow, after accounting for marketing and other expenses, would be consistent with the revenue approach to brand valuation suggested by the ISO. The problem with this approach is that it assumes a static world; it does not recognize the ever-changing nature of the environment and competitors' activities. It also assumes that the firm's own marketing activities are uniform and have a consistent effect over time.

As Fig. 7.2 makes clear, a variety of factors influence the value of a brand. Among the more important factors is the consumer, whose awareness, attitude, and preference for the brand drive purchase. An important goal of marketing expenditures and activities is to influence the consumer in the context of a changing environment and competitors' actions. Such influence may take the form of reinforcing existing preferences for a brand or creating and strengthening preferences relative to competitors' offerings.

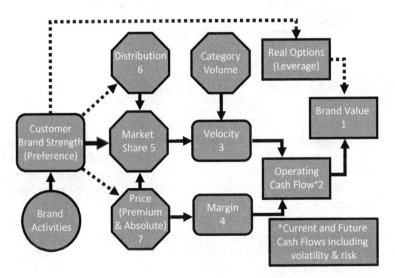

Fig. 7.2 Measuring the value of branding. (Adapted from: Meier et al. 2018)

Ideally, there would be a measure of an intermediate marketing outcome you could easily track to provide information about changes in
brand strength over time and in response to marketing efforts by the firm,
similar to what is shown in Fig. 7.3. This intermediate marketing outcome
would be demonstrably linked to drivers of cash flow, such as customer
acquisition and retention, which feed into the business model of the firm.
The measure would be empirically validated as a predictor of cash flow.

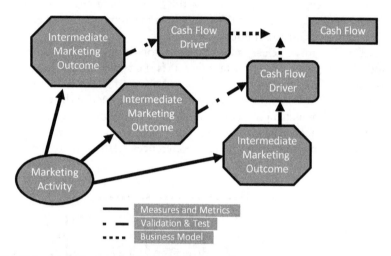

Fig. 7.3 Identify the causal links of marketing activities. (Adapted from: Stewart
2009)

As the discussion in Chap. 5 made clear, there are many measures of intermediate marketing but not all predict sales. The absence of well-accepted
and validated measures of brand value within firms is a particular challenge
to marketing and finance teams who must justify sizeable expenditures on an
ongoing basis. Despite the fact that prior research strongly suggests that a
single brand preference metric is the best way to quantify total brand strength
(Hess and Kuse 2016), there has historically been significant resistance to
and skepticism regarding the use of a standard measure of brand value across
highly varied products in dissimilar industries. A major reason for this resistance and skepticism is that any standard measure of brand preference must
be validated. It must be mathematically linked to both financial outcomes
and to the measures of overall brand awareness and attitude commonly used
by brand teams. Such validation requires time and resources and must be

updated often to remain current. Nevertheless, it is possible, and when done well, validation provides a powerful tool for planning. The next section of this chapter provides an illustration of how such validation is carried out.

VALIDATING A MEASURE OF BRAND PREFERENCE

Findley (2016) reports the results of one of the largest and most comprehensive efforts to validate a measure of brand preference against the financial performance of brands. Sponsored by The Marketing Accountability Standards Board (MASB), this validation effort involved a multi-year longitudinal study to validate a measure of brand preference across more than 120 brands in multiple industries. Six major corporations participated in the study.

The focal products of this study ranged from frequently purchased consumer packaged goods to expensive consumer durable products. Individual unit prices ranged from just under $1 to over $30,000. It is important to note that while some of the product categories lend themselves to spontaneous purchase, others typically involve a significant degree of deliberation that could include third-party influencers in the decision-making process. The product categories involved ranged from highly fragmented, with many competing brands, to relatively concentrated categories with relatively few competing brands. Consumer purchase cycles within the product categories varied from a single week to as long as a decade. Thus, the range of products in the study was highly varied and provided an opportunity for a robust test of brand metrics that was not specific to a particular brand, firm, product category, market, or industry.

All of the corporate participants in the study provided analytical data, including unit sales, market share, pricing information and distribution data for both their own and competing brands within the markets in which their brands compete. Several of the corporate participants also provided higher level brand awareness and attitude data from their own proprietary brand tracking systems. While each tracking system included category-specific measures, seven common classes of measures of "brand health" were provided by these organizations: unaided awareness, aided awareness, advocacy, loyalty, purchase intent, reference, and value.

To provide a benchmark against which all other measures of brand health could be compared, and to provide a common link between measures of brand health and measures of financial performance, brand preference data for each brand was provided by MSW•ARS Research (http://www.mswresearch.com). This patented measure of brand preference has been demonstrated to be highly reliable and predictive of business results (Stewart et al. 2016). Figure 7.4 provides an illustration of the measure, which involves a simple choice task. The measurement exercise is operationalized as an opportunity for survey participants to win a prize that includes the respondents' preferred brand. Brand preference is calculated as a percentage of all individuals choosing a particular brand of product. The measure has the advantage of isolating brand strength by holding product factors that may influence financial performance, such as price and distribution coverage, constant.

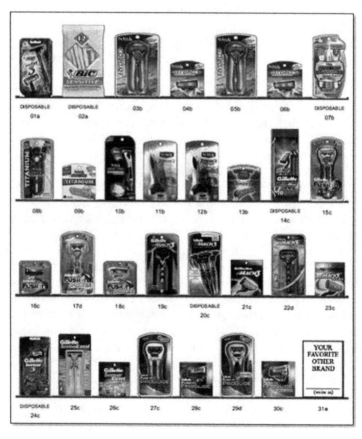

Fig. 7.4 Measuring brand preference. (Adapted from: Meier et al. 2018; Sourced from MSW•ARS Research Brand Preference)

Researchers collected the MSW•ARS measure of brand preference on a monthly basis for 18 months from a representative sample of 400 online panelists in the United States. The MSW•ARS brand preference measure was validated against sales data provided by Nielsen. Across all product categories in the study, the brand preference measure explained over 75% of the variance in unit shares among the brands in the study (see Fig. 7.5). In addition, the same strong relationship was also found within each of the 12 individual product categories (see Fig. 7.6).

While these results explain much of the variability in sales over time, and are consistent with the powerful influence of brand, brand preference does not explain all of the variability in sales over time. Previous research and common experience suggest that there exists a relationship among preferences, product price, and product availability (Jones 1999; Aaker 1996a, b; Farris et al. 1988). For example, while a single consumer may prefer a specific product, he or she may still choose to purchase a less expensive alternative to save money. Similarly, products that are relatively

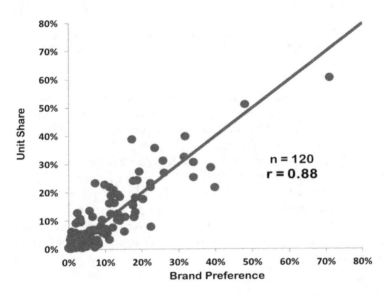

Fig. 7.5 Link between brand preference and unit share market share, all categories. (Adapted from: Meier et al. 2018; Source of data: MSW•ARS Research Brand Preference)

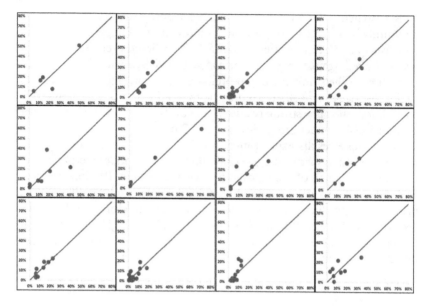

Fig. 7.6 Link between brand preference and unit share market share, within category. (Adapted from: Meier et al. 2018; Source of data: MSW•ARS Research Brand Preference)

more difficult for consumers to acquire because distribution is more limited can lose sales to more readily available alternatives. A consumer may prefer a particular brand but does not want to devote substantial time and effort to the task of obtaining it.

When brand preference is combined with relative price and distribution, the variance explained in unit shares increases to 89% across all product categories examined in the study (see Fig. 7.7). Such explanatory power is formidable and provides a very useful tool for planning. For example, the change in the measure after exposure to an advertisement compared to a baseline obtained prior to exposure can provide insight into the incremental effect of the advertising message on sales.

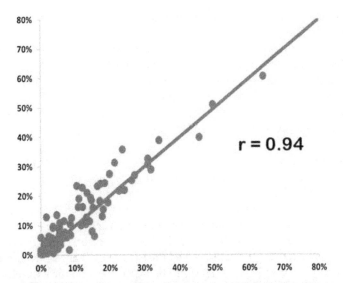

Brand Preference, Price and Distribution

Fig. 7.7 Prediction of unit share with brand preference, price and distribution. (Adapted from: Meier et al. 2018; Source of data: MSW•ARS Research Brand Preference)

OTHER INTERMEDIATE MARKETING OUTCOME MEASURES

The results of the brand preference validation study raise questions about other intermediate marketing outcome measures: (1) How well do they predict sales? and (2) How are they related to brand preference? The MASB study examined these two questions. A correlation analysis was carried out using awareness and attitudinal tracking data provided by the corporate participants in the project:

- Awareness (Unaided)—a report of brand name when prompted within a category, with no brand list given to a respondent.
- Awareness (Aided)—a report of brand names as recognized against a list of available brands.
- Brand Loyalty—an indication that the given brand is one that respondents plan to consistently purchase and/or use when a particular need arises.

- Value—an indication that a given brand provides value for the money being asked.
- Purchase Intent—the likelihood that a respondent is likely to purchase a product or service from a given brand in the future.
- Brand Relevance—a metric identifying how a brand fits into a respondent's particular lifestyle and/or needs.
- Advocacy—an indication as to whether or not a given brand is one a respondent would recommend to others.

These measures were available for 33 brands in 6 product categories. For each of these seven core concepts and brand preference, the correlation and variance explained in unit share of sales was calculated. Given the fact that all of these measures are widely used in managing brands of all types, it should come as no surprise that they ultimately show mean and median correlations to unit share at or above 0.30 (see Table 7.3). On the other hand, none of these other measures predict as well as the brand preference measure that was tested in the MASB study. This is to be expected given the nature of the measures. The brand preference measure mimics what consumers do in the market when they make a purchase; they make a choice. In contrast, the other measures involve other types of processes and behaviors, such as memory, perception, intention, and recommendation.

This does not mean that these other measures are not useful; they are just not as useful as brand preference for predicting sales. They are helpful diagnostic tools. In other words, brand preference is more valid as a predictor of sales. Such a measure provides an opportunity for both brand

Table 7.3 Link between brand preference and other marketing metrics

	Mean unit share variance explained	*Median unit share variance explained*
Awareness-unaided	48%	44%
Brand loyalty	45%	43%
Value	32%	44%
Purchase intent	27%	26%
Brand relevance	19%	18%
Awareness-aided	18%	26%
Advocacy	15%	13%

Adapted from: Meier et al. (2018)

and marketing teams to not only improve the sales predictability of their research tools but also to increase the speed at which they are able to identify a means for improving brand strength. In point of fact, this phenomenon has actually been anticipated since at least the late 1980s by researchers assessing the predictive capabilities and theoretical underpinnings of pre-test, post-test, and brand tracking systems. For example, Stewart and Furse (1986) advanced the idea that:

> *Future research efforts would be more insightful if the focus were on measures of persuasion, or behavioral change, rather than exclusively on cognitive measures such as recall or attitude change. This is not to suggest that these other measures are unimportant but that they should be treated as intervening variables influencing the primary measure of consumer choice.* (pp. 185–186)

The implication of this statement is that measurement of persuasion using behavioral change, and more specifically measurement that is founded on an observation of a consumer choice of brands, provides the most direct and predictive insights into very similar choices that consumers make among brands in the marketplace (see also Stewart and Koslow 1989). Vakratsas and Ambler (1999) made a similar recommendation:

> *we have classified and reviewed prior research of intermediate and behavioral effects of advertising using a taxonomy of models … Although such models have been actively employed for 100 years, we find them flawed on two grounds: the concept of hierarchy (temporal sequence) on which they are based cannot be empirically supported, and they exclude experience effects … We also suggest that behavioral (brand choice, market share) and cognitive and affective (beliefs, attitudes, awareness) measures be compiled in a single-source database to enable researchers … to test the interaction of context, intermediate effects, and long-and short-term behavior. In this effort, we also must relieve measures of affective responses from cognitive bias.* (p. 38)

There, of course, numerous variations of brand preference measures that include choice, in addition to the MSW•ARS measure illustrated in this chapter. A number of commercial research firms offer such measures and some firms have developed their own propriety measures. Regardless of the measure used, however, it is critical that the validity of the measure as a predictor of sales be established and routinely tested. Such a measure provides a means for testing the effects of marketing activities on brand value in advance of expensive implementation in the market and for tracking the value of a brand over time. It also provides a means for determining where the best return on marketing investment can be obtained in the context of decisions involving multiple products, a topic that will be examined in Chap. 10.

THE FOUNDATIONAL PREMISES OF A BRAND VALUATION MODEL

As discussed in earlier chapters, at its most basic level, the value of a brand can be translated into financial terms by using the discounted net present value of future cash flows attributable to the brand (Fischer 2016). While such a computation is possible based on a straightforward extrapolation of current sales that accounts for future market growth, such a computation does not account for marketing activities that may enhance or diminish the value of a brand in the future. Determination of the returns on marketing activities and expenditures requires a valid metric, such as the measure of brand preference discussed in this chapter, that is a leading indicator of future sales and that can be used to examine the potential future impact of marketing actions and that provides an ongoing measure of overall brand strength that can be used to gauge whether brand value is increasing or declining.

The Marketing Accountability Standards Board has developed a model for assessing brand value (Young et al. 2006; Findley 2016; Meier et al. 2018) based on the model of cash flow introduced in Chap. 4 and discussed earlier in this chapter. The MASB Brand Investment and Valuation Model, shown in Fig. 7.8, specifically incorporates a behavioral measure of brand strength. The model also includes mathematical linkages from customer brand strength to brand monetary value. These linkages provide bridges from customers (brand preference) to their behavior in the marketplace (market share, category volume, price vs. competition, relative distribution) and to resulting internal corporate financial metrics (velocity, margin, cash flow).

Read from left to right, the model shown in Fig. 7.8 describes how branding translates into value for the firm. The brand engages in activities such as advertising, packaging, product quality initiatives, and customer relations that make it distinct from competitive offerings. If these activities prove effective, more people will prefer the brand versus others. External activities, such as competitive advertising and social media conversations, can also influence preference for the brand. Increases in customer brand strength can translate into several potential advantages in the marketplace: a higher unit market share as people will choose it more often over other

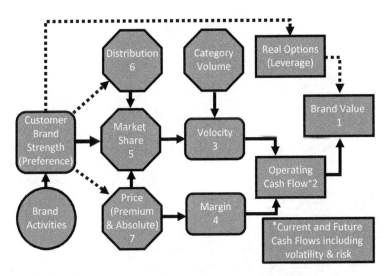

Fig. 7.8 Measuring the value of branding (revisited). (Adapted from: Meier et al. 2018)

options, a higher price point as customers will be willing to pay more for it, and increased distribution as retailers are apt to carry the brands people want most. This results in a greater velocity of sales given the size of the category and a higher margin for each of these sales. Together these lead to greater operating cash flows for the firm. The quantification of this stream of cash flows enables the calculation of a brand's value. By applying a discount rate to a future stream of cash flow, a ***present value*** can be readily calculated. This present value represents its contribution to the firm in terms of today's value of money.

THE FINANCIAL IMPACT OF HIGHER PRICES FOR BRANDED GOODS

Table 7.4 illustrates the financial impact of higher prices for brand-named products. It is based on research that compared the prices of brand-name consumer products to "no-name" alternatives. In this example, brand-name bratwurst sold for $4.35 a pack while the generic bratwurst sold for just $2.96.

Table 7.4 Higher prices drive brand value

			Example: Bratwurst	Brand name	Generic
Wholesale price	0.7	Of retail			
Cost of marketing—branded product	20%	Of wholesale revenue			
Cost of marketing—generic product	1%	Of wholesale revenue			
			Unit price at retail	$4.24	$2.96
			Units sold	10,000,000	10,000,000
			Retail revenue	$42,400,000	$29,600,000
			Wholesale revenue (70%)	$29,680,000	$20,720,000
			Unit cost	$1.00	$1.00
			Cost of goods sold	$10,000,000	$10,000,000
			Gross margin	$19,680,000	$10,720,000
			Cost of marketing (branding)	$5,936,000	$207,200
			Other operating expenses	$5,000,000	$5,000,000
			Total operating expenses	$10,936,000	$5,207,200
			EBITDA	$8,744,000	$5,512,800
			EBITA of branded vs. generic	37%	

Assuming that both types of bratwurst have the same manufacturing costs and wholesale pricing (which is unlikely in real life, but is useful for illustration), we see that the sale of 10 million units translates into revenue of $30 million for the branded product and $20 million for the generic. Even after factoring in the much higher marketing costs associated with the branded product, the brand-name bratwurst still has a 37% higher level of earnings before taxes, interest, debt, and amortization (EBITDA). EBITDA is a measure of cash flow that is essential for NPV and valuation.

What is the value of a shift in brand preference? Table 7.5 takes the same bratwurst scenario and models a hypothetical increase (or decrease) in price based on changes in brand preference. The assumption here is that the bratwurst company has conducted research that correlates brand preference to the price consumers are willing to pay. In this case, we hypothesize that a 1% increase in brand preference (over a 50% baseline) will translate into a 0.5% increase in price. Thus, if brand preference rises from 50% to 55%, the price per pack of bratwurst climbs from $4.24 to $4.35.

This 11-cent price increase may not seem like much, but it makes a big difference in the bottom line. The 2.5% higher retail price translates into a differential of 41% in EBITDA between branded and generic products. Higher EBITDA and brand premium over generic results in higher brand valuation.

NET PRESENT VALUE OF A BRAND

Determination of the value of a brand can be calculated using the model in Fig. 7.8 and the accompanying formulas in Table 7.6. The computation is, in fact, just a variation of the example in Chap. 4 except that a brand preference measure is employed. Computing a value of a brand involves the following steps:

1. **Decide on a discount rate.** Most organizations have a discount rate, typically referred to as "cost of capital," that is used for investment decisions based on the firm's unique situation. If one is not available, a weighted industry average cost of capital can be obtained and used. A useful source of such information is the *Valuation Handbook—US Industry Cost of Capital* (Grabowski et al. 2017). When using industry averages, care must be taken that category-specific inflation/deflation factors are considered.

Table 7.5 The value of a shift in brand preference

Example: Bratwurst	Brand name	Generic
Unit price at retail	$4.35	$2.96
Units sold	10,000,000	10,000,000
Retail revenue	$43,460,000	$29,600,000
Wholesale revenue (70%)	$30,422,000	$20,720,000
Unit cost	$1.00	$1.00
Cost of goods sold	$10,000,000	$10,000,000
Gross margin	$20,422,000	$10,720,000
Cost of marketing (branding)	$6,084,400	$207,200
Other operating expenses	$5,000,000	$5,000,000
Total operating expenses	$11,084,400	$5,207,200
EBITDA	$9,337,600	$5,512,800
EBITDA of branded vs. generic	41%	

Parameter	Value	Note
Wholesale price	70%	Of retail
Cost of marketing—branded product	20%	Of wholesale revenue
Cost of marketing—generic product	1%	Of wholesale revenue
Percent of consumers who prefer brand	55%	(50% = no price impact)
Impact of 1% gain/loss in preference on price	0.50%	(Determined through research)
Impact of preference on price	2.50%	
Baseline retail price	$4.24	
Price after impact of brand preference	$4.35	

Table 7.6   Brand investment/valuation model: predictive equations & terminology

Brand value = Present value of cash flows = $\sum$ {net period cash flows/$(1 + R)T$}
    + terminal value
Operating cash flow = Period cash flows = brand sales—brand costs
Velocity = Category size × average brand unit price × unit market share
Brand costs = Costs associated with producing sales for the brand
Unit share ~ Brand preference × distribution factor/relative price factor distribution
    factor = f (B0 ⊦ B1 × ln (distribution))
Price ratio = f (B2 × average brand unit price/average category unit price)

Where
R = Discount rate which represents the opportunity cost of capital
T = The time of the cash flow
Terminal value = Net present value beyond measured times ($\sum$ T)
Brand costs = Cost to produce, delivery, and service continued brand sales
Category size = Number of units sold for the category as a whole per period
Brand preference = The percent of consumers who choose brand among competitive offerings of the
    category regardless of other market factors
Distribution = A measure of the presence of the brand across possible outlets
B0 and B1 = Beta weights which calibrate category's elasticity to distribution (empirically derived) average
    brand unit price = average price across all units sold
B2 = Beta weight which calibrates the category's elasticity to price (empirically derived)
Adapted from: Meier et al. (2018)

2. **Extract historical financial results from accounting systems.** In most categories, this will mean using the last 12 months of financials. The use of a year's worth of data will help minimize seasonality and other short-term effects. This information provides a starting point for estimating future cash flows.

3. **Determine future cash flow implications.** Most often the current year's cash flow will not be a good estimate for future years. Current year cash flow usually represents a very conservative estimate of brand value because it assumes no growth. However, if a brand is troubled or facing intensified competition, current cash flow may overestimate future cash flows. Thus, estimates of future cash flow need to be adjusted based on assumptions about how the future will differ from the present. The model in Fig. 7.8 identifies four particularly important factors that should be considered:

Category Size Are the category and the specific segments in which the brand competes static, growing, or declining? Many brands exist in categories that grow predictably with population. In such cases, population growth estimates can be used to adjust cash flows up accordingly. Inevitably, some brands exist in categories or segments that are declining. In these cases, cash flow estimates should be lowered. There are also emerging categories where demand will grow substantially. For such categories, cash flow estimates need to be raised in alignment with conservative, documented growth estimates since the sustainability of growth must be considered. Finally, some categories with long purchase cycles may face a saturation point where initial robust demand is followed by lower replacement demand in future time periods. Again, cash flow estimates should be adjusted accordingly.

Brand Preference This is where a valid measure of brand preference is critical. It is important to know the brand's current brand preference level, or baseline. Also important is knowing whether brand strength has been increasing or declining over time and how brand preference stacks up among growing population groups. Brands with higher preference and marketing support tend to be more stable over time, giving confidence to the use of existing cash flow. However, if a brand is experiencing a downward trend or is losing ground among growing population groups (e.g., exhibiting lower preference among younger age groups), then cash flow estimates need to be lowered accordingly. Another situation requiring the lowering of cash flow estimates is when a brand previously supported by substantial marketing efforts is reducing that support going forward.

Pricing If a brand has a sustainably lower price than the competition, that will help maintain a steady cash flow and even growth in times of economic recession. On the other hand, premium priced brands can be vulnerable to future declines unless brand preference is maintained or grown. This is especially likely in highly fragmented categories where competitors use price reduction strategies to sustain or grow their share of market.

Distribution In most instances, a brand's distribution will be high (readily available to 80%+ of market) and stable. It is only in cases where a brand faces a substantial growth or a drop in distribution that cash flow will need to be adjusted.

Based on these factors it should be determined whether the cash flow will be growing, sustainable or unsustainable. It is also possible in the case of emerging categories or segments that a solid determination can't be made. In these cases, a brand value can be calculated but it is unproven, and that caveat should be noted.

4. **Set a time horizon.** Once the future cash flow implications are determined, an assessment should be made of the time horizon for the brand. While mathematically it is possible to treat a brand as a perpetual annuity, brands typically have a shorter expected life. Therefore, a finite time horizon is most often used for the calculation. If the cash flows are sustainable, a good rule of thumb is to use a 10–15-year time horizon. If the cash flow is expected to be unsustainable, a shorter lifespan should be chosen, including making the choice of assigning no value at all. Also, if for strategic reasons the brand is expected to exist only for a limited time, then that should be chosen as its time horizon. Finally, if a brand is expected to be sustainable over a much longer time period than the rule of thumb, a terminal value of a predetermined percentage can be added to the present value calculation to denote the added potential.

5. **Apply the present value formula.** Using the estimated cash flow stream for the given time horizon and the predetermined discount rate, calculate the present value. This will produce a realistic estimate of the brand's value.

CONCLUSION

An especially important set of marketing activities focuses on the creation and management of brands. Successful brands create financial outcomes for the firm by generating cash flow through greater numbers of sales and higher margins. Thus, brands are an especially important asset that the firm should carefully manage. Such management should include the routine measurement of indices of brand health and efforts to determine whether the value of the brand is static, increasing, or declining. The latter requires a valid measure of brand preference that can be used to monitor the strength of a brand in real time and that can be used to test the potential effects of new brand building efforts and investments.

Exercises

1. Identify a well-known brand. What do you associate with the brand (perceptions, beliefs, feelings, etc.)? How did these associations come about? How do these associations create value for the brand?
2. How would you design a survey to validate a measure of brand preference? Who would you include as respondents? What would you

ask of respondents? How would you demonstrate that the measure can predict future sales? How accurate would you want the forecast to be?

3. Many factors can influence the future demand for a product or service. For each of the following products name at least five factors that may influence future demand: Craft Beer, Air Travel, Cookies, Refrigerators, Mobile Telephones. How many of the factors that you identified can a marketer influence?

Points to Ponder

1. Marketing activities are often thought of in terms of building a brand. How would you determine whether a marketing activity really contributes to building a brand? Can some marketing activities reduce the value of a brand? What activities could reduce the value of a brand and how would they do so?

2. Unlike tangible assets, brands are not included on the firm's balance sheet. Why do you think this is the case? Can you think of any advantages to putting the value of brands on the balance sheet? Any disadvantages?

REFERENCES

Aaker, D. A. (1991). *Managing Brand Equity*. New York: Free Press.

Aaker, D. A. (1996a). Measuring Brand Equity Across Products and Markets. *California Management Review, 38*(Spring), 102–120.

Aaker, D. A. (1996b). *Building Strong Brands*. New York: Free Press.

Aaker, D. A., & Joachimsthaler, E. (2009). *Brand Leadership: Building Assets in an Information Economy*. New York: Free Press.

Cayanyab, I. (2012, February). *Growing the GE Brand*. Presentation to the 2012 Winter Summit of the Marketing Accountability Standards Board. St. Petersburg. https://themasb.org/wp-content/uploads/2012/02/D.-GE_Brand-Cayabyab-2.12F.pdf

Crowe, P. (2016, January 17). The 20 Most Valuable Brands Ever Acquired. *Business Insider*. https://www.businessinsider.com/brand-names-are-in-demand-like-never-before-here-are-the-20-most-valuable-ever-acquired-2016-1

Farris, P. W., Oliver, J., & de Kluyver, C. (1988). *The Relationship Between Distribution and Market Share* (Marketing Science Institute Working Paper No. 88–103). Cambridge, MA: Marketing Science Institute.

Findley, F. (2016, March). *Brand Investment and Valuation: A New, Empirically-Based Approach.* Marketing Accountability Standards Board White Paper. https://themasb.org/resources/white-papers/

Fischer, M. (2016). Brand Valuation in Accordance with GAAP and Legal Requirements. In D. W. Stewart & C. T. Gugel (Eds.), *Accountable Marketing: Linking Marketing Actions to Financial Performance* (pp. 182–200). New York: Routledge.

Gelles, D. (2015, March 25). Kraft and Heinz to Merge in Deal Backed by Buffett and #G Capital. *The New York Times.* https://www.nytimes.com/2015/03/26/business/dealbook/kraft-and-heinz-to-merge.html

Givon, M., & Horsky, D. (1990). Untangling the Effects of Purchase Reinforcement and Advertising Carryover. *Marketing Science, 9*(2), 171–192.

Grabowski, R. J., Nunes, C., & Harrington, J. P. (2017). *2017 Valuation Handbook – U. S. Industry Cost of Capital.* New York: Wiley.

Hess, M., & Kuse, A. R. (2016). Measuring Brand Preference. In D. W. Stewart & C. T. Gugel (Eds.), *Accountable Marketing: Linking Marketing Actions to Financial Performance* (pp. 52–59). New York: Routledge.

Horsky, D., & Simon, L. S. (1983). Advertising and the Diffusion of New Products. *Marketing Science, 2*(1), 1–93.

ISO. (2010). *Brand Valuation – Requirements for Monetary Brand Valuation,* ISO 10668. Geneva: International Standards Organization. https://www.iso.org/standard/46032.html

ISO. (2018). *Brand Evaluation – Principles and Fundamentals,* ISO/TC 289, ISO/DIS 20671:2017(E). Geneva: International Standards Organization. https://www.iso.org/committee/5065082/x/catalogue/

Johnson, M. (2016). *Branding in Five and a Half Steps.* New York: Thames and Hudson.

Jones, J. P. (1999). *International Advertising: Myths and Realities.* Thousand Oaks: Sage.

Keller, K. (2013). *Strategic Brand Management: Building, Measuring and Managing Brand Equity* (4th ed.). Boston: Pearson.

Knapp, D. E. (2000). *The Brand Mindset: Five Essential Strategies for Building Brand Advantage Throughout Your Company.* New York: McGraw-Hill.

Meier, J., Findley, F., & Stewart, D. W. (2018, May). *Applying the MASB Brand Investment & Valuation Model,* Marketing Accountability Standards Board White Paper. https://themasb.org/wp-content/uploads/2018/05/MWP_ApplyingBIVModel_MeierFindleyStewart2018.pdf

MolsonCoors. (2016). *Form 10-K filed with the United States Securities and Exchange Commission.* https://s21.q4cdn.com/334828327/files/doc_financials/2016/annual/cfbd1a46-0f56-4f1d-8338-bb71d674c943.pdf

Sinclair, R. (2016). Reporting on Brands. In D. W. Stewart & C. T. Gugel (Eds.), *Accountable Marketing: Linking Marketing Actions to Financial Performance* (pp. 168–181). New York: Routledge.

Stewart, D. W. (2009). Marketing Accountability: Linking Marketing Actions to Financial Results. *Journal of Business Research, 62*(June), 636–643.

Stewart, D. W., & Furse, D. H. (1986). *Effective Television Advertising: A Study of 1000 Commercials.* Lexington: Lexington Books.

Stewart, D. W., & Koslow, S. (1989). Executional Factors and Advertising Effectiveness: A Replication. *Journal of Advertising, 18*(3), 21–32.

Stewart, D. W., Blair, M. H., & Kuse, A. R. (2016). The Marketing Metric Audit Protocol. In D. W. Stewart & C. T. Gugel (Eds.), *Accountable Marketing: Linking Marketing Actions to Financial Performance* (pp. 226–232). New York: Routledge.

Vakratsas, D., & Ambler, T. (1999). How Advertising Works: What Do We Really Know? *Journal of Marketing, 63*(1), 26–43.

Young, Roy, Allen Weiss, and David W. Stewart (2006), Marketing Champions: Practical Strategies for Improving Marketing's Power, Influence and Business Impact, (New York: Wiley Interscience)as.

CHAPTER 8

Customer Lifetime Value: The Significance of Repeat Business

There is an anecdote that is told every year at a well-known business school. A regional chain of coffee shops hired one of the school's better-known professors to advise the firm on improving customer service. The professor spent several days watching the chain in operation. Every morning, he saw customers coming and being met with blank looks and indifference from the staff. There were few smiles, nor many "good mornings" or "thank you's" being uttered.

The professor suggested that management call a meeting of the workers from the coffee shops. At the meeting, he posed the following hypothetical situation to the employees. "Ok, let's say a customer comes in on Monday and orders a coffee and a bagel. You ring up the sale, which is four dollars. You say thank you and the customer comes back on Tuesday and orders another coffee and bagel for four dollars. You say thank you and the customer comes back on Wednesday and orders another four-dollar coffee and bagel."

At that point the professor stopped talking and looked around the room. Everyone was staring at him, stumped. "Why am I telling you this?" the professor asked. Shrugs all around. No one had much of an idea. He decided to clue them in. "That four dollars you get each day ... that's the money the chain uses to pay your salary."

Thunderclap! Truly, this had not occurred to the workers. They had never associated the money they took at the cash register with the

© The Author(s) 2019
D. W. Stewart, *Financial Dimensions of Marketing Decisions*,
Palgrave Studies in Marketing, Organizations and Society,
https://doi.org/10.1007/978-3-030-15565-0_8

money they got in their pay checks. It was a revelation that provided a great opportunity to talk about how good customer service encourages repeat business ... which in turn helps with job security, raises, benefits, and the like.

Following up on Chap. 7, which examined the value of brands and the contribution of branding activities to the firm, this chapter explores the topic of customer loyalty. Customers who are loyal buy over and over again. This reduces the firm's future costs of customer acquisition, which in turn increases the value of the brand through higher margins, and, if you don't have to spend so much on acquiring new customers, you have more money left over in profits.

Customer loyalty is also generally accompanied by a willingness of customers to pay a price premium for the brand, or at minimum, it makes customers more resistant to competitors' price discounts. The effects of such loyalty also extend to other stakeholders, such as members of the distribution channel. Retailers and other distributors prefer to stock those products for which there is strong customer demand and for which customers will pay a premium.

In many ways, brands serve as the nexus of a relationship between the customer and the firm, especially in those markets like consumer packaged goods where there is no close, direct customer interaction. The identities of individual customers are unknown to the firm. For a firm in this position, it's necessary to study consumer behavior to determine the value of a loyal brand customer.

Other businesses enjoy substantial and direct interaction between the firm and customers or at least between personnel and/or machines working on behalf of the firm and customers. In such cases, the identities of customers may be known to the firm. The firm may also know other information about the types, amounts, frequencies, and timing of purchases, among other things. In such businesses, it is possible to examine the history of a customer's purchases and forecast future purchases based on this history. Such history and subsequent analyses allow the firm to determine the value of each individual customer. The value of a customer over time is often referred to as the *lifetime value of a customer*. The aggregation of this value across all customers is frequently referred to as *customer equity*. These concepts are the focus of this chapter.

The Importance of Repeat Business

As the coffee shop anecdote illustrates, repeat business is good business. An objective of many marketing activities is to create repeat business. This objective can be achieved by delivering a quality product or service at a competitive price while making it widely available. While simple in theory, encouraging repeat purchases is a complex challenge. The quality of the product or service must be sufficiently high to create a disincentive to switch to competitors' offerings. Price must be attractive enough, when coupled with the quality of the offering, that customers have little incentive to switch to competitors' offerings. Making a product or service widely available frequently requires partnering with distributors whose own self-interests determine whether they will or will not stock a product.

Despite these challenges, there can be significant advantages to the firm if customers engage in regular repeat purchasing. One advantage is lower customer acquisition costs. It requires far less effort and investment to find and educate repeat customers about a firm's offerings.

How much does it cost to acquire a new customer? You might be surprised to learn how high it can be. As was discussed in Chap. 4, if you sign up for a new credit card, the credit card company could have easily spent over $300 getting you to sign up for the card. Why is this? Well, consider how many times they tried to get you interested in a card before. You probably saw dozens of television commercials and received dozens (hundreds, thousands?) of mailers. All of that cost money … a lot of money. Credit card companies spend billions of dollars finding new customers. Why do they spend so much? Because a customer is worth it, if they remain a customer. It is generally estimated that it takes two to three years for a new credit card customer to generate sufficient revenue to pay for their initial acquisition cost (Reichheld 1994). This means retention of the customer is critical to the success of the firm.

A loyal repeat customer may also be willing to pay a higher price to obtain the firm's offering either because they find the offering superior or simply do not wish to take the risk of switching away from a known offering. Loyal repeat customers may also be willing to put more effort into finding and obtaining their preferred product or service.

Repeat purchasers offer two other advantages to the firm, especially if the firm can identify and track them. They enable the firm to better forecast future sales volume and to more individually tailor marketing activities toward them. Thus, the firm might devote more attention and resources to retaining its most loyal customers, who purchase most frequently and/

146 D. W. STEWART

or in the greatest volume. The business can simultaneously identify customers who purchase less often or in lower volumes, but who are expensive to reach and serve. Similarly, the firm may be able to use information about the characteristics of its current best customers to identify potential new customers with similar profiles. Marketing activities and resources could be more carefully targeted at such potential customers.

A key intermediate marketing outcome is a measure of the propensity of a customer to make repeated purchases over time. Such an intermediate outcome measure is loyalty. Brand or customer loyalty is an important asset of the firm because it influences cash flows.

Consider the case of a large discount shoe store chain. The company's marketing consisted of Buy One Get One Free, or "BOGO" marketing. This approach was simple and it worked, up to a point. It encouraged families to come and buy multiple pairs of shoes. Yet, management started to believe they could do better. Point of Sale (POS) data told them that certain customers came back again and again and bought in high volume. These were the loyal customers. The problem was that the firm didn't know who these loyal customers were. They implemented a rewards program that encouraged repeat purchases. With data from the rewards program, they were able to target customers who had demonstrated loyalty and send them special offers and announcements of sales.

The rewards program was a limited success. It did improve sales, but the company still felt it was missing a much bigger opportunity for growth through customer loyalty. Senior management believed they were wasting a great deal of money sending out BOGO coupons and targeting BOGO ads at huge numbers of indifferent or low volume customers. The company engaged with a specialized marketing agency that did psychological profiling of consumers. The agency spent time in the chain's stores and observed the shoppers. They observed families buying shoes. They analyzed sales data and correlated high-volume, loyal customer to demographic and psychographic categories.

The agency's study revealed that a certain type of person was the chain's best and most loyal repeat customer. The loyal customer profile was a woman, typically a mother, in a particular age range. Most importantly, the agency identified that the loyal customer embraced a positive, personally ambitious life attitude, that is, she wanted to be successful as a mother and sought success and happiness for her children. The chain now understood the personality and psychological yearnings of its best customers. They adapted their marketing creative and messaging to reach this kind of person. They changed their in-store displays and wall posters to match this buyer persona. Now, the loyal customer would receive promotions that matched her views on life. The store itself would reinforce this image. The process worked extremely well. The company focused its marketing on this group and de-emphasized marketing to less profitable segments. Sales and profits rose accordingly.

What Is Loyalty?

Although loyalty seems like a straightforward notion, it has been defined and operationalized in many different ways. The link between loyalty and cash flow is highly dependent on how loyalty is defined and measured. Some measures of loyalty are measures of attitude, that is, how positively consumers feel about the product—the shoe store example shows how this works.

Other measures of loyalty focus on behavior, such as the frequency of purchase of a specific offering relative to all purchases in a category. Loyalty may also be manifest in consumers' willingness to make a greater effort to find and obtain the product or service. Still other measures of loyalty focus on customers' willingness to pay a price premium or resist discounts offered by competitors. Finally, some marketers define true loyalty as a customer's willingness to recommend a product or service to others. These latter types of loyal customers are especially valuable because they not only purchase the product but also they become an extension of the firm's marketing efforts.

Loyalty can be measured in numerous ways. Table 8.1 describes some common types of measures of loyalty. The many definitions of loyalty illustrate a point made in Chap. 5; measures with the same name are often

Table 8.1 Measures of customer loyalty

Attitudinal measures
    How likely is it that you will purchase brand next time you shop?
    Which brand do you prefer?
    Which brand do you intend to purchase?
Search measures
    % of customers willing to leave a without a product if their favorite brand is unavailable
Behavioral measures
    % of past purchases accounted for by a brand
Willingness to pay measures
    % of customers willing to pay a specific price premium
Share of requirements measures
    % of all purchases by a customer within a category captured by a specific brand

---

operationalized in very different ways. This does make any particular measure of loyalty wrong. In fact, the various measures can be quite complementary. A behavioral measure, which tracks actual purchases, may be especially useful as predictor of immediate sales but may indicate little about impending problems until the customer stops purchasing. In contrast, attitudinal measures, especially if tracked over time, may indicate a gradual weakening well in advance of a customer's decision to stop purchasing or to switch to a competitor. In addition, repeated purchases over time may not always reflect loyalty.

There are many reasons a customer may continue to purchase a particular product or service that has little to do with loyalty. The consumer's choices may simply be limited. Purchases may just reflect habit or consumers may not care about which product they buy, so it is easier just to repeat what the consumer has done in the past. Sometimes, there may be barriers to change, that is, switching costs. It may be a lot of trouble to change products or providers. The price of a competitive alternative may be so low as to override preference based on other factors. A particular offering might be more convenient to obtain than another offering that would otherwise be preferred. Thus, repeat purchase alone may not be an indication of loyalty.

While loyalty is important and desirable, it is not the only factor that needs to be considered when thinking about the value of a customer. A customer who only buys one particular brand of a product may be loyal, but if that customer only buys the product once a year, they may be less valuable to the firm than a customer who buys 12 times a year and divides his purchases equally among three different brands. The shoe store case demonstrates how this works.

For this reason, many firms consider not only loyalty but other characteristics of purchase behavior. Among the most common of these characteristics are recency, frequency, and volume. *Recency* refers to the amount of time that has elapsed since the customer's last purchase of the focal brand or product. It is a measure of how active the customer has been in the recent past. In contrast, *frequency* refers to how often the customer has made purchases during some fixed time period, say within the last year. Finally, *volume* refers to how much, on average, the customer purchases on each purchase occasion in either units or money.

When thinking about the meaning of recency, frequency, and volume, it is important to appreciate that their meanings and relevance will vary by product category. Expectations about what is typical for these three measures vary widely across categories. Coffee may be purchased frequently, perhaps multiple times a day, while a refrigerator may be purchased once in a dozen years. Thus, the benchmark for what constitutes a good customer will be dependent on the purchase cycle that is typical in the relevant product or service category.

CUSTOMER RETENTION

The value of repeat purchasing to the firm means that customer retention is an important objective of marketing activities. Retention is important in any industry, but it is a particular focus in industries where there is a reasonable expectation of an ongoing relationship between the firm and the customer. Such industries would include those where contracts between buyer and seller exist, where customers purchase subscriptions, and/or where the customer's use of the product or service tends to be continuous and ongoing, for example, financial services, telecommunications, and health care, among others.

Generally, there is a distinction in terminology between industries where the purchases tend to be discrete and industries where there is a formal or implied ongoing relationship. Thus, in the former industries there is a tendency to focus on *repeat purchase* and *brand switching*, while in the latter industries the terms used are *retention* and *churn*. The underlying processes are the same, that is, the degree to which customers tend to buy the same product over and over or switch among competitive offerings in the market.

There is strong evidence that higher retention rates are related to higher profitability (Lawrence 2012; Grunberg 2016) in most if not all industries. Thus, retention and its inverse, attrition or churn, are important metrics. Retention rate is often used as a measure of higher customer loyalty. It is expressed as percent and is computed as:

$$\text{Retention rate}(\%) = \left[\begin{array}{l} \text{Number of customers retained} \\ \div \text{Number of customers at risk} \end{array} \right] \times 100$$

In contrast, churn rate if computed as:

$$\text{Churn rate}(\%) = \left[1 - \text{Retention rate} \right]$$

There are a variety of diagnostic measures that can provide insight into the likelihood of a customer being retained or lost, well in advance of the loss of a customer. Table 8.2 provides a list of some of these measures. Obviously, renewal of a contract or subscription is a clear signal that a customer intends to remain in a relationship with the firm. However, there are other clues that suggest the relationship is healthy or in trouble. The longer a customer goes without purchase or other interaction, the more likely there is a retention problem. For example, most dissatisfied credit card customers do not cancel their card; rather, they just stop using the card. In addition, trends in purchasing and usage over time may be stable, increasing, or decreasing with respect to frequency and/or size. Much of this type of information is routinely captured as a part of ordinary business transactions with customers. What is required to make use of this information is regular analysis. Even analysis can be relatively easy. For example, the statistical package SPSS has a "direct marketing" module that is designed specifically for the analysis of recency, frequency, and volume/money data, or *RFM analysis*.

Table 8.2   Indices relevant to customer retention

Retention	Subscription, contract, etc.
Recency	Most recent event date
Frequency	Average gap/# events over period
Longevity	Start date/total # events
Amount	Average per order over period
Referrals	Customer get a customer promo/acquisition source

The power of such data is that it can provide insights about both what is happening in the customer base as a whole and for each individual customer. It is also possible to identify market segments using such data. Online retailers now have extensive databases on what customers ordered and when. Amazon's "Your Orders" data contains hundreds of millions of customers' transactions.

Loyalty programs provide a means for gathering such data, as was the case with the shoe store chain. Such data are simple and easy for managers to understand. And, while these data can provide a history of the spending of individual consumers, it becomes even more powerful when used to estimate future spending and guide the design of marketing programs to influence future spending.

Analysis of these data will be most useful when past behavior is a valid predictor of future behavior. This is very often the case. For example, customers who have purchased recently are more likely to purchase in the future and in response to marketing actions; frequent buyers tend to respond more favorably to marketing actions than less frequent purchasers; and customers who buy more are likely to respond more favorably to marketing actions than those who spend less (Reynolds 2012).

CUSTOMER LIFETIME VALUE

Like the many measures of brand health discussed in Chap. 7, measures such as retention rate, recency, frequency, and volume are useful diagnostic measures that can be tracked over time to gain insights into the health of customer relationships. For this reason, these measures can suggest occasions when marketing interventions may be needed. However, like brand health measures, these measures of customer interaction do not provide information about the value of any particular customer or the financial performance that may accrue as a result of interacting with a customer over time. They also fail to provide a clear measure for the value of a particular customer, especially when multiple products or services are part of the firm's offerings. They do not indicate whether a high frequency customer is more profitable than a high-volume customer. Different products and services may have quite different margins. A customer who buys a small volume of high margin products is almost certainly more valuable than a customer who buys many low margin products or only loss leaders that have a negative margin.

Fortunately, there is such a measure of customer profitability, *customer lifetime value* (CLV) (Kumar 2008; Bejou et al. 2016). Like the validated brand preference measure described in Chap. 7, CLV offers a way to summarize the value, or profitability, of a customer. In concept, customer lifetime value (CLV) is a simple concept. It is based on the notion that customers represent annuities, that is, customers may be viewed as a stream of cash flows over time. Thus, rather than focus on individual transactions, the focus is on the many transactions in which a customer may engage over their lifetime as a customer.

As shown in Fig. 8.1, CLV can be computed by taking all customer revenue in a period of time, most often a year, and first subtracting the costs of serving the customer. If one begins with the gross margin of all transactions, the support costs are simplified and include only general marketing costs and other costs that are allocated to the customer. This annual revenue figure is then multiplied by the number of periods the customer is expected to continue to do business with the firm, again, usually measured in years. The result of this computation is the profit that can be attributed to the customer over the relevant time period.

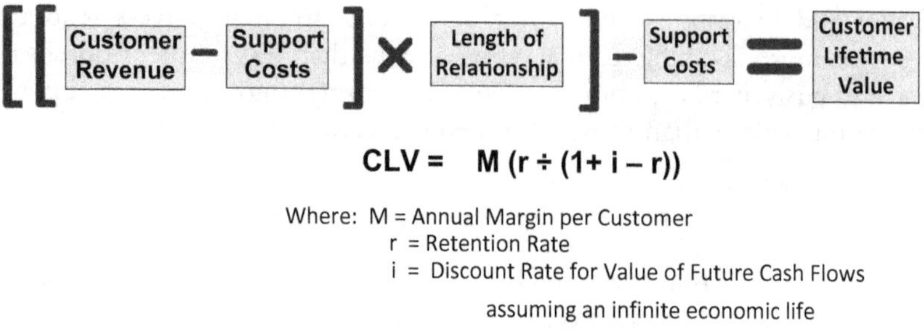

$$CLV = \quad M\,(r \div (1 + i - r))$$

Where: M = Annual Margin per Customer
r = Retention Rate
i = Discount Rate for Value of Future Cash Flows
assuming an infinite economic life

Fig. 8.1 A simple model of customer lifetime value

Of course, as was discussed in earlier chapters, money earned in the future is worth less than money earned today. Thus, to correctly assess the value of a customer today, it is necessary to discount the future cash flows attributable to the customer in the future. This is not only the appropriate way to analyze future cash flows, it is also a way to make the value of customers who may differ in their expected lifetime as customers comparable. Without such an adjustment, two customers who differed in how much they purchased in each of a different number of total years could appear to be equally valuable. Clearly a customer who spends a great deal in a relatively short time period is more valuable than customers who spend rather modest amounts over a much longer time period. Discounting the cash flow attributable to each customer corrects for these differences in the amount and timing of cash flow receipt. The formula in Fig. 8.1 provides a means to determine these discounted cash flows.

There are numerous calculators and other online resources available to assist with the computation of CLV (see for example, http://www.clv-calculator.com/customer-lifetime-value-formulas/clv-formula/example-customer-lifetime-calculation/ and https://hbswk.hbs.edu/Documents/archive/docs/lifetimevalue.xls). Note that the data have to come from historical information or forecasts of customers' purchasing behavior. This is why it is important for a firm to have information systems that not only capture the requisite data but also make the data readily accessible.

Table 8.3 provides an example of some simple computations. In this example, Customer A purchases $500 of products each year. The gross margin on the products purchased is 50% or $250, and other general support costs each year total $50. The customer does business with the firm for ten years. Over this ten-year period the firm incurs another $1000 in support costs. As shown in Table 8.3, the undiscounted value of this customer is $1000:

Table 8.3 Example of computation of customer lifetime value

Total sales revenue	Gross margin	Other support costs	Average length of relationship	Other support costs	Undiscounted CLV		Retention rate	Discount rate	Discounted CLV
$500	$250	$50	10 years	$1000	$1000		80%	8%	$571.43
						Total number of customers			
$50,000,000	$2,500,000	$500,000	10 years	10,000,000	$10,000,000	100,000			$5,720,000

$$CLV = \left[\left(\$500 - \$250 - \$50\right) \times 10 \ \text{years} - \left(\$1000\right)\right] = \$1000.00$$

Assuming the firm has 100,000 customers and they all have the same profile as Customer A, the undiscounted value of these customers to the firm is $10,000,000:

$$CLV = \left[\left(\$50 \ \text{million} - \$25 \ \text{million} - \$500,000\right) \times 10 \ \text{years} - \left(\$10,000,000\right)\right]$$
$$= \$10 \ \text{million}$$

Of course, the firm is likely to lose some customers over time, so the total value of its customers must be reduced by its rate of attrition. In addition, it is necessary to discount the future projected revenues. For the firm in this example, the attrition rate is 20%; in other words, the retention rate is 80% and the firm's discount rate is 8%. Thus, using the formula in Fig. 8.1:

$$CLV = M\left(r \div \left(1 + i - r\right)\right)$$

The discounted value of Customer A is

$$CLV = \$200\left(0.9 \div \left(1 + 0.08 - 0.8\right)\right) = \$571.43$$

Where the contribution of this customer ($200) is obtained by subtracting the support costs ($50) from the gross margin ($250).

And the discounted value of all of the firm's customers is:

$$CLV = \$2,000,000\left(\left(0.9 \div \left(1 + 0.08 - 0.8\right)\right)\right) = \$5720.000$$

Note that the example of the aggregate CLV, while useful for illustrative purposes, is based on an average across all customers. Much of the power of the CLV metric is based on its ability to provide a customer by customer analysis.

Implementing CLV

Although CLV is simple in concept, it is often complex in practice. Most customers do not spend the same amount each year. What a customer has spent in the past is a good starting point, but how is it possible to forecast what a new customer with little or no history will spend in the future? Customers' purchasing patterns often change over time. Some customers increase their purchases over time, while others decrease their purchases over time. And, it is not just the amount purchased that changes; the assortment of items purchased over time changes, and different items in these changing assortments may have different margins and support costs. Some customers are short-timers, while others may literally be life-long customers.

Not all customers are equal, as the shoe store case suggests. Different customers are rarely of the same financial value to the firm. This not only means that some customers will produce more cash flow than others but also that some customers are worth larger investments than others because they are more valuable in the long run. Thus, it may make sense to invest more in the acquisition of some potential customers than others and to invest more in retaining some current customers relative to others.

The differences in the value of customers to the firm imply a need to manage customers as a portfolio. Such management is often referred to a managing the customer life cycle or, more generally, *customer relationship management* (Buttle and Maklan 2016). Figure 8.2 provides a conceptual illustration of the customer life cycle.

The life cycle of a customer begins as a prospect in a target market. This implies that the firm has identified the customer or at least the profile of a likely customer before any transaction has occurred, though clearly a first contact could be an opportunistic sale to the customer. Once the customer has been identified, they must be activated, that is, the customer must be motivated to engage in some behavior. This could be a sale, but in many cases may be something short of an actual sale such as a visit to a website or retail outlet, a request for information, or a request for a sales call. Obviously, the goal of such preliminary steps is to move the prospect to a purchaser. All of the costs of identifying and converting the prospect to a customer need to be identified and included in the costs of customer acquisition, which will be discussed later in this chapter.

Once the customer has purchased, a formal relationship with the firm has been established and this relationship needs to be managed. Managing the relationship requires resources. Such resources involve some means for

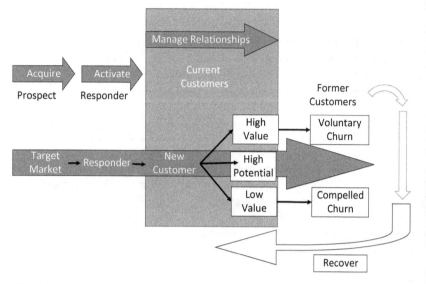

Fig. 8.2 The customer life cycle

facilitating and tracking the ongoing interactions with the customer. Such facilitation and tracking activities may involve automated systems but may also involve account managers or sales and service personnel.

These activities represent the support costs associated with the relationship. These costs may or may not be incorporated into the cost of the individual products or services, but they should be accounted for. They will be accounted for when determining the gross margin if they are included in the cost of the product offering. If they are not included in the sales price but can be assigned to a specific transaction, they should be accounted for when determining the net margin; they are relationship management and marketing costs. Inevitably, there will be some costs of managing a customer relationship that cannot be assigned to an individual sales transaction. Such costs still need to be accounted for and should be subtracted from the overall margin generated from a customer.

A part of managing the relationship with a customer should involve an assessment of the long-term value of the customer. Some customers will prove to be high value. Other customers may not be immediately high value, but they may be recognized as having considerable potential future value. For example, a graduate engineering student or medical student may not appear to be a high value credit card customer while still a student. However, there is a reasonable expectation that such individuals will eventually have substantial future earnings potential that would make them a high value customer in the future.

Another type of analysis may focus on the identification of customers who are underperforming, that is, their profile would suggest that they should be purchasing more frequently or in greater volume than they are. Such customers may be candidates for development efforts designed to move actual purchases closer to their apparent potential.

It is also likely that some customers will prove to be less valuable or even so costly to serve that the firm loses money on them. This can often happen when customers are purchasing low margin products and require substantial support services that are not included in the purchase price of the product or service and the customer is not charged for these services. Such low value customers are candidates for intervention. Such intervention might involve changes in pricing structures, additional charges for services, minimum purchase amounts, or other changes in the relationship that can either increase the value of the customer or encourage the customer to do business elsewhere (*forced churn*).

At the same time, some customers will elect to leave the relationship (*voluntary churn*). Such customers are not necessarily "lost" forever. Indeed, it is often possible to "win back" a formerly loyal customer through proactive marketing efforts. In general, the more valuable the customer has been in the past the more a firm should invest to bring the customer back as a customer. Of course, it makes no sense to spend more on winning back a customer than the expected value of that customer in the future.

Part of the power of CLV at the individual level is related to the ability of the firm to customize offerings based on the value of the customer. This is quite common in many industries. Credit cards, airlines, and hotels, among others, often have "levels" of customer support and rewards that differ depending on the purchase behavior of individual customers, that is, silver, gold, and platinum.

ANALYZING INDIVIDUAL CUSTOMERS

While analysis of the "average" customer can provide some insights, realization of the full power of CLV requires that each individual customer be analyzed to determine their profitability. Further, because the past is not always, or even often, a good predictor of the future, it is important to develop a forecast of the future purchasing behavior of the individual customer. This can be a daunting task given the information requirements. The information required includes the revenue to be received from each customer over some time period, usually annually, the variable cost directly associated with serving the customer, any other costs associated with the customer, and the "life" of the customer as a purchaser of the firm's products or services.

- *Estimating Revenue.* Revenue is relatively easy to estimate. Sales records provide a historical starting point. You can then develop a forecast of future revenue by modeling historical purchase information along with other information about the customer, such as age and life stage in the case of individual consumers, or growth rate and general economic conditions in the case of business-to-business customers. As with any forecast, there will be uncertainty associated with such estimates of future cash flow as well as with future purchasing of individual customers, depending on the amount and quality of information available. The degree of uncertainty should be a part of the considerations of any decisions regarding the individual customer.
- *Determining Costs.* Determination of the costs of serving an individual customer is far more challenging. Firms typically do a poor job of allocating costs. Accounting costs are unlikely to be helpful because they are often aggregated over multiple customers and are often based on accounting rules that may not reflect actual costs attributable to an individual customer. The variable cost of each product sold or service performed may be the easiest cost to determine, but even variable costs may differ if there are economies of scale that change the cost structure of producing the product or delivering the service. There are also costs that are not so easily associated with the sale of a specific product or service. These are real costs, but they are shared across many products. Such costs include the costs of machinery, staff, and office and/or production space, among others. These costs must be allocated, but as pointed out in earlier chapters, such allocations need to be clearly understood and recognized as potentially distorting the actual return on specific marketing expenditures.

One approach to such cost allocation is the use of *Activity Based Costing* (ABC) (Blokdyk 2017). ABC involves the determination of what drives specific costs and allocates them to whatever creates the need for these costs. Thus, building costs might be allocated based on the square footage required to support a particular activity, and staff compensation might be allocated based on the amount of time devoted to specific activities. Inevitably, some costs will be so distant from any customer-specific or transaction-specific activities that an arbitrary allocation rule will need to be adopted.

The allocation of costs is, in part, a political decision. There are many ways to allocate costs and cost allocation decisions influence the profitability of customers. It is often helpful to examine customer profitability based on different cost allocation rules. There is no "right" answer to the allocation decision, but an understanding of how particular allocation rules influence customer profitability can often provide insights into both the contribution of the customer to the firm's cash flow and suggest ways to manage costs that benefit the firm.

- *The "Life" of a Customer.* Some formulas for CLV assume customers have an infinite life. This is unrealistic, of course. Even the best and most loyal customers die or go out of business. Churn is a fact of business life. Thus, there is a need to determine how long an individual customer will remain engaged.

Attrition and retention rates are obtained at the aggregate level. If a firm starts with 100 customers and loses 10 over the course of a year, the attrition rate is 10% and the retention rate is 90%. When analyzing the value of an individual customer such figures are not particularly helpful. Rather, what is required is information about the probability that the customer will continue to be a customer over time, or the probability that the customer may leave at any particular point in time in the future. A simple approach is to assign the aggregate retention rate to each customer, but this ignores important information about individual customers. A customer with a long-term, multi-year contract is far less likely to disengage than a customer without such a contract. A customer who is dependent on the firm for a key product that is not available elsewhere also has a very low probability of disengaging. Such information, along with information about the customers' recency, frequency, and volume of purchases, may be used to develop a statistical estimate of the probability that a customer will disengage or still be "alive" at any point in the future.

Adding to the complexity of individual customer level analysis, and especially the problem of estimating the "life" of a customer, is the question of how the "customer" should be defined. Customers are not always individuals. In business-to-business contexts a firm may do business with multiple individuals, units, or departments within the same organization. In such circumstances it may not be useful to define the larger organization as the unit of analysis for purposes of customer definition. Such aggregation has the potential to mask the dynamics of purchase decision-making within the component organizations. Indeed, one customer in a large organization may disengage even as another emerges. At the organization level, it would appear that the organization has been a consistent customer, when, in fact, there has been a significant change in the customer base. Similarly, for some products and services the best unit of analysis may be the household, but for other products and services, the individuals who make up the household will be the best unit of analysis. One solution is to break down business-to-business customers by product line or business unit. Determination of the best unit of analysis, or how best to define the customer, requires a deep understanding of the purchase process(es) employed by the customer, as well as determination of who and where purchase decisions are made.

Even small variations in revenue and cost can make a big impact on the CLV. Table 8.4 and Fig. 8.3 show a simple modeling exercise. In this case, the historical revenue per customer is $100 per year, with costs per customer of $50. If there are no changes in revenue or cost, the net present value (NPV) of future earnings per customer will be $353.51. This assumes an 8% cost of capital (discount rate).

If we introduce a variation of between −1% and 1% growth in revenue and costs, the NPV changes dramatically. With low (−1%) revenue growth and high (1%) cost growth, the ten-year NPV (or CLV) shrinks to $302.83. At the other end of the spectrum, modeling high (1%) revenue growth and low (−1%) cost growth, the NPV jumps to $405.12. Figure 8.3 shows the earnings trend over ten years based on each assumption. It also includes a random model, where the growth in revenue and costs fluctuates between 1% and −1% randomly each year—this is probably what happens in reality, in any event.

Table 8.4 Small variations in revenue and cost can make a big difference

	Range			NPV	
Variability in revenue estimate	1%	−1%	1%	Case 1: baseline—no changes	$353.51
Variability in cost estimate	1%	−1%	1%	Case 2: negative revenue growth, high cost growth	$302.83
Historical purchase history (annual sales per customer)	$100			Case 3: high revenue growth, negative cost growth	$405.12
Historical cost (annual per customer)	$50			Case 4: random growth	$365.04
Historical earnings per customer per year	$50				
Cost of capital	8%				

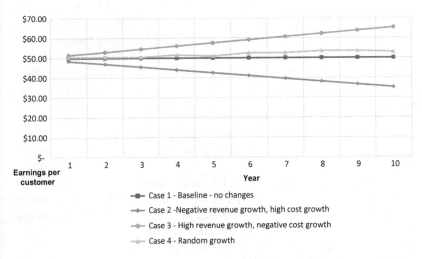

Fig. 8.3 Earnings per customer assuming small differences in revenue and costs. Effect of a 1% positive or negative variation on growth and cost in earnings per customer over a 10-year period

Customer Acquisition

The objective of many marketing activities is to acquire customers. In the context of CLV a key question is whether acquiring a customer will be worth the effort and investment of resources that are required. Answering this question requires an assessment of the value of the customer: will they be profitable? How profitable? Will they be more profitable than other potential customers in whom the firm might invest scarce resources? There is also a need to determine the cost of acquisition.

In order to estimate profitability, there is a need to forecast what a customer might purchase in the future. This might be achieved by developing profiles of current customers who are similar to the candidate for acquisition. The purchasing histories and forecasts for these customers can then be used to estimate future sales to the new customer. In the spirit of CLV, such estimation should take the long-term perspective. A new customer might not be immediately profitable but may have significant long-term potential. Such a customer might well be worth acquiring, especially if the cost of acquisition in the present may be lower than the cost of acquisition in the future.

There is substantial debate in marketing about whether acquisition costs should be considered when computing the CLV of a customer. It is often the case that acquisition costs are subtracted before reporting CLV. This is a practice that can be very misleading. The reason for this is that acquisition costs are a sunk cost. Some acquisition costs do not result in a successful acquisition of a customer. These costs are clearly sunk. But, what of the case where there is a successful acquisition. Clearly if the customer is worth less than the acquisition cost it would be prudent not to spend on the acquisition in the first instance. But, once the funds are expended and the acquisition of the customer is completed, the inclusion of acquisition costs can make an otherwise profitable customer appear unprofitable.

Consider a customer for which the cost of acquisition is $500 and the expected future cost of serving the customer is $1000. The expected future revenue from the customer is $1200. Thus, the contribution of the customer is $200, which makes the customer a profitable customer and asset to the firm worth $200. However, if the cost of acquisition is subtracted ($200 − $500 = −$300), the customer suddenly appears unprofitable. If this negative value is used to justify "firing" the customer, the firm has lost $200. Of course, had all of this been known in advance, there would have been no reason to recruit the customer in the first place, but once the acquisition cost is expended, it makes sense to retain the customer.

This is one reason why decisions about acquiring customers need to be carefully considered. It generally makes sense to invest in the acquisition of a customer if the net present value of the future cash flows is equal to or greater than the cost of acquisition. Determination of acquisition costs and strategy is often facilitated by analysis of the efficiency of these expenditures. Some acquisition strategies produce more inquiries, some produce more qualified prospects, and some are more effective in converting a prospect into customer.

Table 8.5 is an illustration of a cost of acquisition analysis. The analysis compares the efficiency of four channels of communication for acquiring customers. Selecting the cheapest approach is seldom wise because different approaches produce different outcomes. Thus, in the illustration in Table 8.5, each of the channels reaches a different number of prospects, ranging from 30,000 for direct sales to three million for newspaper inserts. However, each of these channels produces quite different response rates, that is, inquiries and/or store visits. The channels also differ in the number of qualified prospects that are identified, that is, the number of prospects for whom the product or service is a good match in terms of benefits and price. In the illustration, all four channels are equally effective in converting qualified prospects into customers. This is not always the case, and different approaches often have different conversion rates.

Table 8.5 Customer acquisition analysis

Channel	Prospects	Response rate	Number of responses	% Qualify	Qualified prospects	% Convert
Direct mail	300,000	2.0%	6000	66.7%	4002	80%
In-store	2,000,000	1.5%	30000	33.3%	9990	80%
Direct sales	30,000	50.0%	15000	66.7%	10005	80%
Inserts	3,000,000	1.0%	30000	33.3%	9990	80%

Channel	Customers	Effectiveness index	Cost per prospect	Total cost	Cost per customer
Direct mail	3202	1.1%	$1.50	$450,000	$140.55
In-store	7992	0.4%	$0.25	$500,000	$62.56
Direct sales	8004	26.7%	$18k/person	$225,000	$28.11
Inserts	7992	0.3%	$0.15	$450,000	$56.31
	27190	0.5%		$1,625,000	$59.77

The four approaches produce quite different numbers of customers, ranging from 8004 for direct sales to 3202 for direct mail. The data in the illustration allows for the computation of various indices of effectiveness. The one shown in Table 8.5 is obtained by dividing the number of customers by the number of prospects. Finally, it is possible to determine the cost per customer acquired. In the illustration, the lowest cost of customer acquisition is direct sales, though clearly the most effective channel will vary by product and market. This does not mean that only the lowest cost approach to customer acquisition should be employed. It would be important to determine whether the various channels were producing different prospects and the value of the newly acquired customers produced by each channel.

The average cost of customer acquisition across all four channels is $59.77. At minimum, this campaign illustrated in Table 8.5 should produce new customers whose net present value exceeds this figure. A common rule of thumb is that the net present value of new customers is ideally at least three times the costs of acquisition (Foster 2017).

Similar types of analyses may be carried to explore the return on development activities involving current customers. In general, a firm should invest no more in customer development and retention than the amount, at the margin, of the increase in customer value attributable to changes in volume, margin, and duration.

Making It Work

CLV is a powerful tool, but its use can be challenging. It requires that the firm be able to track sales transactions at the customer level and have a defensible method of assigning costs to both individual transactions and to customer support costs that are not included in sales transactions. Estimating the "life" of a customer can be difficult. All of this means that in many industries the approach is somewhat impractical. However, when a firm has the requisite data, CLV can be a powerful tool for valuing customers and for making decisions about investments in the acquisition and development of customers.

Conclusion

One way to think about firms is as a bundle of customer relationships. The value of the firm is sum of customer relationships, or more specifically, the net present value of cash flows that arise from the relationships over time. The value of these cash flows is often referred to as customer equity.

Exercises

1. Identify three subscription services with which you are familiar. Examples include streaming music or video services, online games, shopping services such as Amazon Prime, box subscription services, and fitness clubs, among others. What factors influence the recency, frequency, and volume of purchases from these services? What marketing activities might influence recency? Frequency? Volume?

2. Assume a customer purchases $1000 of a firm's services each year. The firm's margin on its sales is 40%. There are other annual support costs associated with the customer that cannot be linked to individual sales transactions. These costs are $100 per year. There are no other costs associated with serving this customer. Assume that the customer will remain active at the same level of purchasing activity for five years. What is the undiscounted CLV of this customer? If the firm has a discount rate of 10%, what is the present value of the customer. What would have been a reasonable acquisition cost for this customer?

3. Assume a firm has 20,000 customers who on average purchase $500 of product each year with a 50% margin. There are no other support costs associated with serving these customers. The annual retention rate is 75% and the firm has an 8% discount rate. What is the net present value of the cash flows associated with the firm's customers? If the firm could increase its retention rate to 80% what would the increase in total CLV be? How much should the firm be willing to invest to increase its retention rate to 80%

Points to Ponder

1. CLV provides a means for identifying high value and low value customers. Should different customers be treated differently based on their value to the firm? If so how? Is there a downside to this practice? What about firing customers? What are the potential disadvantages of firing customers?

2. Should some customers be valued more or less than the sum of their net cash flows to the firm? Why might some customers be more valuable than the sum of their cash flows? Can you identify examples? Why might some customers be less valuable than the sum of their cash flows? Can you identify examples?

REFERENCES

Bejou, D., Keiningham, T. L., & Aksoy, L. (2016). *Customer Lifetime Value: Reshaping the Way We Manage to Maximize Profits*. New York: Routledge.

Blokdyk, G. (2017). *Activity-Based Costing ABC*. Scotts Valley: CreateSpace Independent Publishing Platform.

Buttle, F., & Maklan, S. (2016). *Customer Relationship Management* (3rd ed.). New York: Taylor and Francis/Routledge.

Foster, T. (2017). *Why Your Sales Leader Needs to Understand CAC and CLTV*. Sales Benchmark Index (SBI). https://salesbenchmarkindex.com/insights/why-your-sales-leader-needs-to-understand-cac-and-cltv/

Grunberg, J. (2016, September 14). A Forbes Insight Study: Linking Customer Retention with Profitable Growth. *Forbes*. https://www.sailthru.com/marketing-blog/a-forbes-insights-study-linking-customer-retention-with-profitable-growth/

Kumar, V. (2008). *Customer Lifetime Value: The Path to Profitability*. Boston: Now Publishers.

Lawrence, A. (2012, November 1). Five Customer Retention Tips for Entrepreneurs. *Forbes*. https://www.forbes.com/sites/alexlawrence/2012/11/01/five-customer-retention-tips-for-entrepreneurs/#56751e735e8d

Reichheld, F. E. (1994). Loyalty and the Renaissance of Marketing. *Marketing Management, 2*(4), 10–21.

Reynolds, R. (2012, July). To Sell More, Focus on Existing Customers. *Harvard Business Review*. https://hbr.org/2012/07/to-sell-more-focus-on-existing

CHAPTER 9

Anticipating the Future: Managing Risk and Real Options

Eastman Kodak introduced Advantix film and cameras to consumers in 1996. Based on the new "Advanced Photo System" (APS), Advantix was intended to be a bridge between traditional film-based photography and the looming threat (or opportunity) of digital photography. Fuji also had its own version of APS, as they were as concerned about the future as Kodak.

Advantix was a hedge against future risk. It was fairly clear in 1996 that photography was about to undergo a radical change. Computers were making digital photography more popular, but the quality of digital images was low and the costs were high. Film and photographic paper were still the cheapest ways to get amazing color photo prints. Advantix, which used a reloadable cartridge of film instead of a disposable container, included a magnetic strip on the film which enabled it to record data about each photo like time and date.

The Advantix cartridge was designed to make it easy to scan the film images onto a computer. The industry perspective, at this time, was that film would always be the basis of the photographic image, no matter if the ultimate destination of the image was a paper photo print or a computer disk. The camera and film cartridge came to market accompanied by a host of new photographic lab machines designed for Advanced Photo System. The one-hour photo store had to change along with the new film format.

© The Author(s) 2019   167
D. W. Stewart, *Financial Dimensions of Marketing Decisions*,
Palgrave Studies in Marketing, Organizations and Society,
https://doi.org/10.1007/978-3-030-15565-0_9

It was a pretty good idea, but as we now know, it was hopelessly doomed to failure—doomed by the unexpectedly fast rise of low-cost digital photography. It was further doomed by a fundamental change in the way consumers took and shared photos. Within a short period of time, between 2005 and 2010, millions of consumers stopped taking pictures in order to get paper prints for albums. They took photos on their phones and shared them online. Virtually none of the assumptions Kodak had made over the previous 130 years held up any longer. Kodak's two core businesses, film and photographic paper, were devastated.

Kodak filed for bankruptcy in 2012, unable to compete in a market that had changed so profoundly and quickly that there was nothing the company could do to survive. It was a shocking event. Kodak, which was one of the world's best-known and highly respected brands, had a long history of dominance in the photographic industry. They had enjoyed market shares approaching 80% in the United States at their peak.

What happened? What happened was an incredible demonstration of future risk. That is the focus of this chapter. Chapters 2–4 described the linkages among a firm's marketing actions, business model, and the timing and size of cash flows generated by the firm's products and service. Chapters 5–8 focused on linking marketing outcomes to financial performance. In all of the discussions to this point there has been an assumption of relative certainty about the future.

The future is not certain, of course. There are risks and opportunities that may impact the outcomes of the best-laid plans. This chapter describes how the models, tools, and techniques developed for the case of certainty can be adapted to address more realistic situations in which marketing planning occurs under uncertainty. The chapter will also address the means by which firms may leverage existing marketing assets or real options.

The purpose of this chapter is to present and evaluate the techniques that firms use to incorporate risk into their budgeting processes. The chapter will first review some fundamental concepts of risk and discuss several ways in which risk may be measured. The chapter then turns to the use of sensitivity analysis for the evaluation of profitability that is associated with variations in key assumptions and shows how risk can be incorporated within a marketing budgeting process that includes present value analysis. The chapter will show how staging decisions can be used to evaluate the outcomes of alternative marketing and cost assumptions. Finally, the chapter describes how a firm may identify, evaluate, and leverage its marketing assets to create and develop future opportunities, that is, the firm's real options.

MEASURING RISK

In marketing, risk is often a fuzzy concept that can refer to any number of quite distinct factors: changes among customers, changes in competitors' behavior, and changes in technology, among others that can adversely impact a firm's performance. While these factors can certainly affect the performance of the firm, they are more the reasons risk exists than risk itself. In economics and finance, risk is typically measured in terms of the variability of possible returns.

The variability in a firm's returns is influenced by a variety of factors. General macroeconomic factors affect all firms to a greater or lesser extent. These factors include changes in the rate of growth in the economy, the unemployment rate, consumer spending, the inflation rate, and the size of real interest rates. Other risk factors may be more specific to an individual firm or specific market offerings by the firm. Such factors include competitors' actions, changes in consumer tastes and demand, technological innovations, changing costs and prices, and legal and regulatory changes. The same factors that affect the variability of returns in the stock market also affect the variability of returns from a firm's market offerings, though there are some significant differences between investments in the stock market and investments in a firm's products and services. Chapter 10 will explore these differences in more detail.

Economists refer to risk that arises from macroeconomic factors as *systematic* or *beta risk*. Risk factors that are firm specific are referred to as *unsystematic risk*. Both types of risk are important. In general, firms have far greater opportunities to influence unsystematic risk than systematic risk, but both must be accounted for in the planning process and managed to the degree possible.

An advantage to defining risk in terms of potential variability in returns over time is that such a measure is directly linked to changes in cash flow. Thus, it lends itself to modeling changes in cash flow associated with different assumptions about risk factors. However, even such a well-defined concept is not unambiguous. Variability in cash flow needs to be considered in relation to some benchmark. There are three commonly used benchmarks. Depending on the benchmark employed, risk can take one of three forms:

- **Total risk** associated with a given product or service, based on the variability of returns of the product or service. This measure of risk contrasts the returns of a product or service with its history over time.

- **Firm-level risk** is measured by the contribution of any specific product or service to the variability of the total returns of the firms. Some products or services are just more important to the overall performance of a firm. Thus, changes in the returns of such offerings can have a large impact on the overall financial performance of the firm. For other offerings, even large variations may have a very modest impact on the overall variability of the firm's total financial performance.
- **Systematic risk**, which is measured by the correlation between product/service returns and returns on a diversified portfolio of stock market holdings.

Each of these types of risk has different implications for marketing planning and budgeting.

Product/Service Risk

The degree of business risk associated with a product or service is primarily determined by the variability in its sales and costs. The latter include the initial investment cost, subsequent production or operations costs, and ongoing costs of marketing.[1] While such risks are significant, whatever their origins, it is critical to understand the degree to which these risks can be magnified by operating leverage.

Operating Leverage Operating leverage refers to the costs of any assets for which a firm must pay a fixed cost regardless of the volume of production. Examples of such assets are production and distribution facilities, headquarters buildings, and many personnel, at least in short term. Such fixed costs also include the opportunity cost of the funds invested in these assets, depreciation, property taxes, insurance, management expenses, and even a portion of the utility bills. As observed in Chap. 2, variable costs—raw material, component parts, direct labor, energy, sales commissions, and most utility bills—vary directly with the level of production and sales.

Once a production facility, distribution center, or website is built, the opportunity cost of funds is no longer a relevant fixed cost; it is a sunk cost, unless the firm can find a willing buyer to whom it might consider selling

[1] Other factors may be important in some industries. For example, among natural resource companies there may be uncertainties related to exploration for mineral deposits.

the asset. There are two important management issues related to such fixed assets. First, there is the question of how to best leverage them. A distribution outlet that sits idle for 12 hours a day is losing 12 hours of opportunities for sales each day. For this reason, a number of fast food restaurants began serving breakfast and late-night snacks. This was a way to leverage a fixed asset, the building in which restaurant was located, by making it open, and hence able to make sales, over a longer period of time during each day. Note that this decision was not just a simple matter of opening the doors to the store early and later. Rather, there was need for a menu appropriate for the new day-parts being served and for marketing to make consumers aware of the new hours and new menu items. At least a portion of the costs of the new menu and marketing campaign then become a part of fixed costs.

Second, firms must address the issue of operating leverage when deciding on the types of investments they will make in fixed-cost assets. Among other things, they will need to decide the extent to which they might invest in more automated, capital-intensive facilities with lower unit costs or more labor-intensive facilities with higher unit costs. For example, in the fast food example above, the firm might need to determine whether to staff the restaurants by investing in automated order processing kiosks or by hiring more counter personnel.

Firm Risk: Putting Product Risk in Perspective

Most risk analyses, especially those undertaken by marketing planners, focus on the risk of a product or service standing on its own. Such an approach is usually problematic. In most firms, any individual offering is just one part of a portfolio of offerings by the firm. While each offering has its own uncertain return, it is the overall riskiness of the entire portfolio— what is called firm risk—with which top management is concerned, not so much the riskiness of any individual offering. Firm risk is important to senior management because it is what determines the financial health and solvency of the firm. For this reason, the risks associated with individual offerings will be of concern to top management only to the degree that they influence the variability of the firm's total returns.

From the perspective of a well-diversified investor, the firm itself is just one of numerous firms, each with its own portfolio of offerings. What matters to the well-diversified investor, therefore, is an offering's contribution to total portfolio risk. Of course, the product or service manager charged with managing the offering and who is evaluated based on the results he or she produces will be appropriately concerned with the risk of the product or service offering for which they are responsible. Such concern can sometimes lead to risk-averse or risk-seeking behavior that is suboptimal from the standpoint of the firm.

This is not to suggest that senior management ignores the risk associated with individual offerings. Senior managers pay attention to the risk associated with an individual offering because it provides information about the offering's contribution to the overall risk of the firm. In general, the riskier an offering is on its own, the more risk it is likely to contribute to firm risk.

The Influence of Firm Risk

Marketing managers are often blissfully ignorant of risk at the firm level. This is unfortunate because the financial health of the firm creates both opportunities and constraints. A financially healthy firm is more likely to have the resources to support innovation, growth, and customer satisfaction and retention. In contrast, a financially distressed firm often faces the prospect of reducing personnel, cutting costs and failure to deliver a high-quality customer experience with its offerings.

Firms engage in a variety of risk-reduction activities, including purchasing insurance, signing long-term contracts for raw materials and supplies, entering into long-term contracts for distribution, and forward purchasing, among others. There are many reasons for this behavior. One is that lower risk is often associated with a lower cost of capital, which gives the firm greater access to additional financial resources. A second reason, which should resonate with marketers, is that reduction in total risk can increase expected cash flows. Total risk may increase the financial instability of the firm, which may, in turn, influence the willingness of customers, suppliers, and employees to enter into relationships with the firm. Such unwillingness may then affect future sales, operating costs, and financing costs. A reduction in total risk can facilitate marketing efforts by offering assurance to customers that the firm will still be present in the future to service and upgrade its products and services. Purchasers of long-lived products and services are especially concerned about the seller's longevity. They want to be sure that the manufacturer will be there to service equipment and supply new parts as old ones wear out. If the original supplier goes out of business, parts and repairs may become a problem.

In addition, the cost of doing business is, in part, related to the degree a firm's suppliers have a favorable view about its long-run prospects. A firm struggling under financial pressures is not likely to find suppliers who are enthusiastic about providing it with products or services, especially if those products or services are customized and useful to only the firm in question.

It is axiomatic in marketing and consistent with the precepts of customer life time value, that the value of investing in a long-term relationship with a customer depends on whether and how long that customer is expected to survive in the long run. The greater the probability of a firm's potential for failure, the greater the costs of its relationships with customers and suppliers because it will have to bear more of the costs of these relationships with customers, pay higher prices to suppliers, and obtain products and services that are less customized for its unique needs. In addition, high-risk firms usually have a more difficult time attracting and retaining higher-quality personnel.

Finally, higher-risk firms may confront greater constraints related to obtaining financial resources from lenders. Such constraints may not be restricted to higher interest rates. Lenders may impose constraints on operating policies and the types of investments that a firm may make. Such constraints can reduce the flexibility of the firm and even prevent the firm from investing in what appear to be promising new markets or products.[2]

This discussion of firm risk should make clear why marketers need to be concerned with the broader risk of the firm, as well as the risks that may be unique to the individual product or services for which he or she is responsible. It is especially important that marketers be cognizant of how the market offerings for which they are responsible influence the greater risk of the firm and how this risk influences their access to resources for the products and services they manage.

Systemic Risk

As described above, systemic risk is associated with general factors in the macro-environment. Such risks are real but not under the control of management or investors. In an ideal world, the risk associated with investing in an individual offering should be independent of the firm's total risk and the

---

[2] While beyond the scope of this chapter, it is also worth noting that other benefits accrue to financially healthy, lower risk organizations, including numerous tax advantages related to depreciation, tax credits, and interest expense write-offs.

rate of return demanded by an investor for making an investment in an individual offering should not affect the expected return required by an investor. For reasons we will discuss in Chap. 10, this is not the case. All that should matter to a well-diversified investor is the offering's contribution to the risk of the investor's portfolio. Of course, relevance of the risk associated with any given market offering depends on where one stands. The amount of risk that is of concern to an investor who is well-diversified across many firms is less than the degree of risk that is relevant to senior corporate management, which, in turn, is less than that of the managers of the individual offering.

An important point is that the required return on an individual product, service, or even marketing campaign should be a function of the riskiness of market offering itself, not the riskiness of the firm. An implication of this, and one that is important for marketers to understand, is that each product may be treated as having its own cost of capital, independent of the firm. Thus, when Amazon entered the motion picture business, its required return on this investment should have been determined by the risk of making films, not the risk of being in the online retailing business or the cloud services business. Nevertheless, total risk can affect cash flow by influencing the perceptions and expectations of customers, suppliers, employees, and creditors. Thus, even the well-diversified investor should be interested in the total risk associated with an individual product or service to the extent that it may influence the offering's actual return.

Accounting for Risk

Accounting for risk is an important part of informed and responsible marketing budgeting and planning. Simple net present value (NPV) analysis uses the expected values of sales and costs and ignores any variations in these numbers. There is an elegant simplicity to this approach that makes comparisons among alternative investments relatively easy and decision-making straightforward. If NPV is positive, the investment should be undertaken; if it is negative, it should be rejected. However, the single NPV number often hides important information about the riskiness of candidate investments.

The future is unknown and unknowable. In the words of economist John Kenneth Galbraith: "There are two kinds of forecasters: those who don't know, and those who don't know they don't know." Simply stated, virtually all forecasts are wrong, but some are more wrong than others. It is a near certainty that today's estimates of future sales volumes, prices, costs, and competitor's actions are going to be wrong. However, just because they may be wrong is not a reason to ignore them. Rather, it is useful to acknowledge the likelihood of error and examine how changes in assumptions and potential estimation errors might affect the NPV of a particular investment. Two marketing actions that produce the same net present value when risk is ignored may differ substantially in the degree of risk involved. Prudent management decision-making would select the less-risky action in such a circumstance. Thus, there is a need to make some adjustment for risk when comparing alternative marketing investments.

As a first step, it is useful to ask whether risk will have a significant impact on an investment's net present value. Many marketing investments carry very modest risks. This is because results can often be monitored in real time, at least by means of intermediate marketing outcomes, and can be modified or eliminated quickly. There is little point in doing a comprehensive risk analysis if the risk is negligible. A useful method for going beyond the information conveyed by a risk-adjusted NPV is *sensitivity analysis*.

There are various ways to adjust for risk. The simplest approach is to make a subjective assessment of risk based on what is known. Such "guesses" are fraught with problems. It is difficult for a manager to cognitively determine how the many factors that influence risk may interact to produce an outcome. Information that is already uncertain leads to even greater uncertainty when combined. Human judgment is fraught with biases (Musashi 2016; Montibellar and von Winterfeldt 2015). The optimism bias described in Chap. 4 is particularly problematic when evaluating risk. Table 9.1 describes a number of common biases.

BEST, WORST, AND MOST LIKELY CASE ANALYSES

A better and less subjective alternative for considering risk in decision-making is to create alternative scenarios of potential outcomes based on different assumptions about demand, competitors' action, and other factors. While any number of scenarios might be identified and investigated, a particularly useful approach is to estimate the best-case scenario, the worst-case scenario, and the most likely case scenario.

Table 9.1   Common biases in risk estimation and decision-making

---

Affective bias: an emotional predisposition for, or against, a specific outcome or option that influences judgments.

Ambiguity Aversion: a preference for outcomes with explicitly stated probabilities over gambles with diffuse or unspecified probabilities.

Anchoring: estimation of a numerical value is based on an initial value (anchor) that is not sufficiently adjusted when arriving at a final answer.

Availability bias/ease of recall: the probability of an event that is easily recalled is overstated.

Certainty bias: a preference for sure things; tendency to discount uncertain events.

Confirmation bias: a desire to confirm one's belief leading to unconscious selectivity in the acquisition and use of evidence.

Conjunction fallacy: The joint occurrence (conjunction) of two events is judged to be more likely than the constituent events.

Conservatism bias: failure to sufficiently revise judgments after receiving new information about an event under consideration.

Endowment effect: the disutility for losing is greater than the utility for gaining the same amount.

Equalizing bias: decision makers assign similar weights to all objectives' or similar probabilities to all events.

Gain/Loss Bias: descriptions of a decision and its outcome(s) may result in different decision depending on whether the outcome(s) are described as gains or as losses.

Gambler's fallacy/the hot hand: tendency to think that irrelevant information about the past matters when predicting future events, for example, that, when tossing a coin, it is more likely that "heads" comes up after a series of "tails"

Ignoring base rate: ignoring base rates when making judgments and relying instead on specific individuating information.

Motivated Reasoning: the desire for a particular outcome or the desire to avoid a particular outcome leads to select use and weighting of information consistent with the desired outcome

Myopic problem representation: an oversimplified problem representation is adopted based on an incomplete mental model of the decision problem.

Omission of important variables: one or more important variables are overlooked.

Subadditivity/super-additivity bias: When judging individual subevents, the sum of the probabilities is often systematically smaller or larger than the directly estimated probability of the total event.

Sunk Costs: considering sunk cost when making prospective decisions.

Adapted from: Montibellar and von Winterfeldt (2015)

Such an analysis provides a means for bounding likely outcomes and for creating contingency plans for the best and worst cases. Table 9.2 provides a simple illustration of such an analysis for the first year of a hypothetical new product launch. The three case scenarios, best, worst, and most likely, differ in assumptions about the size of the market, the market share the

Table 9.2 Example of best case, worst case, most likely case analysis (first year sales)

	Best case	Worst case	Most likely case
Market size	10,000,000	3,000,000	6,000,000
Market share	25%	10%	20%
Sales in units	2,500,000	300,000	1,200,000
Price	$ 12/unit	$ 8/unit	$ 10/unit
Gross revenue	$30,000,000	$2,400,000	$12,000,000
Margin	60%	40%	50%
Gross contribution	$18,000,000	$960,000	$6,000,000
Marketing expense @ 10% of Gross revenue	$3,000,000	$240,000	$1,200,000
Net contribution	$15,000,000	$720,000	$4,800,000

firm is likely to capture, the price the firm will be able to charge, and the margin the firm will obtain. The scenarios also assume that the firm will spend a fixed percent of gross revenue on marketing.

The results for the first year do not look promising in the example, but the firm does not lose money in the first year, even in the worst case, assuming that other overhead costs are not greater than $720,000. The firm might well decide that given the required upfront investment and the risk in the worst case, it cannot justify the launch of the product. However, note that one of the big differences in the scenarios is the estimated size of the market. This difference might well be attributed to assumptions about how fast the market might develop, which is always a question for new-to-the world products. The firm might well ask what the worst-case scenario would look like in five years assuming the size of the market increased over time. Table 9.3 provides this analysis.

In Table 9.3 all of the assumptions about market share, price, and margin remain the same as in Table 9.2. The only difference is that the market size grows over time, reaching ten million in the fifth year. Now the worst case does not look so bad. Indeed, assuming costs of developing and launching the new products, which are not included in these analyses, was two million dollars, the new product launch appears justified. Note that any of the parameters in the examples could be changed to determine the impact of the change. Other parameters could be added to the examples. For example, rather than just assuming marketing expenditures are a fixed percent of sales revenue, different levels of expenditures might be considered along with the influence of these expenditures on such factors as product awareness, distribution, and market share. Indeed, such analyses,

Table 9.3 Example of best case, worst case, most likely case analysis (five year sales with annual growth)

	Year 1	Year 2	Year 3	Year 4	Year 5	NPV of cash flows over 5 years
Market size	3,000,000	4,000,000	6,000,000	8,000,000	10,000,000	
Market share	10%	10%	10%	10%	10%	
Sales in units	300,000	400,000	600,000	800,000	1,000,000	
Price	$ 8/unit	$ 8/unit	$ 8/unit	$ 8/unit	$ 8/unit	
Gross revenue	$2,400,000	$3,200,000	$4,800,000	$6,400,000	$8,000,000	
Margin	40%	40%	40%	40%	40%	
Gross contribution	$960,000	$1,600,000	$1,920,000	$2,560,000	$3,200,000	
Marketing expense @ 10% of gross revenue	$240,000	$320,000	$480,000	$640,000	$800,000	
Net contribution	$720,000	$1,280,000	$1,440,000	$1,920,000	$2,400,000	
Discounted net contribution (8% discount rate)	$720,000	$1,185,185	$1,237,997	$1,524,158	$1,764,072	$6,431,412

while extremely useful for answering questions about "what if?", can become quite complex. Dealing with such complexity necessitates the use of computers and the application of *sensitivity analysis* and *computer simulations*.

SENSITIVITY ANALYSIS

Sensitivity analysis is a procedure used to systematically study the effect of changes in the values of key assumptions and parameters—including market size, market share, price, R&D expenditures, production costs, and plant construction cost—on the NPV of an investment. It provides a means for answering a series of "what if" questions that are framed in terms of "What would happen if X changed?" where X is any assumption or parameter. If a change occurs when an assumption or parameter changes, the analysis can also answer the question of how big a difference the change makes. Use of a spreadsheet or other computer program can make it easy to substitute one assumption or variable for another to see what happens.

Sensitivity analysis can be taken to a more complex level using computer simulation. Such simulations can create a probability distribution for the NPV of a marketing investment rather than a single number. In order to conduct a simulation analysis, it is first necessary to estimate probability distributions for each factor that is expected to influence the cash inflows and outflows. For example, for a new product introduction, these factors would include the initial investment for product development and launch, market size, growth of the market, price, market share, variable costs, fixed costs, and the life of the new product, as well as assumptions about competitors' behavior and other environmental factors that may influence demand and cost. Some of these probability distributions can be estimated based on internal information about the firm's cost structure and the costs of R&D, while others such as price, distribution coverage, and market share may be informed by market research.

Once these distributions have been identified, a computer program can be used to randomly select one value apiece from each of the probability distributions associated with relevant factors. These values—for market size, distribution coverage, market share, variable costs, and so forth, are then combined to calculate the net cash flow for each period. This process may be repeated hundreds or even thousands of times to generate a distribution of NPVs. As each scenario is generated—a scenario being a particular set of values for the relevant project variables—

the project NPV associated with that particular combination of parameter values is calculated and stored. This process is repeated, say, 600 times by the computer. The stored NPVs (all 600 of them) are then printed out by the computer in the form of a frequency distribution, along with the expected NPV and its standard deviation. The mean and standard deviation of this distribution of NPVs provides a most likely outcome and an indication of the likely size of variation, respectively. The latter is a measure of risk.

Software tools for sensitivity analysis are widely available. There are macros available for spreadsheets, such as Excel and there are numerous specialized software packages for sensitivity analysis. A useful resource for identifying such software is https://www.capterra.com/budgeting-software/.

One limitation of simulation analysis is that it can become quite complex, especially when there is an effort to create a complete and realistic replication of the market. There are interdependencies among the variables and what happens in one period is often related to what has happened in previous periods. Demand and price often move together, in opposite directions, within a period. Increasing marketing costs may be accompanied by increasing sales volume. A higher market share in one period is likely to mean a higher market share in the next period. Identifying and specifying such interdependencies are difficult, but the value of a simulation will be reduced if they are not built in.

A second limitation of simulation analysis has both practical and theoretical dimensions. A simulation analysis produces a frequency distribution for the NPV of a given investment; it does not provide a decision rule for trading off risk versus return. On the other hand, the NPV rule is quite specific: if NPV is positive accept the project; otherwise, reject it. A third problem is that the analysis of risk produced by a simulation does not involve consideration of opportunities for managing risk or to diversify away a portion of the risk. If the returns on a particular marketing investment are not highly correlated with returns on the firm's other assets, the incremental risk of the investment to the firm may be lower than the risk of the marketing investment.

A fourth, but significant, difficulty with simulation is that it rests, at some basic level, on assumptions made by human beings. No matter how good the math, nothing can make a bad assumption good. In the case of Kodak, they surely had modeled the Advantix product line and determined that it would have a high NPV. The assumptions held that film cameras would be popular for another 20 years, when, in fact, their market lifespan was far more limited. It's easy to see that error now. Only a genius could have predicted the arrival of a device like the iPhone in the early 1990s when Kodak was developing Advantix. However, most people in the industry knew that something like the iPhone was going to come along at some point; they just didn't know when and most executives were too intellectually and emotionally invested in traditional film based photography to contemplate that their entire business would be wiped out in a matter of years.

BREAK-EVEN ANALYSIS

A very common analysis used to evaluate and manage risk is *break-even analysis*. A significant concern associated with any investment is the possibility of losing money. In many, but not all, businesses, production or operations costs are relatively predictable. Thus, a critical determinant of whether a firm will make money or lose money on a product is the amount of sales revenue. The price and margin of any given product or service is generally easy to estimate. Thus, the largest contributor to uncertainty about revenue is uncertainty about sales volume. One method for addressing this uncertainty is break-even analysis. Break-even analysis involves determining the amount of sales required to just cover costs or break even. Marketers often use break-even, which can be obtained using the following formulas (In reality, other factors such as depreciation and taxes also need to be considered, but these factors are frequently idiosyncratic to the firm and are ignored here):

$$\text{Break-even}(\text{in units}) = \text{Fixed Costs} \div (\text{Price per unit} - \text{Variable Costs})$$

$$\text{Break-even}(\text{in revenue}) = \text{Fixed Costs} \div (\text{Contribution Margin} \div \text{Unit Sales Price})$$

Note that the denominator in the first formula is the gross contribution of the sale. This formula indicates how many units must be sold to just cover the costs associated with the product. In the second formula the denominator is the ratio of the contribution margin to the unit sale price. An advantage of break-even analysis is that it is usually easier and requires less information to determine whether sales are likely to be greater or less than the break-even than to estimate actual sales.

182 D. W. STEWART

While marketers frequently employ break-even analysis in marketing planning, they often ignore the time value of money when making the computation. This is sometimes called the accounting profit break-even. From a financial planning perspective break-even volume should be the volume of sales at which the product's NPV is zero. The financial break-even must take into account the timing of sales and the resulting cash flow over time. It is usually higher than the accounting break-even.

Adjusting for Risk

The focus of this chapter thus far has been on how to assess risk. There remains the important question of how risk can be factored into a budget analysis. There are three widely used methods for incorporating risk into investment planning: (1) changing the payback period, (2) using a risk-adjusted discount rate, and (3) modifying the cash flows.[3]

- *Changing the Payback Period.* Many firms deal with risk by requiring that riskier investments have a shorter payback period. Thus, an investment with an above average level of risk might be required to have a payback period of two years, compared to an investment of average risk. Alternatively, a low risk investment might be assigned a payback period of five years. While there is a certain intuitive appeal to such treatment, it is quite subjective. It is unclear how the payback period should be adjusted or what the relationship is between the realities of risk and the length of time for payback. This approach is at best subjective and arbitrary and at worst misleading.
- *Using a Risk-adjusted Discount Rate.* Another common approach for dealing with risk is to adjust the discount rate to account for the riskiness of the investment. While theoretically correct, its use in practice is often arbitrary. Too often, it is applied in an ad hoc manner. The practical question is one of how much the discount rate should be changed to account for risk. If a firm ordinarily requires a return of 10%, what rate of rate of return should be required for a risky investment and how is the amount of adjustment related to the degree of risk. In practice, decision-makers also often fail to distinguish between an investment's total risk and the systematic compo-

---

[3]A fourth approach, calculating certainty equivalents for the cash flows, is found in the finance literature but exists largely as a theory without a practical means for implementation.

nent of the risk, which would be inherent in any investment. This leaves open the question of which type(s) of risk are relevant, and how the various types of risk should be reflected in the discount rate.

- *Modifying Cash Flows.* When modeling distributions of cash flows, by using a simulation or other method, there are alternatives regarding which of the cash flows is taken to be most likely or representative. The mean of such distributions has the undesirable property that it can be affected, sometimes quite significantly, by a few extreme values. For this reason, many firms discount the most likely (modal) cash flow rather than expected (mean) cash flow. If a significant new risk arises, the modal value of the probability distribution of future cash flows will be significantly above the mean. For example, consider a pharmaceutical firm for which both the mean and mode of future cash flows from a particular drug are projected at $50 million annually. Suppose now that a change in government regulation raises the possibility that the drug might be withdrawn from the market as a result of some adverse effects among some users. If the probability of withdrawal is 25%, the mean value of future annual cash flows will decline to $37.5 million ($50 million × 0.75 + $0 × 0.25); the modal value will remain at $20 million.

In such situations, firms will use the modal value and either shorten the payback period or raise the discount rate. Neither of these adjustments lends itself to a careful evaluation of the actual impact of a particular risk on investment returns because a comprehensive analysis of risk would include consideration of the size and timing of the relevant risk and its influence on projected future cash flows. A change in the payback period and use of the risk-adjusted discount rate both ignore timing. Withdrawal of the drug, in the example, in five years has less impact than immediate withdrawal.

The preceding discussion makes clear that there is no simple approach to accounting for risk. It is important for marketers to understand the traditional financial perspective on risk presented above. There are two reasons marketers need this understanding. First, it is the way financial managers think about risk. Discussions of risk will likely be more productive if marketers have an appreciation of the financial perspective. A second reason marketers should understand the financial perspective is because some marketing projects do involve large initial investments with long payback periods, that is, R&D, product development, branding, and opening new distribution channels. But, as will be discussed in Chaps. 10 and 11, marketing investments, indeed investments in most intangibles, involve ongoing investment rather than a one-time, upfront investment.

MARKETING PROCESS AS RISK MANAGEMENT

There are other ways to account for risk. Many marketing expenditures are designed to produce both short-term results and long-term results. The short-term results provide feedback that can indicate whether the marketing activities are achieving the intended results. Indeed, this is an especially important role for the intermediate measurement outcomes discussed in Chap. 5. Such feedback provides information that allows the firm to adjust, increase, or reduce spending or stop a particular marketing activity altogether. Such a process is really a form of risk management. Indeed, unlike a large capital expenditure on an asset like a building or production facility, which cannot easily be started and stopped, marketing activities and expenditures can be adjusted on a regular basis in response to changing market conditions and new information. Such management requires proactive monitoring of marketing outcomes using appropriate measures of both intermediate marketing outcomes and financial results.

A good example of such a risk management process is found in the widely used *stage and gate product development process* shown in Fig. 9.1. Rather than make an all or nothing, upfront decision about investing in a

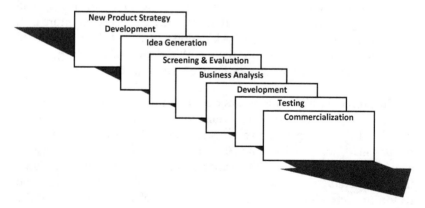

Fig. 9.1 Stage and gate product development process. (Source: Booz et al. 1982)

new product, the stage and gate approach breaks the development process into discrete stages. Each stage concludes with a decision point, or "gate" that determines whether the project continues to the next stage. Thus, the first stage is idea generation. Once ideas are generated, the process proceeds to the next step where the ideas are evaluated based on available information. Many ideas may be eliminated at this stage and those ideas would not progress to the next stage. For example, if it were determined that a product could not be profitable even if every imaginable customer bought one, the idea could be easily dismissed. Ideas that make it through the screening stage might then be evaluated more systematically based on market research and cost analyses. Promising candidates that make it through the business analysis stage then progress to actual development. Note that at each stage there may be a decision to expend more resources in the next stage, a decision to end the project, or a decision to defer continuation of the development project to some future date. The final decision to launch only occurs for products that have been repeatedly vetted through multiple stages with increasing amounts of information. The risk of failure and of expending resources on failures is thus managed through this process.

Many marketing programs can be structured using a similar process. In addition, the use of intermediate feedback once a decision is made to launch provides further information about risks and the need for appropriate adjustment. In this way, marketing management is a type of risk management process.

The popularity of venture-backed startups can be found, at least partly, in this gate-based model of risk management. A startup and its investors bear the risks of the first several stages of the product development and commercialization cycle. If the product is successful, then a larger firm will acquire the venture. Or, the company will go public, which is another way of selling the product to other investors. Though the acquiring company pays a premium for the successful startup, it is worth it because they have delegated the risk of investing in an untested idea and picked a proven winner of the gating process. (Most of the time.)

Summary of Risk Management

The management of risk is a critical element in marketing management. There are numerous techniques for identifying risk and for evaluating the effects of risk on future outcomes. While no technique for assessing risk and for incorporating risk in an analysis is perfect, each can provide some useful information. Using multiple techniques in combination with one another is a practical approach to a difficult task.

FUTURE OPPORTUNITIES: REAL OPTIONS

The stage and gate product development process described earlier in this chapter is an example of a firm creating opportunities or options for itself. At each gate the firm has the option to continue, discontinue, or defer. Such a process is actually more typical of decision-making than the use of discounted cash flow (DCF) analysis. DCF treats expenditures and expected cash flows as given at the outset of a marketing project with all of the operating decisions made in advance. In reality, the opportunity to make decisions at some point in the future, when more and better information is available, is characteristic of many investment decisions, and most especially marketing decisions.

Depending on a marketing project's initial outcomes (e.g., indicators such as intermediate marketing outcomes described in Chap. 5) and contemporaneous environmental factors (e.g., level of demand, competitors' actions), further marketing expenditures and activities can be increased, decreased, or eliminated altogether. The capacity of a firm to alter course in reaction to environmental changes establishes what are called real options, or growth options. In addition, certain actions by the firm may create such options. For example, once a firm has created a brand it has the option to extend it into new product categories. This is just what Procter and Gamble did with its Crest brand. The brand was originally built around a tooth paste, but in recent years has been expanded to include a whole range of dental hygiene products. Similarly, Canon has been able to leverage its technological expertise in lasers, fine optics, micro-electronics, and precision mechanics into a wide array of quite different products, ranging from copiers and printers, to cameras, to cell analyzers, to laser imagers.

Many marketing activities have the effect of creating real options. Opening a new distribution channel, creating a website, and even attracting a first-time customer can be viewed as the creation of options for growth in the future. Such options have value even if they are not immediately pursued. The ability of a firm to increase its profitability by expanding its product or service line or by entering new product or service categories represent important growth opportunities. This is one reason why new firms that may not even have a product in the market have value—the value rests in the opportunities for future growth.

The greatest real options of firms rest largely on their intangible assets—brands, contracts, technological expertise, and managerial talent. This is why the largest percent of the value of firms, is, by far, found in their intangible assets, as was discussed in Chap. 2. This is one reason why traditional discounted cash flow models often underestimate the real value of marketing actions. Many actions are but a first step in a chain of potential opportunities. Because of the uncertainties associated with forecasting, it is difficult to place a specific value on real options. However, marketers sell themselves short if they do not explicitly recognize the value created by real options. Marketing plans and programs that might not appear justifiable using a strict DCF approach may not only be justifiable but also highly lucrative once the value of real options is accounted for.

Much of the value associated with real options arises from simply identifying them and incorporating them into the planning process. At a minimum marketing planning and budgeting should identify and qualitatively assess the value of the real options that proposed marketing actions may create. In some cases, a rough approximation of the value of an option may be estimated by considering the size of potential new markets that may be opened as a result of exercising an option. Obviously, any marketing action that can be justified based on a DCF analysis should probably be pursued. However, there are circumstances in which the NPV of a marketing activity may be negative but where the value of the options it creates compensates for what otherwise appears to be a poor investment. Marketers, and their organizations, would benefit from explicit consideration of the options they create.

Conclusion

Traditional financial planning models assume a greater degree of certainty than is usually present when making business decisions. As a result, discounted cash flow analyses and determination of the net present value of investments are, at best, estimates that are at least as fuzzy as many marketing estimates. This does not mean that these tools are without value. There is a need for some means for making well-informed and disciplined investment decisions. However, it is important to consider the risks and opportunities that the future may hold. Marketers can add enormous value to planning process of the firm and increase their credibility by being knowledgeable and active participants in the estimation of cash flow, the analysis of risk, and identification of growth opportunities.

Exercises

1. When thinking about the risk of a marketing investment, what factors should be identified and evaluated? How do these factors influence cash flow?
2. Risk can be divided into systematic risk, firm risk, and risk associated with a specific product or project. How are these types of risk different? How would a marketing manager estimate each? What actions might a marketing manager take to manage each type of risk?
3. In the best, worst, and most likely case analyses illustrated in Table 9.2, which factor is the most important determinant of the outcomes obtained? What would the result be if the market size in the best case was 50 million units? What would the result be if the market size was 3 million units but the firm obtained 100% market share? Do these analyses suggest anything about risk?

Points to Ponder

1. Financial analysis is often seen as more rigorous, objective, and precise than marketing analysis. Why is this the case? In light of the discussion in this chapter, is financial analysis more rigorous, objective, and precise than marketing analysis? Why or why not?
2. How can marketers contribute to the identification of risks and opportunities related to future cash flows? What tools and techniques can marketers use to help identify risks and opportunities? How can the results obtained with these tools and techniques be translated into financial performance?

REFERENCES

Booz, Allen and Hamilton. (1982). *New Product Management for the 1980s*. Booz, Allen and Hamilton Inc.: New York.

Montibeller, G., & von Winterfeldt, D. (2015). Cognitive and Motivational Biases in Decision and Risk Analysis. *Risk Analysis, 35*(7), 1230–1251.

Musashi, K. (2016). *The 25 Cognitive Biases: Understanding Human Psychology, Decision Making & How to Not Fall Victim to Them*. CreateSpace Independent Publishing Platform/Virtual Publisher.

CHAPTER 10

Managing Portfolios of Products

Would you like to own a billion-dollar business? The answer depends on who you are and what else you're doing with your time and money. For most companies, a profitable, billion-dollar business would be a dream. For IBM in 2012, a company with $104 billion in revenue, their billion-dollar-a-year Point of Sale (POS) business was a distraction at best. It was a slow-growing, highly mature market. Profits were acceptable but flat. They sold the division to Toshiba so they could focus on their core business lines of hardware, software, and IT services.

There was absolutely nothing wrong with the IBM POS business. Practically every major retailer in the United States ran IBM cash registers. It was, in fact, a legacy of the company's very first products in the early 1900s. By 2012, though, the company had changed. Their market had changed. Their strategy had changed. It was time for POS to go. The divestment provides a good example of the challenges of marketing portfolios.

Much of the discussion in this book so far has focused on the individual product or service. Most firms, of course, offer multiple products and/or services. Such portfolios of offerings add to the complexity of decision-making because management must not only identify profitable strategies for individual products but also seek the optimal allocation of resources among all of the products in the portfolio.

This chapter focuses on the management of portfolios of products and approaches for making decisions about resource allocations and activities

© The Author(s) 2019
D. W. Stewart, *Financial Dimensions of Marketing Decisions*,
Palgrave Studies in Marketing, Organizations and Society,
https://doi.org/10.1007/978-3-030-15565-0_10

in the context of multiple offerings. In such contexts, the objective is not profit maximization for any single product. Rather, profit maximization is sought at the portfolio level. This means that what may be an optimal allocation of resources for an individual product is often not the optimal allocation across multiple products.

Managing Product Portfolios

The management of portfolios of offerings has been the subject of considerable work by academic researchers, practicing managers and management consultants. For example, the Boston Consulting Group (BCG) has suggested the use of a two-dimensional matrix for classifying product offerings based on the growth rate and market share. Figure 10.1 provides an illustration of the *BCG Growth-Share Matrix.*

In the BCG matrix, products are plotted based on the rate of growth of the market and their market share. Most often a high rate of market growth is defined as 10% annual growth and high relative market share is defined as twice the share of the nearest competitor, but different organizations often employ different definitions.

The underlying premise of the BCG approach is that different products, with different market characteristics, should be managed differently. Thus, a "cash cow" is a product with a high relative market share in a mature market that generates more cash than is needed for reinvestment back into its support. Therefore, such cows throw off cash that the firm can use for other purposes. Although the good people in Redmond might

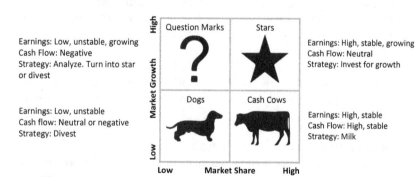

Fig. 10.1 Boston Consulting Group Growth-Share Matrix. (Adapted from Henderson 1970, 1979, p. 165)

disagree with this assessment, Microsoft Office is a great example of a cash cow. The product line throws off somewhere along the lines of $12 billion a year. This cash flow is not going to slow down any time soon. The product doesn't cost much to support. It has almost no competitors.

In contrast, a "star" has a high relative market share in a growing market. The need to support growth means the firm must reinvest the cash generated by the star in order to sustain its market share, and, hopefully, as the market matures the star will become a cash cow. Smart phones provide an interesting case example of a product that is transitioning from star to cash cow. The iPhone is still a star, for sure, but the market is maturing and the innovation cycle is slowing down. There's a perceptible decline in excitement about new iPhone models. Most people who want one already have one. It's gone from a land rush market to a replacement market. Cash cow status is around the corner. Thus, Apple is looking for its next star. The Apple Watch was a candidate, but it may not become a star for a variety of market-based reasons, for example, not everyone wants an iPhone on their wrists.

"Dogs" have a small market share in a market that is not growing. Such products are typically not profitable and often are net consumers of resources. For this reason, dogs are candidates for divestiture. In the BCG view, the IBM POS business was a "dog." It was not going to be a star, at least not at IBM. Another company might turn the cash register business into some cutting-edge mobile app wallet business, for instance, but that was not going to happen at IBM. POS needed to be divested.

Finally, there are "question mark" products, products in growing markets that have a small market share. The key question to ask of question marks is whether they can be turned into stars by increasing market share. If they cannot be transformed into stars they too should be divested.

The BCG matrix is based on the premise that market share drives margins and cash flow. Thus, it is important to invest in acquiring market share in growing markets so that as a market matures, and growth slows, the firm will have a product that generates more cash than is needed to support the product. It is simple and easy to understand. On the other hand, it is often criticized for being too simple. In addition, it is not always clear how a market and how market share should be defined. For example, is *Coca-Cola* in the soft drink business or the beverage business? The assumed relationship between market share and profitability is not always present. Competitive pressures can neutralize margins as a market expands. The history of the hard disk drive industry presents a terrifying example. In the 1990s and 2000s, hard drive manufacturers put each other out of business making smaller, faster, and cheaper hard drives. Margins were flat. Capital investments were high. The market was exploding but few companies made any money. Finally, many products fit into a mid-range that is neither high nor low with respect to market growth rate and relative market share and therefore do not easily fit within the product definitions identified by four cells of the matrix.

In order to compensate for the limitations of the BCG matrix, a number of organizations have developed more complex matrices that provide for greater numbers of product types, and therefore strategies, and that consider a variety of factors other than market share and market growth. Figure 10.2 illustrates one such matrix, the *General Electric/McKinsey Matrix*. This matrix provides for nine types of products that are described by the multidimensional factors called Business Position and Market Attractiveness. These two factors are obtained as weighted composites of a variety of factors, as shown in Fig. 10.2.

Tools for product portfolio analysis aid in thinking about the portfolio and can provide some general direction with respect to marketing strategy. The usefulness of such models is well documented by the amount of attention they have received from corporate management and in the academic literature. However, they do not provide much help in making specific budget decisions or in identifying specific marketing actions that can generate positive cash flow. All are classification systems, and the rules for classification are often vague and ambiguous. They may make more sense when applied to a specific company which can assign its products to the various slots on the chart and compare their potentials.

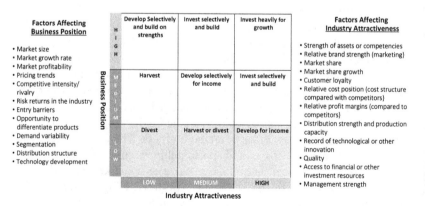

Fig. 10.2   General Electric/McKinsey Matrix. (Source: Allen 1979)

In addition, different portfolio models appear to produce different managerial implications. One reason for this state of affairs is that the analogy of the investment portfolio was borrowed from the financial investment literature, but without the conceptual rigor of this literature. As a result, these tools do not help in making trade-offs among marketing investments for products located in the same space on the matrix and often fail to clearly define where a product even fits in the matrix.

THE CAPITAL ASSET PRICING MODEL (CAPM)

In an effort to bring more of the rigor of financial analysis to the product portfolio management, a number of academics and consulting organizations have attempted to employ the *capital asset pricing model* (*CAPM*). CAPM is designed to provide guidance for investors in financial securities and it describes the relationship between the risk and expected return from assets, particularly stocks. The general conceptual frameworks of CAPM rest on the notions of the time value of money and risk. As such, the earlier discussion of the net present value (NPV) and risk are quite consistent with the CAPM perspective.

The basic idea underlying CAPM is both simple and elegant: that investors want to be compensated for the time value of money and risk. Compensation for risk is generally defined as a premium over and above the rate of return that could be obtained from an investment with no risk of loss. In reality, no investment is ever truly risk free, but in practice it is usually defined as the rate of interest on current long-term treasury bonds, T-bills. T-bills are considered almost risk free because they are fully backed by the US government. As such, they provide a useful benchmark for the return that should be expected from riskier investments.

CAPM can be used to calculate the expected return of an asset given its risk using the formula:

$$\text{Expected Return} = r_f + B\left(r_m - r_f\right)$$

Where

r_f = the risk-free rate
B = Beta
r_m = return on the market

The risk-free rate in the formula (r_f) represents the time value of money and represents the minimum compensation investors expect for placing money in any investment over time. The other half of the formula B ($r_m - r_f$) represents risk and provides an estimate of the compensation an investor expects for taking on additional risk. The risk measure, Beta, can be calculated by comparing the returns of the specific asset to the return for the market over time and to the price premium ($r_m - r_f$): the return of the market in excess of the risk-free rate. Beta reflects how risky an asset is compared to overall market risk and is a function of the volatility of the asset and the market, and the correlation between the two.

Remember from Chap. 9 that risk is defined as the variability in return, or cash flow, over time. A stock with the same risk as the market as a whole would have a Beta of 1; a stock that is twice as risky as the market would have a Beta of 2. For stocks, the S&P 500 is usually used to represent the market, but other indices can be used. The CAPM model says the expected return of a security or a portfolio equals the rate on a risk-free security plus a risk premium. If this expected return does not meet or beat the required return, then the investment should not be undertaken.

This simple idea has been extrapolated from the securities market to product portfolios. The basic notion assumes that investments in products or marketing should return the risk-free rate plus a premium that represents the riskiness of the marketing actions. This makes a lot of sense conceptually, and as noted above, much of the thinking about financial risk management, which was described in Chap. 9, follows from this idea. While still a useful way of thinking about investments in general, and investments in marketing more specifically, the practical application of CAPM to marketing investments is problematic. The reason for this difficulty is related to the differences between securities markets and product markets.

WHY PRODUCTS DIFFER FROM SECURITIES

A number of scholars have pointed out the significant differences between investments in products and investments in securities (e.g., Devinney and Stewart 1988). A portfolio of products is not the same as a portfolio of pure financial market investments. The market may correctly value a bundle of products known as the firm, but there is no reason to believe that this aggregate valuation carries any information about the individual products. The "market" in which a firm's products trade is restricted.

Decisions about investments in products and marketing actions are made within the firm; there is no broader market that can assess the value of individual investments of a firm that are largely unknown to outsiders.

Product markets are structurally different from financial markets in terms of the factors that influence profits or returns. There are at least six differences: (1) managerial control, (2) the relationship of risk and return, (3) the availability or lack of availability of external investment alternatives, (4) unique knowledge, (5) economies of scale and scope, and (6) the temporal characteristics of investments and return. It is important for marketing planners to have an appreciation of these differences and their implications for marketing planning.[1]

Managerial Control An individual investor in financial instruments rarely has control over the risk and return of his or her investment. Indeed, current models of financial markets assume investors have no such control. In contrast, firms exercise a significant degree of control over the risk and return characteristics of their products and services. Managers have numerous means for influencing the risk and return of products within a product portfolio and for the portfolio as a whole. It is possible to shift investments within the firm to more or less risky products or to products with a greater expected return. For any individual product or service, the management of a firm can adopt more or less risky strategies. Finally, the management of a firm may elect to reduce or eliminate investment in all or parts of its product portfolio and choose to return funds to shareholders or invest in some new external venture. For example, Amazon decided to purchase Wholefoods. This move took Amazon into a new category, grocery products, that is at once both very large and highly competitive. Simply stated, managers, especially marketing managers, have a degree of control not available to investors in traditional securities markets.

The Relationship of Risk and Return It is fair to say that there is a general association between risk and return across products. However, it is not difficult to find examples where risk and return are independent for a single product over some specified range and time frame. Investment of a fixed percentage of revenue in the marketing of a mature, high market share brand is unlikely to carry large risks, at least in the short-term. Such an investment may not be the best use of resources, but the risk is not large.

---

[1] There following discussion is based on Devinney and Stewart (1988).

The relationship between risk and return in financial markets grows from assumptions about such markets, but these assumptions do not necessarily hold for individual products or marketing programs within the firm.

Availability of External Investment Alternatives Many approaches to managing product portfolios assume that investment opportunities are constrained to the firm's current product line or lines. This is obviously not the case. A computer company named Apple chose to enter the music business, the telephone business, and the watch business, businesses that at the time would have been considered mature. Netflix decided to move from the distribution business into the creation of original content, two very different business with quite different business models. Similarly, Computer chip maker Broadcom purchased CA Technologies, thereby expanding its business from hardware to software. There is nothing to inhibit a firm's thinking about investment opportunities beyond its current products and services. Considerations of risk, current technological expertise, and market knowledge might suggest some advantage to focusing on current product lines, however, assuming there was still some growth opportunity in the market for such products.

The need to consider external investment opportunities might suggest that investment decisions should always be reduced to a simple net discounted present value rule. However, there are two other characteristics of product and marketing investments by the firm that necessitate consideration of factors beyond simple net present value calculations.

Specific Knowledge Among the most important intangible assets of a firm is knowledge, especially knowledge specific to technology, markets, customers, and processes. Use of such knowledge can make investments less risky and more profitable, for any given amount of investment, than external investments where the firm does not possess such specialized knowledge. Such specific knowledge may permit a firm to judge the opportunities for return and the risks associated with an investment more quickly and precisely or to more rapidly enter and efficiently produce and market a product or product line. Thus, returns on such products are, in part, a return on the intangible asset of managerial knowledge.

Economies of Scale and Scope Finally, unlike investments in securities and other financial instruments, firms may possess economies of scale and scope. Economies of scale are a proportionate savings in cost associated with increased levels of production or operations. Economies of scale occur for two reasons. The variable cost of producing the one-millionth unit may be less than the cost of producing the first unit because the cost per unit of production declines with volume. Such reductions in cost may be associated with "learning" from repetition, from lower costs of supplies due to larger bulk purchases or other operational factors. The second reason for economies of scale is associated with the ability to spread fixed costs and overhead, such as production facilities, equipment, and labor across a larger number of sales.

Economies of scope are economic savings that arise when the cost of simultaneously producing multiple products is less than the cost of producing each product independently. Thus, on average, it is less costly for McDonald's to produce both hamburgers and French fries than it would be for two different firms to produce these two products independently. This is because McDonald's can use the same physical space, cooking equipment, and storage space for both hamburgers and French fries.

Such economies of scale and scope create interdependencies among product and marketing decisions. Interdependencies mean that analysis of investments in one product or marketing program cannot be evaluated separately. For example, a retail trade promotion targeted at a large retail chain may have effects on dozens of products that a large firm sells through the chain. Advertising for a particular model of a printer may have its greatest financial impact on the sales of the ink cartridges used by the printer. A discount on admissions to Disneyland may increase movie box office receipts or create revenue streams from merchandising and licensing agreements.

Interdependencies mean that the profits of a specific set of products or marketing actions will be related. Were it not for such interdependencies, the management of product portfolios would be more similar to traditional financial investing. The presence of such interdependencies can dramatically change both the return and risk of a marketing investment. Interdependencies also violate a fundamental assumption of CAPM, that is, that the risk and returns of individual investments are independent. Arguably, it is the presence of such interdependencies that make the modern firm a necessary viable economic entity.

There are two types of product interdependency: demand interdependency and supply interdependency, that is, interdependencies that arise from characteristics of the market and interdependencies that arise from characteristics of the producer. There are three types of demand interdependency:

Demand Substitutes, where the demands for two products are negatively related; that is, if the demand for one of the products increases the demand for the other will decrease. For example, when a consumer purchases one brand of a firm's several detergents he or she is less likely to purchase the firm's other brands of detergent.

Demand Complements, where the demands for two products are positively related; that is, if the demand for one of the products increases the demand for the other will increase as well. For example, purchases of printers tend to increase the demand for ink cartridges.

Demand Neuters, where the demands for two products are independent; that is, possess a zero covariance. Changes in the demand for one product will not affect the demand for the other.

Similarly, there are types of supply-side interdependencies:

Supply Substitutes, where a resource must be used exclusively to produce one or the other of two products. For example, an automobile manufacturer may be able to use a production facility to make four-door sedans or pick-up trucks but not both at the same time. Usually there are substantial conversion costs associated with changing what is produced. Supply substitutability implies that there are joint diseconomies of scale.

Supply Complements, where the joint cost of producing the products is less than the sum of the costs of producing the products individually. For example, a fast food restaurant can produce hamburgers, French fries, milk shakes, and an array of other product offerings at less cost than if a separate facility were used to make each product individually. Supply complementarity implies that there are joint economies of scale or scope.

Supply Neuters, where the joint cost of producing the products is not different from the sum of the costs of producing the products individually. In other words, there is no interdependency with respect to product and/or operations.

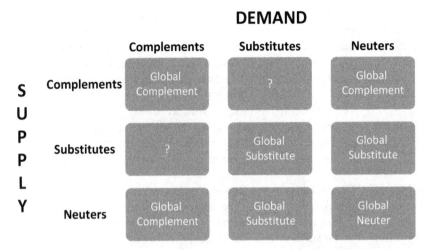

Fig. 10.3   Interdependencies among marketing investment decisions. (Source: Devinney and Stewart 1988, p. 1089)

The various combinations of these supply and demand characteristics are shown in Fig. 10.3.

It is obvious that a firm would prefer complements to substitutes. Ideally, a firm would seek global complements and avoid global substitutes. At a minimum, a firm would seek to organize in such a way that it enjoys either a demand or supply complement with the other interdependency being neutral. Similarly, a firm would avoid a situation in which there is either a demand- or supply-side substitute where the other interdependency is neutral. The complex case, in which one interdependency is a complement and the other is a substitute is more common than it might seem. Such circumstances might occur, and be useful to a firm when markets are highly segmented, but distribution and production are complementary. For example, different flavors of soft drinks may appeal to different groups of consumers, who buy one product instead of another (a demand complement) but the bottling operations and channels of distribution are shared by both products.

It's useful to understand such interdependencies because they create problems for applying standard financial metrics to investments. An NPV computation based only on the revenue and costs of one product will not reflect the correct return across multiple products. An advertising campaign that drives sales of printers inevitably results in an increase in revenue from ink cartridges. An update of a computer operating system likely increases demand for more powerful hardware and upgraded software. Such interrelationships are not a reason to avoid financial analysis. The influence of interdependencies can be estimated as part of any financial evaluation, though they are likely to be idiosyncratic to the individual firm and even marketing program. Marketers can play an especially important role in identifying and accounting for such interdependencies, not only with respect to demand through analysis of customer behavior but also through analysis of such supply-side activities as distribution.

Temporal Characteristics of Investments and Return Unlike many capital investments, where there is a one-time upfront investment and an assumed cash flow over time, marketing investments usually take the form of multiple investments over time. Once a product or service is launched, there is usually a need for continuing investment in marketing communications, distribution, service, and other support. These continuing investments are intended to influence demand, revenue, and ultimately cash flow. However, such investments do not always increase demand. In many cases, such expenditures are necessary responses to competitors' actions, changes in consumers' behavior, the dynamics of the market environment, and other factors that may influence demand. Indeed, this is one reason baseline, discussed in Chap. 6, is important. When analyzing the return on marketing investments it is important to ask what would happen if the investment were not made.

Like interdependencies, the temporal characteristics of investment and returns adds complexity to any analysis of financial outcomes. Chapter 11 will address some approaches for dealing with these complexities. As with interdependencies, the fact of complexity is not a reason to ignore the need for estimation of financial outcomes associated with marketing investments.

SELECTING ALTERNATIVE MARKETING INVESTMENTS

Even in a firm with a single product, there is a need to evaluate alternative marketing and operational investments. Inevitably, in any multi-product firm there is a need to make decisions about what products to invest in, how much to invest, and how to invest. Despite the need for assumptions and the complexities associated with applying a net present value rule, it remains the most robust method for selecting among alternative actions. Other things being equal, after adjusting for risk, actions with a higher net present value of future cash flows are preferable to those with a lesser NPV. Nevertheless, many firms have developed simple rules of thumb for evaluating alternative investments.

Payback Period

As noted throughout this book, marketing investments and activities may produce both short-term and long-term outcomes. Some marketing actions may have almost instantaneous outcomes. For example, a direct marketing offer in an infomercial may produce orders even during the time the infomercial is running. In contrast, other marketing actions may have effects that not only occur immediately but also occur over a relatively long period of time. Brand-building activities often fit in this latter category. Thus, in making comparisons among alternative marketing actions, there is a problem of comparability when costs and benefits occur at different times. A common approach for addressing such comparability issues is the use of the *payback period*, which was briefly introduced in Chap. 9.

The payback period is a simple concept; it is the period of time required to recoup the funds expended in an investment. Payback period is expressed in units of time, such as weeks, months, or years. It is quite easy to calculate. If a marketing investment, such as an online advertising campaign, is $100,000 and generates $20,000 in incremental income each month, the payback period is five months: Payback period = $100,000 ÷ $20,000.

When used for marketing decision-making, the shorter the payback period the better. Thus, when comparing two potential marketing investments, the payback period for each would be computed and compared. For example, if a firm were contemplating two investments in a marketing program, each requiring $25,000, and one program (MktProg1) would generate $5000 per month and the other program (MktProg2) would generate $2500 per month, the first investment has a payback period of five months and the second investment has a payback period of ten months. Clearly, investment in the first program would be preferred.

While the payback period is a useful piece of information, it is incomplete and can be misleading when used alone. It ignores any cash flow after the payback period. If the benefits of MktProg1 in the example above ended after five months, while the benefits of MktProg2 continued on for two years, MktProg2 is clearly superior. An NPV analysis would reveal the superiority of MktProg2.

The popularity of payback period as a means for comparing alternative investments rests on its simplicity, the short-term nature of many marketing outcomes, the scarcity of resources in many businesses and the general risk aversion of many managers. In addition, managers can place a maximum payback period on investments, which serves as a further heuristic for decision-making. Simply stated, when resources are scarce, getting them back quickly can be both desirable and less risky. Nevertheless, use of payback period alone is likely to produce myopic and suboptimal investment decisions.

Internal Rate of Return (IRR) and Hurdle Rates

Two related rules of thumb for evaluating investments are the *internal rate of return (IRR)* and a *hurdle rate*. Stated simply, the IRR is the interest rate at which the net present value of all the cash flows (both positive and negative) from an investment equal zero. If the IRR of a new project exceeds a company's required rate of return, that project is desirable. If IRR falls below the required rate of return, the project should be rejected. A hurdle rate is the minimum rate of return on a project or investment required by a manager or investor. The hurdle rate signifies the appropriate compensation for the level of risk present; riskier projects generally have higher hurdle rates than those that are less risky. As such, the hurdle rate includes explicit consideration of the riskiness of an investment.

The formula for IRR is:

$$0 = CF_0 + \frac{CF_1}{(1+IRR)} + \frac{CF_2}{(1+IRR)^2} + \frac{CF_3}{(1+IRR)^3} + \ldots + \frac{CF_n}{(1+IRR)^n}$$

Or

$$0 = NPV = \sum_{n=0}^{N} \frac{CF_n}{(1+IRR)^n} \mid$$

Where

CF_0 = Initial Investment/Outlay
CF_1, CF_2, $CF_3 \ldots CF_n$ = Cash flows
n = Each Period
N = Holding Period
NPV = Net Present Value
IRR = Internal Rate of Return

There are three ways to carry out the calculation of the internal rate of return:

1. Use the IRR or XIRR function in Excel or other spreadsheet program;
2. Use a financial calculator, such as the Hewlett Packard 12C or the Texas Instruments BA II Plus; or
3. Use an iterative process where the analyst tries different discount rates until the NPV equals to zero (Goal Seek in Excel can be used to do this).

Generally, when computing an IRR a firm will use its cost of capital or its expected rate of return. The hurdle for typical projects will be set at this rate. For riskier projects, some value greater than the firm's cost of capital or its expected rate of return will be used to compensate for risk. The value used will depend on the amount of risk that is perceived to be associated with the project. There is no single best adjustment for risk; firms often establish a standard set of rules for such adjustments based on past experience, perceptions of the degree and type of risk, and the risk aversion of managers. Fortunately, as noted in Chap. 9, for many marketing investments, there are other ways to manage risk.

IRR is commonly used by firms, and, for this reason, marketers would do well to understand it. It is easy to use for comparing alternatives, since investments with higher IRR are preferred, subject to adjustment for risk. However, IRR is not without its problems and limitations. The timing of cash flows can create problems for the computation of IRR. In fact, in some cases, more than one IRR may be obtained for the same project, based on assumptions about the amount and timing of cash flows. IRR assumes an initial cash outlay followed by one or more cash flows. The need for additional investment at later points in time also creates problems for finding a unique value for IRR.

In addition, IRR ignores the size of the investment and the amount of return. As a result, IRR favors investments with high rates of return even when the amount of the return is very small. For example, a $10 investment returning $30 will have a higher IRR than a $1 million investment returning $2 million. Finally, IRR *cannot* compare proposed projects with different durations. Thus, although IRR is frequently used, it is inferior to NPV and far less relevant to most of the types of investments that involve marketing activities.

EVALUATING ALTERNATIVES

Ultimately, marketers are best served by use of NPV combined with careful evaluation of the factors that can influence future cash flows, future costs, and risk. Table 10.1 provides a list of the more important and common of these factors. Putting actual numbers to these factors is, of course, important, but even a ballpark estimate can provide a good indication of the viability of a proposed marketing investment. Some of the factors in Table 10.1 may be more relevant or important to investments such as launching a new product or opening a new market, but most would apply even in the context of advertising and promotion campaigns. For example, increasing advertising in a market where there is limited distribution is unlikely to pay off.

Some firms make consideration of such factors more formal and explicit by applying criterion and/or ratings for each of these factors. For example, for current market size there may be a rating scale of 1–5 where each point represents a particular dollar size of the market:

Selection criteria	5	4	3	2	1
Market size today	>$500 M		>$100 M		<$20 M
Market growth (do not consider <=10%)	>30%		>20%		>10%

Similarly, market growth could be rated and even include a criterion for unacceptable growth rates:

Selection criteria	5	4	3	2	1
Market growth (do not consider <=10%)	>30%		>20%		>10%

Use of such formal ratings, along with NPV analysis can add discipline to the evaluation of marketing investments and activities. Rating scales require careful discussion of the criteria for evaluating alternative investments and activities, in advance of consideration of specific proposals. Such standards provide guidance for the initial screening of proposals, create stronger proposals for formal consideration, and remove at least some of the subjectivity and politics from marketing investment decisions.

Table 10.1   Factors for evaluating marketing alternatives

Market Potential

Current Market Size. What customers currently spend per year to satisfy the need addressed by the product or service

Market Growth. Estimate compounded annual growth rate (CAGR) of the market size over the next 5 years (or other relevant time period)

Upside Market Potential. The upside market potential (in 5 years) for the product. Small, unestablished or emerging markets, whose projected growth is significant, explosive growth in existing, emerging or new markets made possible through use disruptive technology, and/or emerging geographies with great potential should there be an increase in per capita spending or infusion of external funding from loans, grants or foreign credits

Potential for Proliferation. Opportunities to increase business by selling products/service to additional customers with adaptation to specific needs or based on establishment of a new customer relationship

Competitive Environment

Intensity of Competition. The amount and type of competition. A sellers' market where demand exceeds supply, current suppliers are just taking orders, and customers pay (almost) any price; or, a buyers' market where only the strongest competitors make any profit

Strength of Competition. Dominant, where one competitor with significant resources owns more than half the market; Strong, where there are two or three well financed and competent competitors; or weak, where current competitor(s) are not very competent in the market or have little resources to defend their shares

Importance of Market to Competitors. High, where the market is the major source of revenue for the major competitors. Their existence depends on maintaining their share and the likelihood of a major competitive response is high; medium, where a major competitor(s) will not easily give up the market and there is a likelihood of a significant competitive response, or weak, where the business is not core to the competitors and competitors neglect the market

Competitive Advantage

Differentiators. What kind of differentiation could be established/delivered to potential customers: compelling, some, none (me too product)

Potential Sustainability of Differentiator(s) or Barriers to Entry. Inherent in the capability and culture of the organization or strong defensible intellectual propriety (patents, copyrights, etc.) or easily imitated by competitors

Brand Loyalty & Competence Recognition. The firm is well-known to customers and potential customers and is recognized for its competence in serving their specific need with similar products; or, customers may or may not know the name and would never expect the firm to offer a product of this type

Strategic Fit

Fit to Organizational Strategy and Competence. This business will further strengthen the firm's position and/or is required or highly desirable to complement other programs or products; or, it is a poor fit

(*continued*)

Table 10.1   (continued)

Required Investment. New resources required

Accessibility of Necessary Competencies. Includes financial resources, organizational capabilities, manufacturing, operations, distribution, service delivery, and people skills. Ranges from high, for example, all competencies are in place or readily available to low, for example, something completely new and different

Availability of Necessary Competencies

New Product/Service Generation ($M for R&D & Marketing). The total cumulative R&D and marketing investment needed to design and develop the product/service or marketing program

Time to First Sale. The duration from the time of deciding to take an action until the first (incremental) revenues are received

Order Fulfillment. All activities required to sell a product: ordering & billing, product/service planning, supplier and materials management, production, shipping, physical distribution, installation, and service delivery. Ranges from everything is in place, to all new

Channels of Distribution. Ranges from existing distribution channels are adequate to requires new distribution channel(s)

Risks

Departure from Current Business or Brand Image. Degree to which firm is undertaking something unfamiliar or inconsistent with prior markets served, technologies used, and/or current brand image

Barrier(s) to Adoption/Customer Action. Any barriers customers or potential customers face in adopting a new product/behavior, or in taking the desired action. Examples for such barriers include: loyalty to existing products, switching costs, customers forced to behave in a new way, unproven cost savings or equivalence/superiority competitors' products, and/or long-term contractual arrangements

Technology Feasibility. Ranges from all technology elements can be demonstrated today to a technological breakthrough would be required to achieve the desired differentiator(s) or respond to competitors' strong position

Interdependencies. Entities outside of the firm's direct control (e.g. major partners, suppliers, or distributors) who must buy-in for the idea to be successful

Potential Market/Industry Shifts. Likelihood of a market shift (a significant change in customer priorities or in the number and/or kind of customers) or an industry shift (a change in the underlying structure of an industry resulting from consolidation/fragmentation and/or new unexpected entrants) will occur and be disruptive

Regulatory Hurdles. More important in some markets than others. Usually based on the degree of product risk, but may also include issues related to pricing, distribution, or manufacturing. Generally associated with the need for government approval or other forms of certification such as ISO

Intellectual Property/Product Liability/General Litigation. Vulnerability to litigation

Conclusion

Among the more difficult decisions confronted by marketers are decisions involving trade-offs among alternative investments, regardless of whether those investments are for different products or different marketing plans. Simple NPV computations rarely provide complete information about the likely returns on such investments because of the interdependencies among products. Nevertheless, NPV provides the best approach to quantifying financial returns and when used with a well-designed template for evaluation and selection of alternative marketing actions can provide effective direction for marketing decisions.

Exercises

1. Pick any business. Identify the supply-side and demand-side interdependencies. What are the implications for marketing actions? What are the implications for financial returns?
2. What factors might change the amount of ongoing investment required to support a product over time? What factors might influence the cash flow attributable to a product over time. Can the effects of these factors be estimated with any degree of accuracy? Can they be estimated with sufficient accuracy to inform short- and long-term planning and decision-making.
3. Using the factors in Table 10.1, develop a rating scale for evaluating alternative marketing actions. What criteria would you employ for the scale points in your rating scale? How might these criteria be identified? How might you put such scaled items together to arrive at an overall evaluative summary.

Points to Ponder

1. Given the limitations of CAPM and other financial theories that have been applied in a marketing context, why do they continue to be used? What advantages do they offer? What can marketers do to make such financial theories more useful in a marketing context?
2. What does the notions of supply-side and demand-side interdependency suggest about the role of the firm? What do they suggest about how a business should be defined and organized?

REFERENCES

Allen, M. G. (1979). Diagnosing GE's Planning for What's Watt. In R. J. Allio &
M. W. Pennington (Eds.), *Corporate Planning: Techniques and Applications*
(pp. 211–220). New York: AMACOM.

Devinney, T., & Stewart, D. W. (1988). Rethinking the Product Portfolio: A
Generalized Investment Model. *Management Science, 34*(9), 1080–1095.

Henderson, B. D. (1970). *The Product Portfolio.* Boston: Boston Consulting
Group. https://www.bcg.com/en-mideast/publications/1970/strategy-the-
product-portfolio.aspx

Henderson, B. D. (1979). *Henderson on Corporate Strategy.* New York:
HarperCollins.

CHAPTER 11

Marketing Strategy and Financial Performance

The Nasdaq Composite stock market index peaked in value on March 10, 2000. The next day, the "dot-com bubble" burst. The 18 years since the bubble burst has been marked by periods of turmoil, with a housing crisis and "great recession" that was followed by a long period of slow growth. Iconic brands like Radio Shack, Toys-R-Us, and Blockbuster all but disappeared in bankruptcy. Yet, despite a difficult economic environment, Apple, which was nearly bankrupt in 1997, emerged as the world's first trillion-dollar company just a little over 20 years later. Similarly, Amazon, which began as an online book seller in 1995, became the second trillion-dollar company in 2018.

What can explain these divergent, perhaps unexpected business outcomes? This chapter focuses on the role of marketing strategy in determining financial results. It follows earlier chapters of this book, which examined individual marketing programs, measures of marketing outcomes, and the linkages of marketing outcomes to financial performance. The generation of cash flow has been identified as the ultimate objective of marketing activities, though this objective needs to be placed within the context of time and risk management.

Most of the chapters of this book have focused on single products or marketing activities, but Chap. 10 introduced the important issues confronted by marketers when managing a portfolio of products. As was obvious from the discussion in Chap. 10, strategies for managing products

© The Author(s) 2019
D. W. Stewart, *Financial Dimensions of Marketing Decisions*,
Palgrave Studies in Marketing, Organizations and Society,
https://doi.org/10.1007/978-3-030-15565-0_11

must recognize and incorporate complex relationships over time and across products and markets. In this chapter we will consider marketing strategy in greater detail.

SUCCESS AND FAILURE

The differences in the performance of Apple and Amazon versus Radio Shack, Toys-R-Us, and Blockbuster in the same economic environment raise the question of what made their fate so different. Why would a cash machine like Blockbuster go under while a thousand-dollar investment in Apple in 2008, at the beginning of the great recession, would be worth more than $7000 in 2018? Toys-R-Us, an established, innovative retailer, fell apart in this period. Meanwhile, a thousand-dollar investment in the experimental startup Amazon at about the same time would be worth more than $20,000 in 2018 (Carter 2018a, b).

Was it a great brand? Both the winners, Apple and Amazon, and the losers, Radio Shack, Toys-R-Us, and Blockbuster, have, or had, great brands. Was it scale? At its height, Radio Shack was the world's largest telecommunications retailer with thousands of retail stores. Toys-R-Us was considered a "category killer," as the world's largest seller of toys with thousands of retail stores. Blockbuster used a sophisticated computerized inventory management system to become the dominant distributor of video entertainment, also with thousands of retail stores. Was it great distribution? In their day Radio Shack, Toys-R-Us, and Blockbuster were powerful retailers.

Was it superior marketing? Radio Shack, Toys-R-Us, and Blockbuster executed some strong advertising and promotion. Radio Shack advertised during the Super Bowl and filled pages of newspapers with ads for its products. Blockbuster offered a very powerful shopper loyalty program, Blockbuster Rewards, powered by a sophisticated customer database. Toys-R-Us created an iconic "spokes animal," Geoffrey the Giraffe. Was it access to capital and other resources? All three of the now defunct firms had significant cash flow and access to investment funds. Indeed, all three were acquired, in some cases more than once. What, then is the difference between a business winner and a business loser?

While there is no doubt that being lucky, being at the right place at the right time with right product, plays a role in success, the real difference is the ability of managers, including marketers, to create positive net present value (NPV) products and marketing campaigns. Product innovation without positive return produces failure (see DeLorean). Great advertising without positive returns will not be successful (see Kodak). There is no doubt that quality, innovation, creativity, and execution are important. Marketing is important. But, without the discipline of positive financial outcomes, a firm cannot be successful.

Corporate strategy and marketing strategy are about finding positive net present value opportunities. This is not as easy as it seems. If it were so easy, there would not be a history of colossal failures by some of the largest and dominant firms.

Innovative ideas can fail in two ways. The most visible failures are those introduced into the market without success. More insidious are failures associated with good ideas never getting to market because they lacked the resources and management support for implementation.

FINDING MARKET OPPORTUNITIES

The classical economic perspective holds that perfectly competitive markets are characterized by undifferentiated products sold based only on price. Any departure from such a characterization is viewed as evidence of an imperfect market. This view of markets has given rise to strategic thinking that focuses on the identification of market imperfections and the creation of structural barriers to market entry and the creation of supply-side competitive advantage (Porter 1998). This view of markets leads to a focus on avoiding competition. For most markets, at least in relatively affluent developed nations, this view is demonstrably wrong (Dennin 2012; Stewart 2009). This is wrong because it ignores individual differences among both customers and suppliers.

In contrast to the "perfect" markets described by economists, a marketing view of a perfect market is one in which individuals can exercise their idiosyncratic preferences for goods and services. They do this by matching their preferences with the idiosyncratic skills of producers and suppliers. Any "competitive advantage" arises from a producer's unique skills and willingness to serve consumers' idiosyncratic needs. This might be a single customer, if the customer is willing pay enough, but often, it is a group of customers who share similar preferences. Firms that offer a poor match with market needs ultimately leave the market. This is why undifferentiated products rarely succeed in the marketplace.

Of course, differentiation can take many forms. In most markets, there are price sensitive customers who will sacrifice other potential differences in products or services to obtain the lowest possible price. Thus, in most markets there is a low-cost supplier who differentiates its offering based on low price. Note however, that in the long run, there can only be one low-cost provider and that provider must have a cost structure that allows it to still make a profit even when offering a low price to customers. Firms that are not low-cost producers must find other points of differentiation and in many markets there is a large array of opportunities for differentiation: quality, service, convenience, features, and more. Even for such characteristics as quality, there are further opportunities for differentiation because customers differ in how they define quality. Thus, success in business is about finding positive net present value opportunities that match the needs of at least a portion of the market. Or stated in terms described in Chap. 3, success in business is about finding a business model that provides a profitable match with a market segment.

Finding such business models is not an assurance of long-term success, but it certainly helps. There is always the possibility that a competitor will find a better way to serve customers with higher quality, a lower price, greater convenience or some other point of differentiation valued by customers. But the focus is not on being better than a competitor but on better serving customers. Such competitive pressures force firms to constantly innovate, even if in only small ways, in order to better serve customers. While no market is ever really perfect, this process has the effect of creating pressure on producers to offer ever better matches with customer preferences. In this way, customers are well-served by markets that work well. The challenge for a business is to be responsive while finding ways to generate positive cash flow.

Structural Barriers to Competition

It is questionable whether there have ever been real long-term structural barriers to market entry. Certainly, economies of scale provide cost advantages to large-scale producers and high capital requirements may keep some potential competitors at bay. For example, if you wanted to start an international oil company, you would need to have enough capital to produce and refine oil on the scale of ExxonMobil to be viable. That's a pretty big nut to crack, but it can be done.

Economies of scale did not preserve the dominance of the US automobile industry or the photographic film industry. Rather, failure to stay close to customers and innovate in ways to better serve those customers with new technologies, services, and business models were the reasons for the loss of dominance. Dependence on structural barriers to competition is a false hope.

Firms can make it more or less difficult for competitors to enter a market. Product differentiation, branding, advertising and promotion expenditures, access to limited distribution space, production and operations efficiencies, exemplary and responsive service operations, and strong customer relationships can all make it difficult for other firms to compete. But, these so-called structural barriers provide an advantage in the long run only to the extent that they continue to enable and support the effective fulfillment of customer needs. A unique role for marketing, and perhaps the defining role of marketing, is to assure that investments meet customer needs and produce positive cash flow. It is not a mystery how this is done.

Identifying and Meeting Customer Needs and Response

An implication of the importance of meeting customer needs is that well-designed, strategic customer and market research should be an investment priority of the firm. Indeed, as discussed in Chap. 9, such research can be used to manage risks. There are few marketing actions, whether it be the introduction of a new product or service, the development of an advertising campaign, or the opening of a distribution channel that cannot be tested in advance of the large investments that accompany such actions. Indeed, it is usually easier to extrapolate the results of a well-designed and well-controlled test to future financial results than to estimate financial returns after a marketing program has been implemented in the market. The use of validated, intermediate marketing outcome measures, discussed in Chaps. 5 and 6, can play an important role in such tests. However, such tests and intermediate measures will not be complete unless they are linked to the financial return to the firm, or the return on marketing investment.

Assessing Return on Marketing Investment

While NPV is a useful decision tool, and negative NPV actions rarely, if ever make sense for the firm, there are many occasions where NPV may not provide a definitive answer to the question of the best course of action.

As has been discussed, NPV depends on the discount rate and level of risk. It also does not easily deal with risks that change over time, nor does it capture the value of real options. NPV also fails to measure the efficiency of an investment, that is, the relationship between return, as measured by NPV, and how much is invested to obtain that return. It is possible to obtain the same NPV from investments of different amounts. It is always desirable, other things being equal, to obtain the same NPV with a smaller investment than a larger investment. Thus, various measures of the efficiency of a marketing investment are available. The most common are *return on sales (ROS)*, *return on investment (ROI)*, and a *profitability index.*

Return on Sales (ROS)

ROS, which is also called *operating margin,* is a simple measure of the proportion of sales revenue that is profit. It is a widely reported measure in both internal budgeting and in public reports. It is calculated as net profit divided by sales revenue:

$$ROS = \left[\text{Sales Revenue}(\$) - \text{Total Costs}(\$) \right] \div \text{Sales Revenue}(\$)$$

$$ROS = \text{Net Profit}(\$) \div \text{Sales Revenue}(\$)$$

As an example, consider a seasonal discount offered by an airline. If the discount cost the airline $50,000 and brought in $100,000 in incremental sales, the ROS would be calculated as:

$$ROS = \left[\$100,000 - \$50,000 \right] \div \$100,000 = \$50,000 \div \$100,000 = 0.5$$

Note that the Net Profit in the ROS formula is not the gross contribution or even the net contribution after marketing expenses. Rather, it is sales revenue after all allocated costs are included. In most cases, sales revenue and total costs are taken from accounting records, which means that the total costs often include allocated costs that have nothing to do with marketing actions.

ROS is often useful as a tracking measure over time because it provides an indication of what is happening to margins. If ROS shrinks over time it could indicate increasing inefficiency, competitive pricing pressure, or greater price sensitivity among customers. In any case, a shrinking ROS is a cause for concern that requires follow-up.

ROS is also often used as a measure of profitability to compare firms. Such comparisons can be quite misleading with respect to the health and viability of a business. Business models may differ substantially and the meaning of ROS needs to be examined in the context of the underlying business model. No one would consider Walmart an unsuccessful or unprofitable business but its ROS is lower than many other firms. This is because Walmart's business model is built around low margins and high volume. In contrast, Ritz Carlton has a high ROS because its business model is built around high margins (but much lower volume than Walmart).

Return on Investment (ROI)

Often referred to as return on marketing investment (ROMI) or marketing return on investment (MROI), this term has been borrowed from finance where it has a very specific meaning. Unfortunately, ROI is used in many different ways by marketing professionals, and few of these uses have any relationship to the financial meaning. One survey of CMO's reported that a sizeable percent of them claimed to measure ROI using surveys of customers (Moorman 2014). Such a finding illustrates the problems with the use of the term in marketing because there is no information in a survey of customers that can inform the computation of an ROI, at least in the financial sense of the term. Often, when used by marketers, ROI means only that some type of measure of marketing outcome was obtained. Such use of the term is confusing to financial professionals at best and infuriating in the worst case. Needless to say, such loose use of the term does not create credibility for marketers.

In its financial meaning, ROI quantifies the amount of profit relative to the investment required to generate the profit:

$$\text{Return on Investment}(\%) = \text{Net Profit}(\$) \div \text{Investment}(\$)$$

ROI provides a measure of the efficiency of an investment. For financial managers, and for marketing managers, ROI provides a means for evaluating investments of differing amounts. Such a measure is important when there are many alternatives for spending and finite resources are available. Two good ideas for marketing action might generate the same NPV, but one may require less investment; the one requiring the smaller investment is, therefore, more efficient. Everything being otherwise equal, an alternative with a higher ROI, which indicates greater efficiency, is preferred to an alternative with a lower ROI.

Consider the following illustration. The marketing manager at NewCorp is evaluating the relative success of marketing actions to attract new business in order to determine the best course of action for the future. One alternative, participation in a tradeshow, cost $25,000 and generated new business with a net profit of $50,000 the last time the firm participated in the show. A second alternative is to use a Google *Adwords* campaign which cost $15,000 and generated new business with $40,000 in net profits. The ROI for each alternative would be:

$$\text{ROI for tradeshow} = \text{Net Profit} \div \text{Investment} = \$50,000 \div \$25,000 = 200\%$$

$$\text{ROI for Adwords} = \text{Net Profit} \div \text{Investment} = \$40,000 \div \$15,000 = 267\%$$

Thus, the *Adwords* investment is more efficient. Other things being equal, and assuming the future performances of the tradeshow and *Adwords* campaign are similar to their performance in the past, the better, or more efficient alternative would be *Adwords*. However, both alternatives have a very good ROI. If NewCorp had the resources, it might choose to do both again, but before doing so, it might do one more analysis.

NewCorp might ask how much of the profit obtained from the tradeshow could have been obtained using only *Adwords* and vice versa. Now the question is about the *incremental* profit associated with each alternative. Unless all of the new business obtained using each alternative is unique, there is some overlap in the new business obtained. If all of the new business is unique to each alternative, then the ROIs for the tradeshow and for *Adwords* are 200% and 267%, respectively, as computed above. However, suppose that all of the new business obtained from *Adwords* would also have been obtained from the tradeshow and none of the new business obtained from the tradeshow would have been obtained from *Adwords*. Of course, regardless of which alternative is selected, the firm will have to spend $15,000 to obtain $40,000 in net profit. So, the question becomes, what is the incremental return from spending an additional $10,000 for the tradeshow. Consideration of incremental profit and incremental spending changes the equations:

$$\begin{aligned}
\text{Incremental ROI for tradeshow} \\
= \text{Incremental Net Profit} \div \text{Incremental Investment} \\
= \$10,000 \div \$10,000 = 100\%
\end{aligned}$$

Incremental ROI for Adwords
= Incremental Net Profit ÷ Incremental Investment
= $000 ÷ $000 = 0%

This simple example illustrates why it is important to understand the baseline that was discussed in Chap. 6. In most organizations, there will be some sales even if there is little marketing. Current marketing efforts, if they are at all successful, will generate some sales. This means that when thinking about changes in marketing expenditures, the relevant analysis is not the absolute effect of those changes but the incremental change in baseline. The example above focused on new business. Presumably, there would be some continuing business even if neither of the marketing alternatives were implemented. The historical performance of the two alternatives suggests the firm would obtain $40,000 in new profits regardless of which alternative is implemented because all of the profits obtained from the *Adwords* campaign would also be obtained from the tradeshow. Thus, the relevant investment decision for the marketer is how much additional (incremental) profit can be obtained from incremental spending on marketing. In the illustration, this is the $10,000 of additional cost for the tradeshow relative to the cost of the *Adwords* campaign.

Of course, in most marketing situations things are not as clear cut as the illustration. Some customers obtained through the tradeshow might have been obtained with *Adwords* and some of the customers obtained with *Adwords* may not have been obtained at the tradeshow. Further complicating such analyses is the fact that different marketing actions may not only identify different customers but the customers that are identified may differ in what they buy, how much they buy, when they buy, and how profitable they are. These types of differences are what marketers deal with every day as they develop and implement marketing strategies and plans. The key to making these strategies and plans complete, and credible to financial planners, is to link these differences to marketing expenditures and cash flow.

While ROI is useful for comparing expenditures on alternative marketing actions, it should not be the sole determinant of marketing expenditures. Implementing an action with a lower ROI may still result in greater total profits for the firm than would be the case if it were not implemented. Comparisons based solely on ROI ignore the size and risk of alternatives. In addition, when there are interdependencies among marketing actions and outcomes, ROI may be misleading. Finally, ROI compares a single investment with a single return. As was observed in Chap. 10, many marketing-related activities require multiple investments and have different levels of returns and risks over time.

These complicating factors are not a reason for ignoring ROI. They are, however, an opportunity for marketers to contribute to the performance of the firm by helping financial managers understand such complexities and their implications. The ongoing and incremental nature of most marketing expenditures makes ROI less relevant as a measure than incremental cash flow.

Profitability Index

Closely related to ROI is the profitability index. The profitability index (PI) provides an approach to overcoming some of the limitations of ROI by considering the stream of future cash flows associated with an investment. The profitability index is an index that attempts to identify the relationship between the costs and benefits of a proposed activity. It is calculated as:

$$PI = (\text{Present Value of Future Cash Flows}) \div \text{Initial Investment}$$

A profitability index of 1.0 would indicate that the project's present value (NPV) is equal to the initial investment. Thus, any proposed investment where the index is below 1.0 should be unacceptable.

The profitability index obviously requires a forecast of future cash flows. As has been noted repeatedly in earlier chapters, forecasting is difficult and generally wrong. However, for planning and decision-making purposes an approximation is adequate. If under the most optimistic of assumptions the PI cannot reach 1.0, an investment is not worthwhile. On the other hand, if under the most conservative of assumptions the PI is large, making the investment and moving forward makes sense. Precision is seldom possible or necessary when dealing with future events.

It is possible to take the PI one step further by incorporating future costs and investments:

$$PI = (\text{Present Value of Future Cash Flows})$$
$$\div (\text{Present Value of Initial and Future Investments})$$

Of course, forecasting future costs is even more difficult than forecasting future returns. Nevertheless, use of such a ratio can provide useful direction in thinking about multi-year marketing projects, like the launch of a new product or the signing of a multi-year distribution agreement. This modified PI can not only indicate the profitability of a proposed investment but can also be used for various "what-if" analyses that could provide an estimate of how much future investment a firm could make, in total or on an annual basis, and still have a profitable venture.

STRATEGIC PROFITABILITY

Firms cannot survive, at least in the long term, without making a profit. The ways in which a firm organizes itself, manages its costs, and innovates are important determinants of profitability. Nevertheless, the profitability of a firm ultimately rests on how well it meets the needs of customers and what its customers are willing to pay for its products and services. Efficiency only makes sense in the context of customer satisfaction and sales. Indeed, a firm can become so efficient that it destroys some or all of what customers once valued and were willing to pay for. For example, in 2018, airlines have become so efficient by adding more and smaller seats that they have prompted customer complaints and even Congressional hearings. Innovation is important but only to the extent that the new ideas can be linked to the needs of some set of customers.

The long-established role of marketing in obtaining the voice of the customer is, therefore, critical to the strategic success of the firm. Also critical is the ability of the firm, with the help of its marketing professionals, to identify products and services that fulfill customer needs and desires and that can be produced and offered profitably by the firm. Customers often want things that cannot be profitably offered, at least within known constraints related to costs, technology, time, and place. This is the reason that marketing's role cannot stop at identifying opportunities. It is also the reason that marketing is so often perceived as a cost and tasked with tactical activities in many organizations.

The role of marketing does not stop with the identification of potential customers or the service of existing customers. The strategic role of marketing is to create markets by identifying opportunities to match the desires of some set of customers with the skills and resources of the firm. The operational form through which such matching takes place is the business model of the firm. The opportunities marketers should seek to discover do not end with customers; rather, to make market opportunities relevant for the firm, there must be a business model that makes financial sense for the firm.

In the course of successfully executing business models, marketers create intangible assets that have value to the firm. Srivastava, Shervani and Fahey (1998) call these assets "market-based assets." Such assets include brands, loyal customers (an installed base) and partner relationships with distributors, suppliers, and others. These assets, in turn, allow the firm to meet the needs of customer and serve the profit needs of the firm. Figure 11.1 provides an illustration of the linkages between market-based assets and financial performance.

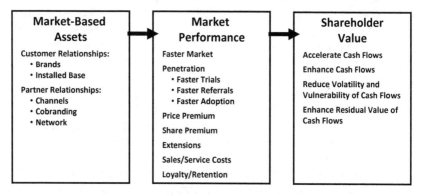

Fig. 11.1 Linking market-based assets to financial performance. (Source: Srivastava et al. 1998)

A Template for Financial Planning for Strategic Marketing Planning and Budgeting

It is certain that successful businesses start with the identification of customers with needs the business can meet. But marketing planning starts with a business model—a statement of how the firm will make money by serving the needs of customers. Marketers who wish to play a strategic role must understand the business model of the firm. Every marketing action needs to be placed in the context of the business model it is designed to support. Indeed, truly strategic marketers will focus on the analysis of existing business models with the objective of making them better or replacing them with a new business model that better serves customers and the firm.

Most actions carried out within a firm are not strategic or at least are carried out by individuals who are not strategic. Most marketing actions are carried out as tactics. Buying media is not, in itself, strategic; producing and distributing products or services, are not, in themselves strategic. R&D can be an exercise in curiosity rather than a strategic activity. However, all of these activities can occur within the context of a strategy. Individual activities become strategic when they serve the broader strategy. Marketing activities become strategic when they focus on the execution of a business model that generates profits for the firm. Thus, analysis and planning of any marketing action should begin with a clear understanding of the business model within which the action will occur.

With the business model clearly in mind, some simple planning principles can guide decision-making and the identification of the potential contribution of marketing actions to the financial performance of the firm. Table 11.1 provides a simple planning template for the budgeting and planning of marketing actions. Each marketing activity and expenditure should be vetted against how it will contribute to cash flow. The link between a marketing action and cash flow is often not direct. As discussed in Chaps. 5 and 6, there may be a need to identify intermediate marketing outcomes and their linkages to financial performance. This should include specification of specific outcomes, time frames, milestones that demonstrate progress (or a lack thereof) and the specific ways relevant outcomes will be measured.

Once the logic, or story, of how the marketing activity will contribute to cash flow is identified, a financial analysis can be carried out. The cost of the marketing action should be identified and a forecast of sales revenue and net contribution after marketing determined. This forecast may be for a single period or for multiple periods. As with any forecasting exercise, assumptions need to be identified, tested, and monitored for changes over time. Finally, relevant risk factors need to be determined to assess the relative riskiness of the marketing action under review. Most of these risk factors will be related to the assumptions that drove the forecast. The riskiness of the project can then be factored into the discount rate used to compute the net present value of the return on the investment in the marketing action. If desirable, for comparing alternative marketing actions or for other purposes, an ROI or profitability index can be obtained.

This planning process can be carried out for a single marketing activity or for an entire campaign. Some actions may be so short term, low cost, or low risk that a full analysis through NPV may not be worth the time and effort. However, thinking through the logic of a marketing action in the context of the business model of the firm is always appropriate. Marketers

Table 11.1 Financial marketing planning matrix

Marketing action	Effect cash flow	Relevant intermediate marketing objective(s)	Expected outcome(s)	Links to cash flow	Cost of marketing action	Net contribution after marketing expenditure	Relevant risk factors	NPV	ROI or PI
	Customer acquisition	Awareness	Quantitative outcomes						
	Customer retention	Brand preference	Time frame						
	Increase in share in category	Store visit	Milestones						
	Increase in frequency of use in category	Web site visit	Measures						
	Increase in share of wallet	Increase in distribution coverage							
		Purchase							
		Other(s)							

who can tell the story of how marketing facilitates and improves the financial performance of the firm will find themselves at the table when strategy is discussed.

CONCLUSION

The financial performance of a firm rests on how well the firm meets the needs of a set of customers. Long-term financial success does not grow from the creation of barriers to entry. Such barriers are usually illusory, and history teaches that they are certainly not permanent. Successful financial performance grows from a firm's ability to create a business model that matches a firm's capabilities with the needs of customers in a way that both satisfies the customer and allows the firm to make a profit. Every marketing activity and expenditure should be evaluated relative to its role and contribution to the firm's business model. When marketing activities are placed within such a context, it is relatively easy to identify how they contribute to financial performance.

Exercises

1. Two of the most common methods for budgeting marketing activities are (1) take what was spent last year and add (subtract) a percentage based on expected sales and (2) allocate a fixed percentage of sales revenue (either gross or net) to marketing. What are the advantages of these approaches? What are the disadvantages of these approaches? What alternative(s) would you suggest?

2. Suppose a small firm's business model involved offering pet sitting and pet walking services in a local community. The firm charges $10 per hour per pet with a minimum charge of $10.00. To date, it has built its business through referrals from current customers. The firm thinks it could generate more business if more people were aware of it. It is considering buying an advertisement in a local community newspaper to increase awareness. The ad would cost $100.00. How many new customers would be needed to justify this advertising expenditure? As a further incentive, the firm is considering including in the ad a coupon for a free hour of service. What are the financial implications of using the coupon? How many new customers would be required to justify the placement of the ad and the coupon? What assumptions are necessary to arrive at your answer? Does consideration of baseline play a role?

3. Select an established business in which you are interested. Identify its market-based assets (brand, current loyal customer, channel partners, etc.). How does the business use these assets in the marketplace to serve customers? How do these assets contribute to the financial performance of the firm?

Points to Ponder

1. What types of customer and market research are most likely to produce positive net present value returns? How would a firm assess the value of its customer and market research investments? Is there value in research that demonstrates an idea is a poor idea? How would you value research with such a negative outcome?
2. Is a measure of return on investment or a profitability index the best measure of marketing's contribution to the financial performance of the firm? Are there other metrics that are also important? If so, how would these complement the financial outcome metrics?

References

Carter, S. M. (2018a, May 28). If You Invested $1,000 in Apple 10 Years Ago, Here's How Much You'd Have Now. *CNBC Make It.* https://www.cnbc.com/2018/05/04/if-you-put-1000-in-apple-10-years-ago-heres-how-much-youd-have-now.html

Carter, S. M. (2018b, May 26). If You Invested $1,000 in Amazon 10 Years Ago, Here's How Much You'd Have Now. *CNBC Make It.* https://www.cnbc.com/2018/04/27/if-you-put-1000-in-amazon-10-years-ago-heres-what-youd-have-now.html

Dennin, S. (2012, November 20). What Killed Michael Porter's Monitor Group? The One Force That Really Matters. *Forbes.* https://www.forbes.com/sites/stevedenning/2012/11/20/what-killed-michael-porters-monitor-group-the-one-force-that-really-matters/#32620d92747b

Moorman, C. (2014, August). *The CMO Survey Report: Highlight and Insights,* p. 66. https://www.slideshare.net/christinemoorman/the-cmo-survey-report?next_slideshow=1

Porter, M. E. (1998). *Competitive Advantage: Creating and Sustaining Superior Performance.* New York: Free Press.

Srivastava, R. K., Shervani, T. A., & Fahey, L. (1998). Market-Based Assets and Shareholder Value: A Framework for Analysis. *Journal of Marketing, 62*(January), 2–18.

Stewart, M. (2009). *The Management Myth: Why the Experts Keep Getting It Wrong.* New York: W. W. Norton & Company.

CHAPTER 12

Measurement Beyond the Firm

Microsoft paid $171 million to acquire a small software company called Groove in 2005. Groove was privately owned, so it's hard to know for sure if their financial performance warranted that purchase price. Most likely, Groove wasn't performing well in the traditional sense. That wasn't the issue, in any event. As *Business Insider* described the decision, "It [Groove] never sold very well, but Microsoft bought Groove in 2005 for $171 million, and Bill Gates later said the main reason was to get Ozzie. The next year, Ozzie took over from Gates as Microsoft's chief software architect" (Rosoff 2012).

Ozzie went on to become a highly successful Software Architect. His Groove engineers contributed significantly to the creation of Microsoft's SharePoint collaboration technologies—a critical addition to the aging Microsoft Office product line. From this perspective, it seems that Microsoft acquired Groove's people and their brains as much as its assets. In a strong sense, those brains were Groove's assets. This chapter explores the issue of non-financial resources like the engineering prowess of Ray Ozzie and the Groove team—what you might call "human capital."

The market seems to have rewarded the decision. Microsoft's stock price ticked up on the day of the acquisition announcement, which is atypical. Investors must have seen the purchase of a questionably profitable but talent-rich company as a good move. Then, after a brief downturn, Microsoft stock rose for the next three months after the Groove deal.

© The Author(s) 2019
D. W. Stewart, *Financial Dimensions of Marketing Decisions*,
Palgrave Studies in Marketing, Organizations and Society,
https://doi.org/10.1007/978-3-030-15565-0_12

The first 11 chapters of this book focused on the financial dimensions of marketing management. The message in these chapters was that marketing is a key driver of financial performance and that it is important for the marketing planning and budgeting processes to explicitly address the linkages between marketing activities, expenditures, and financial outcomes. This means both articulating the contributions of marketing in financial terms and demonstrating an understanding of the responsible management of financial resources in pursuit of marketing and market outcomes.

A deeper analysis reveals, however, that financial resources are not the only resources that firms and marketers within firms must manage and consider when planning. There are a variety of other resources for which managers are responsible: physical resources, human talent, intellectual property, natural resources, and social relationships, among others. This chapter explores the role of these other types of capital and their implications for marketing planning.

Types of Capital

Firms and other organizations make use of many forms of capital. Financial capital is an important and necessary form of capital. Historically, it is the use of this type of capital that public firms have been required to report. Hence, the focus of much of this book is on managing financial resources within the context of marketing. However, financial capital is only one type of capital for which firms are responsible.

Firms are increasingly being asked to report on their use and stewardship of other types of capital. The *Triple Bottom Line* (TBL or 3BL) account framework, which emerged in the 1990s, asks firms to report on their stewardship with respect to people, planet, and profits (Savitz 2013). TBL wants firms to account for how well they manage employees, customers, and suppliers, how the firm manages environmental resources, and the degree to which these elements contribute to profits.

Integrated Reporting, a model of value creation that goes beyond basic finances, asks firms to address use of financial capital, physical or manufactured capital, human capital, intellectual capital, natural capital, and social capital (International Integrated Reporting Council 2013). Table 12.1 lists the dimensions of Integrated Reporting and Fig. 12.1 illustrates the ways in which the Integrated Reporting Framework conceptualizes the relationships of these dimensions to value creation. Other organizations have suggested similar dimensions.

Table 12.1   Dimensions of Integrated Reporting

Financial capital: The pool of funds available to the organization
Manufactured capital: Manufactured physical objects, as distinct from natural physical objects
Human capital: People's skills and experience, and their motivations to innovate
Intellectual capital: Intangibles that provide competitive advantage
Natural capital: Includes water, land, minerals, and forests; and biodiversity and eco-system health
Social capital: The institutions and relationships established within and between each community, group of stakeholders and other networks to enhance individual and collective well-being. Includes an organization's social license to operate

Source: International Integrated Reporting Council (2013)

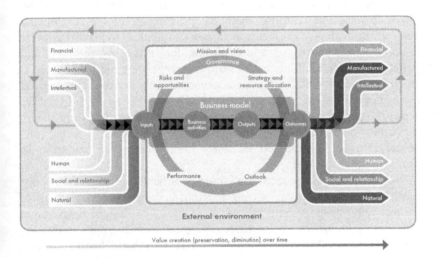

Fig. 12.1   Value creation process as conceptualized by Integrated Reporting. (Source: International Integrated Reporting Council 2013, p. 13)

Both TBL reporting and Integrated Reporting argue that firms are responsible to all "stakeholders," of whom shareholders comprise just one set. This view changes the focus and objective of the firm from maximizing shareholder or owner value to coordination of the interests of multiple stakeholder, including shareholders, employees, customers, suppliers, the local and larger community, creditors and government, among others.

Though noble in principle, there are criticisms of TBL reporting and Integrated Reporting in practice (Robins 2006). Even some of the early proponents have suggested a need to rethink the ideas embodied in these approaches (Elkington 2018). The criticisms range from the arguments that these approaches are impractical to concerns that the approaches do not go far enough. Also, the practical incentive structures of most companies make it difficult to execute business strategies that emphasize TBL or Integrated Reporting objectives over financial performance and share price.

One important element missing from these approaches is explicit consideration of a temporal dimension. The time value of money (net present value (NPV)) provides a means for considering the trade-offs related to the receipt of financial costs and benefits at different points in time. No such measures currently exist for other forms of capital. Making application of these approaches even more difficult is the fact that there is no common metric, such as cash flow, for comparing the costs and benefits of a firm's actions across various stakeholders and for arriving at an overall measure of the firm's performance. This makes it challenging, if not impossible, to make well-informed trade-offs among alternative actions. There are no measures such as NPV that provide a summary of outcomes. An implication of the absence of such measures is that outcomes that are difficult to measure often receive less attention in organizations.

Nevertheless, just because something is difficult to measure does not mean it should not be part of considerations in decision-making. Many of the intangible assets of firms identified in Chap. 2 can also be described as stakeholders—customers, employees, supplier and distributor relationships. Many organizations now engage in various activities broadly defined as *corporate social responsibility*. *Fair trade* and *ethical trade* initiatives seek to spread the profits of sales more evenly across the value chain, while also encouraging sustainable practices. There is active pressure on publicly traded firms to give more thought and action to broader constituencies through *socially responsible investing*. Such investing can influence firms' access to financial capital and their cost of capital. Thus, there is a very real financial dimension of these concerns. At the heart of concerns linked to TBL reporting and Integrated Reporting is the very definition of the firm and its objectives.

THE ROLE OF THE FIRM

The notion of the firm or the corporation has existed for less than 500 years. With roots in the early trading companies, such as the East India Company, the modern business has evolved from a very small part of a largely agrarian economy to a dominant economic and social institution. Coupled with the technology developed during the industrial revolution and more recently, the information revolution, the firm has produced enormous increases in productivity. The effect of the modern firm can be seen in the per capita growth of GDP in Western Europe between 1350 and 1950. During this period, per capita GDP increased by almost 600%, while remaining virtually unchanged in China and India during the same time (Zakaria 2012).

Much has been written about the role and operation of the firm, though a comprehensive theory of the firm remains elusive. There are numerous theories of the firm that differ in focus, emphasis, and scope. Coase (1937), Williamson (1979), and others have argued that firms exist to reduce or eliminate the transaction costs that would arise in production if every transaction involved a market. Grossman and Hart (1986) and Williamson, among others, emphasize the importance of incomplete contracts and decision-making rights that make decision-making easier and faster than would be the case if every new decision had to be negotiated by the parties involved. Both theories can be extended beyond the firm to explain relationships within value chains.

When thinking about accountability and the evaluation of performance, a critical issue is how the boundaries of a firm are to be defined. Triple Bottom Line reporting and Integrated Reporting both expand the boundaries of the firm because they suggest that decisions by a firm should include consideration of factors that can be far removed from the firm or even the value chain in which it operates. Where these factors are only partially under the control of a firm, if at all, and where the value created by a firm is diminished in an absolute sense or relative to competitors, response to these larger issues becomes problematic.

Truly egregious and irresponsible conduct is not difficult to identify, but most decisions regarding the management of resources are subtler. For example, how does a firm make the trade-off between the use of coal and the loss of tens of thousands of jobs, especially in the short term? Similarly, what is the appropriate trade-off between automation and jobs? Does it make sense for a firm to avoid necessary layoffs that would accompany automation and more efficient production in order to support the local community? Does it still make sense when failure to automate makes the firm less competitive, reduces its overall contribution to society and ultimately is forced out of business because it lacks the ability to compete?

Nobel laureate Milton Friedman famously wrote that: "There is one and only one social responsibility of business—to use its resources and engage in activities designed to increase its profits so long as it stays within the rules of the game, which is to say, engages in open and free competition without deception or fraud" (Friedman 2009, p. 55). This appears to be a simple and compelling definition of the role of business. While often quoted, use of the quotation often ignores the latter half of the quote, which talks about activities that are "within the rules of the game." Thus, even a champion of free markets and profit maximization acknowledges that there are appropriate constraints on the maximization of profits. In addition, while profit maximization sounds good, it is a term often used without a temporal dimension—that is, what time period should be recognized when thinking about profits.

There is no doubt that the actions of firms involve externalities, that is, actions that have costs or benefits for parties who did not choose to incur these costs or receive the benefits. These are costs and benefits that are often not reflected in market prices or costs. The over fishing that destroyed the whaling industry in the nineteenth century (mentioned in Chap. 3) was clearly an externality, but one that had specific long-term consequences for the business model. Other externalities, such as air pollution that creates health problems may be regulated by government in order to reduce the cost of an unwanted consequence.

Sadly, much of the focus on the externalities associated with business and marketing is on the negative. To be sure, there are negative externalities associated with business, though arguably, they pale next to the negative externalities of governments. Governments are neither benign nor benevolent, and many of the externalities assigned to business are the result of the complicity of government. The whaling industry still exists largely because it is subsidized by governments. Many constraints on markets exist because one constituency has managed to use government to its advantage relative to other constituencies.

The positive externalities of marketing, economic growth, job creation, innovative new products, life-saving and life-prolonging therapies, among others, are less frequently the subject of discussion. Yet, complete reporting as suggested by triple bottom line and Integrated Reporting requires that these positive consequences be a part of any comprehensive report. The requirements of TBL and Integrated Reporting are related to clearly identifying both positive and negative externalities. This is a measurement issue.

THE ROLE OF MEASUREMENT

Important measurement issues emerge in the various calls for reporting on externalities. Much of the focus of this book has been on the measurement of the outcomes of marketing actions and the resulting financial performance of the firm. Measurement is important because it focuses discussion and facilitates decision-making. Most people want a less polluted environment and want a higher return or income on their time and money. In a more specific market context, most people want higher quality, less expensive, more accessible and more convenient health care. It is easy to articulate such desires in the abstract. But discussions at such abstract levels are not helpful and certainly do not facilitate decision-making because they do not frame decision in terms of the inevitable trade-offs between costs and benefits.

In addition, there is often a difference between what people say they want and will pay for in the abstract and what they will actually pay for. Surveys repeatedly find that consumers want "green" products but will not pay more for them. Such findings are not a paradox. Rather, they represent differences in measurement—when measures ask about abstract wants, consumers may respond in one way, but when the measure is reaching into one's wallet to pay, consumers may respond in another way. This is a well-known phenomenon in marketing; consumers often have a preferred brand but will buy another product if there is enough of a price discount.

Meaningful discussion and decision-making require defining constructs in specific operational terms and the creation and use of measures that are clearly identified. A central thesis of this book is that well-informed decisions require measures that allow the costs and benefits of alternative actions to be summed into a single measure that can be used for comparison purposes. This is the value of NPV, although as has been discussed in earlier chapters, there are subjective elements of even a measure like NPV, such as adjustment for risk and the time period to be considered. Nevertheless, NPV provides a starting point and significantly narrows the focus of further discussions. In the absence of such a measure, discussions merely devolve into political debates and idiosyncratic value judgments. Within the context of an organization, such debates do not further the organization's agenda. It is useful to note that this statement applies to all organizations, including governments and not-for-profit organizations, as well as businesses.

Marketers have a unique contribution to make to the development and use of measures in business and organizational contexts. The rich array of intermediate marketing outcome measures described in Chaps. 5 and 6 attests to the creativity and expertise of the marketing discipline in developing diagnostic and evaluative measures, planning processes, and decision-making rules that inform the management of the firm's delivery of value to customers and to shareholders. As firms move toward greater efforts to capture and report on the externalities of their operations, marketing can contribute in important ways by bringing its expertise in measurement to bear on the issues surrounding such reporting. In a larger context, this means marketing as a discipline can increase its influence and contributions by thinking more broadly about value creation within the context of contributions to the quality of life.

Quality of Life

Marketers, who already have an orientation toward creating value for customers in the markets they and their businesses serve can broaden understanding of that value by focusing more broadly on how marketing actions, products, services, and other market interventions contribute to improvements in the quality of life. Quality of life is not a new topic, even within the marketing discipline (see Sirgy and Samli 1996; Sirgy 2015). Nevertheless, it has not received the attention it deserves. As pressure mounts for firms to report more broadly about their impact on the larger society, marketers would do well to think about how to measure the impact of the firm, generally, and marketing more specifically, on the quality of life of the larger society.

One effort among many to attempt to measure quality of life has been carried out by The Economist Intelligence Unit (Kekic 2012). The Economist Intelligence Unit has used survey research to measure individual's satisfaction with life across 140 cities around the world (Kekic 2012; Economist Intelligence Unit 2018). It has also sought to identify factors that contribute to this subjective measure of satisfaction. Table 12.2 provides a list of these factors.

Table 12.2 The Economist Intelligence Unit's quality of life index

1. **Material wellbeing:** GDP per person, at Purchasing Power Parity in $
2. **Life expectancy at birth in years**
3. **Quality of Family life:** based on divorce rate (per 1000 population)
4. **State of political freedom**
5. **Job security:** based on unemployment rate, %
6. **Climate:** Average deviation of minimum and maximum monthly temperature from 14 degrees centigrade and the number of months with less than 30 mm of rainfall
7. **Personal Physical Security:** based primarily on recorded homicide rates and ratings for risk from crime and terrorism
8. **Quality of Community life:** based on membership in social organizations
9. **Governance:** based on ratings of corruption
10. **Gender equality**

Source: Kekic (2012)

It is perhaps not surprising that more than 50% of the variability in life satisfaction can be explained by GDP per person, both within and across geographic regions: income is important. The wisdom of Henry Ford's decision to pay his workers well, discussed in Chap. 3, seems vindicated. But income is clearly not the only factor influencing life satisfaction and quality of life.

Studies of the quality of life, the influence of the firm, and marketing actions will become more important as firms grapple with how to report the broader dimensions of their performance. Marketers have an opportunity to take a leadership role in measuring such dimensions, even as they become better at linking marketing actions and expenditures to financial performance.

CONCLUSION

Financial performance is important. Marketers clearly must justify their actions and expenditures in terms of their contributions to the financial performance of the firm. However, there is growing pressure on firms to report on broader dimensions of their performance. These dimensions focus on the impact of the firms' actions on the broader society, ranging from the management of human resources to natural resources. Marketers have an opportunity to broaden their contributions and influence by focusing their expertise in measurement on these dimensions.

This book is a call to action. Marketing has its roots in solving an important societal problem: the efficient matching of supply and demand in increasingly urbanized markets with diverse needs and wants (Wilkie and Moore 1999). As producers became more remote from purchasers and purchasers became more segmented and individualized, this matching task became more complex and difficult. Today, this matching task takes place at a global level. Efficiency is an economic concept and therefore must be measured in financial terms. Marketers have an obligation to their firms and the greater society to demonstrate that it is working in their interests to efficiently match supply and demand.

Marketing as a discipline has enormous expertise and skill that it has developed over more than 100 years of practice. As a discipline, marketing has developed a rich literature and body of knowledge on consumers and customers. It has a toolbox filled with methods for studying consumers and customers in great detail and for updating knowledge in response to changes in the marketplace. Finally, marketing has developed an extensive body of knowledge and practice about how to efficiently organize value delivery systems to serve dispersed and diverse customers.

Marketers do their job well. The affluence of modern society, the rich array of goods and services available to consumers, and the improvements in the quality of life of many societies, can be traced, at least in part, to the success of marketing. To be sure, there is still much to be done to improve the lives of many people, but the quality of lives of even the least developed societies has unmistakably improved during the marketing era. Brands are important parts of the lives of consumers. Market relationships are an important part of the social fabric of society. Marketing actions create value for consumers and for firms. The creativity and innovation of marketing has contributed to culture, entertainment, and the health and welfare of society.

Unfortunately, marketing has not received the credit it is due for its important contributions. Ironically, this is largely because marketing has done a poor job of defining its contributions in the very terms that gave rise to it—its economic contributions. This book is a call for a better telling of the story that includes linking all of the many things that marketing does to financial performance. It provides some tools, terms, and techniques to help marketers tell the story.

There is also an opportunity for marketers to increase their contributions and influence by telling the story of marketing's financial contributions and its larger contributions to society.

Exercises

1. Consider the dimensions of Integrated Reporting listed in Table 12.1. To what degree can a firm influence these factors? What specific measures might a firm report to show its influence and management of these factors?
2. Can marketers or the firms that employ them influence the quality of life factors in Table 12.2? If so, how? Are some more easily influenced than others? Should firms be held responsible for these dimensions of the quality of life?
3. List ways in which marketers and their actions contribute to the quality of life. Be specific. Identify specific firms, product/services, or marketing actions that contribute to a higher quality of life.

Points to Ponder

1. What is the obligation of a marketer to serve stakeholders other than business owners/shareholders, if any? How does one make trade-offs among the needs of various stakeholders? Should shareholders be required to give up profits of the firm to serve the needs of others? Are there any advantages or disadvantages to maximizing shareholder value and leaving it to shareholders to decide how they will spend or contribute their profits?
2. Why are governments so often considered the solution to social problems? Are governments and government officials better at allocation of resources than businesses and consumers? Why or why not?
3. How would you describe the contribution(s) of marketing to the firm and society in a compelling fashion? Think about how you might justify the presence of a marketing organization in a firm.

REFERENCES

Coase, R. H. (1937). The Nature of the Firm. *Economica, 16*(4), 386–405.
Economist Intelligence Unit. (2018). *The Global Liveability Index.* https://pages. eiu.com/rs/753-RIQ-438/images/The_Global_Liveability_Index_2018.pdf
Elkington, J. (2018, June 25). 25 Years Ago I Coined the Phrase "Triple Bottom Line." Here's Why It's Time to Rethink It. *Harvard Business Review.*
Friedman, M. (2009). The Social Responsibility of Business Is to Increase Its Profits. In T. L. Beauchamp, N. E. Bowie, & D. G. Arnold (Eds.), *Ethical Theory and Business* (8th ed.). Upper Saddle River: Pearson.

Grossman, S. J., & Hart, O. D. (1986). The Costs and Benefits of Ownership: A Theory of Vertical and Lateral Integration. *Journal of Political Economy, 94,* 691–719.

International Integrated Reporting Council. (2013). *The International Integrated Reporting Framework.* London: The International Integrated Reporting Council. http://integratedreporting.org/wp-content/uploads/2013/12/13-12-08-THE-INTERNATIONAL-IR-FRAMEWORK-2-1.pdf

Kekic, L. (2012, November 21). The Lottery of Life Methodology. *The Economist.* https://www.economist.com/news/2012/11/21/the-lottery-of-life-methodology

Robins, F. (2006). The Challenge of TBL: A Responsibility to Whom? *Business and Society Review, 111*(1), 1–14.

Rosoff, Matt (2012, January 5). The Man Who Bill Gates Once Hired to Replace Him Has a New Startup. *Business Insider.* https://www.businessinsider.com/the-man-who-bill-gates-once-hired-to-replace-him-has-a-new-startup-2012-1. Downloaded 1 Nov 2018.

Savitz, A. (2013). *The Triple Bottom Line: How Today's Best-run Companies Are Achieving Economic, Social and Environmental Success – And How You Can Too.* New York: John Wiley.

Sirgy, M. J. (2015). Measuring the Impact of Social Marketing Programs Using Personal Well-Being Constructs. In D. W. Stewart (Ed.), *The Handbook of Persuasion and Social Marketing* (Vol. 2, pp. 217–238). Santa Barbara: Praeger.

Sirgy, M. J., & Samli, C. A. (1996). *New Dimensions in Marketing/Quality-of-Life Research.* Santa Barbara: ABC-CLIO.

Wilkie, W. L., & Moore, E. S. (1999). Marketing's Contributions to Society. *Journal of Marketing, 63*(3–4), 198–218.

Williamson, O. E. (1979). Transaction-Cost Economics: The Governance of Contractual Relations. *Journal of Law and Economics, 22*(2), 233–261.

Zakaria, F. (2012). *The Post-American World, 2.0.* New York: W. W. Norton.

Index[1]

[1] Note: Page numbers followed by 'n' refer to notes.

© The Author(s) 2019
D. W. Stewart, *Financial Dimensions of Marketing Decisions*,
Palgrave Studies in Marketing, Organizations and Society,
https://doi.org/10.1007/978-3-030-15565-0

CPSIA information can be obtained
at www.ICGtesting.com
Printed in the USA
LVHW080713100822
725606LV00004B/178